# THE SINGING CURE

# THE
# SINGING
# CURE

*An Introduction to*
*Voice Movement Therapy*

## PAUL NEWHAM

### FOREWORD BY ANDREW SAMUELS

SHAMBHALA
*Boston*
1994

Shambhala Publications, Inc.
Horticultural Hall
300 Massachusetts Avenue
Boston, Massachusetts 02115

© 1993 by Paul Newham. First published in the
United Kingdom by Rider, an imprint of Random House Ltd,
20 Vauxhall Bridge Road, London SW1V 2SA

9   8   7   6   5   4   3   2   1
First Shambhala Edition

Printed in the United States of America on acid-free paper ⊗

Distributed in the United States by Random House, Inc., and in
Canada by Random House of Canada Ltd

Library of Congress Cataloging-in-Publication Data
Newham, Paul, 1962–
The singing cure: an introduction to voice movement therapy/
p.  cm.
Paul Newham.—1st Shambhala ed.
Originally bibliographical references.
ISBN 0-87773-997-8 (acid-free paper)
1. Singing—Therapeutic use.   2. Voice—Therapeutic use. I. title.
RZ999.N43   1994        93-34739
615.8′515—dc20        CIP

*To Josephine*

*Whose voice I listened to
but rarely heard*

# CONTENTS

# FOREWORD

Donald Winnicott once said that there is no such thing as originality except on the basis of a tradition. Paul Newham has opened up an entire new field of therapeutic endeavour, yet throughout his book he takes the greatest care to root his ideas and practices in what has gone before. If this means that he strikes a modest note from time to time, then that is all to the good in an age which still believes in the miraculous efficacy of the latest cure programme/therapy.

I have read hundreds of case histories in my time and maybe I am unusually jaundiced. But long ago, in company with many colleagues, I began to realise that case histories prove nothing and are better regarded as rhetorical, suasive projects. That said, I cannot recall being quite as moved as I was when reading two of Newham's accounts – the cases of Jonathan Staves and Lydia Philipson (see pp. 225–227 and pp. 239–243 below). Jonathan was a mentally handicapped man who, in a voice movement therapy group led by Newham, encountered a side of himself, expressed in vocal sounds, that had a numinous impact, not only on the client but on all who witnessed the moment, staff and clients alike. The encounter with the numinous is a meeting with something wholly 'other' to oneself and it inspires awe and fascination; one is quite literally taken out of oneself by such an experience. This process – meeting with the spiritual – lies at the heart of psychotherapy, no matter how tight are the technical rules (the 'frame').

I was equally impressed by the way Lydia, the other client, followed her voice to an empowerment of herself as a woman and as a person with marked social features. In a sense, voice movement therapy led to her *political* individuation.

I have begun this Foreword with clinical commentary because I am keen that Newham's work should not be sequestered into professional areas where he might be well known already. This book should be read by analysts and psychotherapists of every persuasion. We know about the talking cure; we know that it ain't what you say but the way that you say it; we know the unconscious is structured like a language; we know we have to listen with the third ear. But as professional disciplines, psychotherapy and analysis have not paid enough attention to – have not heard – the voice.

Paul Newham is performing valuable acts, if not exactly of synthesis, then of bridging. The voice, whether worded or unworded, stands as a bridge over the gulf we call mind–body or psyche–soma (or whatever phrase is preferred). As the book tells us, the voice's roots are in the functioning and evolution of the human body. Its branches and leaves are in the realms of advanced cognition, spirituality and interpersonal relationships. Hence the voice itself is a crucial mediation between the sensual world and the life of intellect, spirit and love. For, make no mistake about it, therapy (and existence itself) requires the active participation of intellect, spirit and love. What is particularly pleasing about this text is that the intellect is never dismissed in some cheap glorification of the supposedly more 'natural' body. The journey the voice travels as it moves up and out of the body and into communicative realms is not a 'natural' journey. Newham shows us that this journey, while redolent of biology, is also a social and cultural one. So, to the gulf between mind and body bridged by the voice, we have to add that of nature and culture. In a remarkable section on the 'androgyne voice' (see pp. 196–199) Newham destablises and deposes gender verities and certainties (which is part of what I would call his political project). The traditional masculine and the traditional feminine are brought into a new set of relationships (without, I think, there being a denial that difference between the sexes exists).

My previous apperception of voice was very much in communicative terms – that is, communication with another person or with other people. Newham adds a self-referential dimension. I suppose it is still communication when I communicate with myself but there is surely something special about it as well. It never occurred to me so clearly before that, whether speaking or making noises, one might be talking to oneself! On this basis, everything in this book is not only of the utmost relevance to professional practitioners but also to those engaged in self-exploration or self-analysis.

A fascinating section of the book (see pp. 24–35) makes some connections between voice work and infant research. There is a term in infant research called 'proto-conversation'. This term covers all the signals and cues that pass between parent and baby. In the context of proto-conversation, Newham takes therapists on to a challenging track. If work with regressed clients/patients is coloured by patterns mapped out in infancy, then should not a degree of vocalisation akin to the cooing and gurgling of parent and baby be a part of the therapeutic repertoire? Newham uses it already, but I do not think many analysts and psychotherapists do – even those whose patients paint, move, play instruments or receive massage. There is a last barrier or taboo to be broken when two adults stop talking and start vocalising. This is a radical change in how therapy is usually conceived (two adults *starting* to talk). For myself, I do still talk to my children in parent-baby sounds (and also to our cats), but up to now not with patients.

It may be that the relationship between voice movement therapy and infant research will be a two-way relationship and the discoveries made by voice movement therapists will be of interest to infant researchers.

It is significant that from time to time Paul Newham refers to developments in experimental theatre, mostly from the 1960s and 1970s but going back to the 1920s. I can speak from personal experience here as a one-time director of an experimental-theatre company in the 1960s and 1970s and very much aware then of the kinds of things Newham is writing about. This was a period of intense questioning of the nature of performance and the roles of actors and audience.

In the world of analysis and psychotherapy, at the same time, an equally intense questioning was going on over how to understand and handle the practitioner's private experiences in relation to the patient/client. How were we to understand the subjective responses to the patient/client that so often produced disturbances of affect, strange fantasy imagery and uncharacteristic behaviour *in the practitioner*? This is not the place to detail the enormous debate over countertransference that has been going on since then, but I think that, in a sense, these experiences of therapists and analysts can be understood by imagining them as the therapist performing in a script provided by the patient/client: the therapist as actor. Of course, one can just as well conceive of the patient/client as a performer and the therapist as the audience. Either way, performance is an apt metaphor for therapy. I wonder whether voice movement therapy will now become a source of inspiration for performance theory and practice?

I will conclude this Foreword by posing a question which has puzzled me for some time. What does the balance sheet look like when comparing the expressive therapies (and I would count voice movement therapy among these, along with art therapy, dance movement therapy and music therapy) with the more generic psychodynamic and humanistic approaches to analysis and psychotherapy? Is it a question of microcosms and macrocosms (the voice as a microcosm representing the macrocosm of the human being)? In which case, it would not matter all that much which therapeutic modality one uses because, psychotherapeutically speaking, all roads lead to Rome. Or are there specific indications and contra-indications for the various therapies? I do not think that a clear-cut answer exists. My intuition is that voice movement therapy will not only develop to become an important therapeutic discipline in its own right, with specific indications and contra-indications, but will also become a fount of ideas and techniques for people working in a more generic manner.

In sum, I feel that a sense of challenge and opportunity, with attendant feelings of discomfort, is the hallmark of a text that truly is an original contribution. In a few lines, I have tried to demonstrate the value and usefulness of this book on voice movement therapy in the fields of therapy of all kinds, personal growth, socio-political action, infant research and the performing arts.

Andrew Samuels

# ACKNOWLEDGEMENTS

I would like to acknowledge the following people for their contributions to the work which led to this book: Christopher McCullough for ignition; Roy Stevenson for music; Christopher Fettes and Yat Malmgren for analysis; Anne Kilcoyne for a decade of critique; Peter Hulton for Scheersburg; Steve Paxton for stillness; Enrique Pardo for sounding me out; and Andrew Samuels for affirmation.

Thanks also to Anthony Bateman, Michael Blackman, David Garfield-Davies, Marita Günther, Helga Jenkins, Jean McConnell, Maralyn Pietroni, Pat Trueman.

I should also like to express sincere gratitude to my publisher, Tessa Strickland, for consistent on-line support and guidance which served to assuage the unnecessary fear of publishers previously installed in me by popular misconceptions. And to my editor, Kate Parker, whose keen eye for both detail and review made her indispensable to the production of this book.

Warm appreciation goes to Helen, and Ma and Pa Baggett.

Finally, my heartful thanks to Verity, who made it possible for me to write.

Information on voice movement training and therapy may be obtained from:

The Administrator
The International Association for Voice Movement Therapy
7c Ballards Lane
London
N3 1UX

Tel. 081–343 1959

# INTRODUCTION

*Language was originally a system of emotive and imitative sounds –
sounds which express terror, fear, anger, love . . . sounds which imitate the
noises of the elements: the rushing and gurgling of water, the rolling of
thunder, the roaring of the wind, the cries of the animal world . . . and
lastly, those which represent a combination of the sound perceived and the
emotional reaction to it . . .*

*Thus, language, in its origin and essence, is simply a system of signs and
symbols that denote real occurrences or their echo in the human soul . . .*

*The most abstract system of philosophy is, in its method and purpose,
nothing more than an ingenious combination of natural sounds.*[1]

C. G. Jung

The human voice is the primary medium of communication in human
beings. It is an expression of who we are and how we feel. In the timbre of a
person's voice you can hear the subtle music of feeling and thought. The
ever-shifting collage of emotions to which we are all prey colours the voice
with tones of happiness, excitement, depression or grief.

Hearing the sound of our voice is an important way of affirming our self-
image. Moreover, the voice and the psychological state of an individual
mutually influence each other: when we sound good, we feel good and
when we feel good, we sound good. The physical condition of the body is
also reflected in the vitality of vocal expression: illness, faulty posture and
habitual muscular patterns all take their toll on the way we sound.

For many people the voice can, without warning, simply let them down.
They may wish to express a particular emotion, such as anger or sympathy;
they may need to instil confidence or calm; or they may be required to project their voice over a considerable distance. However, the voice simply
clams up, becomes bound by tension and inhibition or else conveys an un-
intended mood or sense.

The factors which cause depleted vocal function are psychological,
physical and political, for the voice is at once an expression of psychological state, a physiological operation and the means by which a person
asserts his or her rights within the social order.

Throughout the world the fundamental right to vocal expression has
existed for centuries in the form of communal singing. At the lakeside, in
the cotton fields, in battle and in love, in the funeral procession and at the
wedding feast, in the mountains of Argentina and in the great gospel halls
of New Orleans, singing has been the most arousing and enlivening communal activity since the earliest of times. However, in the modern era of the
Western world the culture of singing has been lost to a great extent. The
conditioning we receive from parents or teachers who tell us we cannot

sing, the sense of inadequacy instilled in those who do not read music and the overbearing preoccupations of everyday life – all these have led to a silencing of the true voice which in fact everyone possesses.

But because the voice is composed of such complex ingredients, the process of silencing and vocal subjugation, to which so many people are subjected, leads to an inhibitory impairment on a psychological, physiological and social level. To reverse the process and revive vocal function therefore necessitates attention to all these levels. Providing these elements are properly understood, working with the voice can be an enlivening way of helping people overcome difficulties which hinder the acoustic and kinetic expression of self and soul.

With each passing year an ever-increasing number of people find themselves affected psychologically by stress, anxiety and depression, and physically by illness, congenital conditions, injury or bodily misuse and by socially enforced inhibitions. If these effects continue unabated, they often begin to reduce the agility and vitality of body and voice and thereby deplete the capacity for unencumbered expression. Because the primary medium of expressive interaction between human beings is vocal, one of the first instruments to be most severely affected is the voice.

In recent times the act of singing and the creative exploration of vocal sound have enjoyed increased use and popularity among those concerned with the application of artistic media to therapeutic procedures, and the number of different 'voice workshops' available in Europe and the USA is growing.

The increasing attention which vocal work and its self-enhancing potential is receiving necessitates the need for more widespread dissemination and understanding of the means by which unhampered vocal expression may be nurtured, not only in those to whom a voice workshop is financially, socially and physically accessible, but in those whose predicament isolates them from such privileges.

For some time now, medical and educational establishments throughout the Western world have employed an increasing number of non-clinical specialists to contribute to the therapeutic treatment and personal development of those in their care. Painters, sculptors, masseurs, dancers, acupuncturists and dramatherapists are just some examples of the practitioners who have been employed by institutions in the private and public sector. As a result, the patients of hospitals and clinics, whether private or public, the clients of day centres, residential hospices and pastoral foundations for disabled people, and the students of special-education institutes and care units have all been able to benefit from an integrated programme of treatment and health education.

The success of inter-professional collaborations between clinicians and a range of artists and complementary practitioners, coupled with a growing awareness of the therapeutic and educational value of singing and vocal creativity, has led to an increased interest in the application of practical voice work among care-givers and health-workers of all orientations.

I have been very fortunate to have had the opportunity to work with both the staff and the clients of many therapeutically and educationally orientated institutions. Among the clients whom I have seen benefit from vocal work have been people whose ability to express themselves has been impaired by environmental or emotional problems, trauma or mental illness; those whose lives have been turned around by the effects of severe injury or the development of diseases such as multiple sclerosis; and those with congenital conditions such as cerebral palsy and Down's syndrome. In addition, there have been the equally important needs of those whose social or professional position places exceptional demands upon the voice, such as singers, actors, teachers and priests, who often find themselves ill equipped to preserve the health and longevity of their vocal instrument and therefore require re-education and rehabilitation. No less important have been those clients who, while healthy and not overtly inhibited, have none the less discovered an increased potential for self-expression and creativity through singing and sound-making.

In my search to develop a consolidated body of vocal work that would meet such a broad spectrum of requirements, I was confronted with the need to synthesise elements drawn from a range of disciplines including psychotherapy, massage, remedial voice training, stress management, singing and special-needs education.

Delving into the background of remedial, educational and artistic methodologies, I discovered that the therapeutic application of voice, though seemingly a recent concept, has in fact been a part of healing practices among non-Western peoples for thousands of years. In addition, the psycho-physical significance of vocal expression has been an important though little-publicised part of the research carried out by many of those familiar names, such as Freud and Jung, which characterise the medicinal revolutions of the twentieth century in Europe and the USA. As my practical investigations unfolded, so they became rooted in traditions that had gone before me.

The prevalent but hitherto unconsolidated research into the psycho-physical benefits of vocal work carried out during the twentieth century contained an implicit plea for an integration of many diverse principles and strategies into a systematic and analytically grounded practical discipline; it was in response to this plea that voice movement therapy evolved.

Looking for conceptual models upon which to base any practical discoveries, I found myself continually drawn to ideas formulated during the early and middle part of the twentieth century. Although an astounding quantity and quality of clinical and scientific vocal experimentation has been conducted in the last twenty years, especially that achieved by measuring aspects of the voice with electronic instruments, it was the less technological and more interpretative work conducted in the 1940s, 50s and 60s that particularly attracted me. Voice movement therapy therefore originally developed in response to ideas which preceded much of the technological and quantitative analysis of the human voice, and I have therefore confined my historical overview to the period which provided the foundations for my work.

I myself enjoyed the privilege of studying with some of the most perceptive and innovative figures in their fields and from whom I obtained theoretical and practical knowledge of the divergent paradigms which I needed to respond to the complexity of vocal dynamics. Yat Malmgren's adaptation of Rudolf Laban's dance analysis into a psychological framework; Anne Kilcoyne's fusion of social, anthropological and artistic processes; Steve Paxton's research into human movement; Mary Fulkerson's use of the bodily image; and Enrique Pardo's inquiry into the archetypal and synaesthetic aspects of singing – all these have provided catalytic foundations of inestimable importance in the construction of voice movement therapy.

Equally crucial to the development of voice movement therapy has been the practical investigation into and training of my own voice, as a result of which I have found it possible to extend the malleability of vocal timbres far beyond that which people are encouraged to achieve. I have given demonstrations of my voice-dance in a range of contexts: for experimental music festivals, for dance companies and for voice and speech clinicians. Despite the fact that I have been working for some years at this, and regardless of the fact that I have never caused myself or any of my clients so much as a sore throat, there have been some horrified responses from those suspecting physiological damage.

I was therefore very fortunate when David Garfield-Davies, Director of the Middlesex Hospital Voice Clinic, gave me the opportunity to make a video stroboscopy recording of my working larynx in which I was able to demonstrate an extensive range of pitch and timbre. This confirmed that a wide spectrum of acoustic sounds, produced according to the principles of voice movement therapy, can be generated in a manner entirely concordant with the healthy and organic functioning of the vocal instrument. The making of this short film was one of a number of key points in the development of my work, for it was emblematic of the way that the clinical and the non-clinical can work in tandem to the same end, providing that both parties remain responsive to the evidence provided by each other's research. I am indebted to Garfield-Davies for the consistent personal support he has given me.

In the UK such an interdisciplinary perception of vocal work has been encouraged and developed nowhere more thoroughly than in the forum provided by the British Voice Association, which facilitates dialogue between vocal practitioners from fields as diverse as laryngology and folk singing. I gave a paper at one of the first symposia of what was at that time the Voice Research Society, and since then I have seen it grow through these annual events into the most essential and significant national organisation for those working with any aspect of the human voice; indeed, my discovery of this assembly marked another significant moment in the development of my work.

Another important and symbolic occurrence was the publication by the *Journal of Analytical Psychology* of an article which I wrote on the application of Jung's psychological principles to the methodological analysis of the singing voice; this exemplified the increasing interest in the use of non-verbal strategies among clinically orientated psychotherapists.

Despite liaison with and respect for clinicians of psyche and soma, the roots of my work were originally nourished by artistic phenomena and I continue to utilise an essentially creative and artistic view of the human condition. However, I could not have developed voice movement therapy without following a rigorous, consistent and critical study of the physical, psychological and social principles which underpin the operation of vocal expression.

I cannot claim to have invented a new therapy or pioneered a road forward through hitherto unexplored territory; I have merely consolidated the principles which others have discovered into a practicable stategy, so that the therapeutic and educational application of voice work may be disseminated in a form which is accessible but which pays close attention to the complex conceptual and practical frameworks within which an instrument as intricate as the human voice should be analysed.

The first half of this book is an introduction to some of the most important theoretical paradigms which inform the psychotherapeutics of singing and vocal expression. Chapter One describes the significance of pre-verbal sound-making among early peoples and in infants and locates the therapeutic application of vocal sound in a number of indigenous cultures. Chapter Two explains those principles established by Freud and Jung which are relevant to the expressive capacity of the human voice. Chapter Three introduces the work of those who may be described as having pioneered the path towards a psychotherapy of singing, or a 'singing cure'.

Part Two of the book details the various stages of the working process which I have named voice movement therapy, which may be described as a method of helping people overcome difficulties which impair and subdue vocal and physical expression. As I have stated, it is a synthesis of a number of long-established scientific and artistic techniques which release the voice, body and mind from constriction and inhibition.

Voice movement therapy is conducted with individuals and with groups. The clients begin by making their most effortless natural sound while the acoustic tones of the voice are listened to and the muscle-tone of the body observed. In response to an informed analysis of breathing, sound and movement, the therapist massages and manipulates the client's body, gives instruction in ways of moving and suggests moods and images which the client allows to affect and infiltrate the vocal timbre. The voice is thereby sculptured and animated by subjection to a kaleidoscope of shifting moods and shapes, colours and images, by which it increases radically in range, tone and substance. The result is psychologically uplifting, physically invigorating, creatively rejuvenating and serves to release vocal function from constriction.

An understanding of voice movement therapy necessitates an insight into the anatomical and acoustic operations which generate vocal sound, and these are introduced in Chapter Four. The remaining chapters correspond to the three aims, which may be regarded as separate and interrelated, of voice movement therapy. The first is concerned with the release of the voice from fundamental social and psycho-physical constrictions and is dealt with in Chapter Five. The second is concerned with extending the artistic creativity and psychological expressivity of a voice once it is fully liberated; this is dealt with in Chapter Six. The third concerns the application of voice movement therapy techniques to the field of speech and is approached in Chapter Seven. Chapter Eight provides some case studies from my own practice.

Voice movement therapy is not an activity which a would-be practitioner or a willing recipient can learn from a book. It must be introduced in practice. In 1992 I established a professional training programme in voice movement therapy from which fully qualified practitioners would graduate. I also instigated the foundation of the International Association for Voice Movement Therapy in order that non-clinical voice therapists could be part of a nationally and internationally recognised institution.

I hope that this book will provide a useful and thought-provoking contribution to the work of those already exploring the application of voice in divergent settings; that it will assist those who are campaigning for the systematic addition of vocal work to existing programmes in the therapeutic and educational arena; and that it will be a source of inspiration for those who are considering entering a field which is beginning to receive widespread attention that is long overdue.

# PART ONE
## The Singing Cure

# CHAPTER ONE

# Origins – Voice, Music, Language

## *The Vocal Dance of Early Peoples*

'In the beginning was the word,' or was there?

So-called 'primitive' peoples did not speak with words but voiced with sounds. Before the acquisition of language in the development of the human species, communication took the form of a combination of vocal sound and bodily movement, an acoustic gesture, a voice-dance, an act of singing.

To communicate anger, fear, sadness or revenge, people had to represent both vocally and physically the essence of these emotions, which involved a spontaneous translation of affective experience into acoustic and kinetic expression.

The composition and choreography of this primeval song and dance was not an abstract representation of emotions but a direct expression of affect and instinct. We may expect the communication of fear to have combined an increased breathing rate and loud panting with a raised vocal pitch punctuated by a flickering tremor and accompanied by a defensive bodily pose, perhaps crouching with arms covering the head.

Because such communication demanded the total involvement of body and voice, it was necessary to re-enact this involvement even when expressing emotions in retrospect. Moreover, this principle of a communicative song and dance based upon the reproduction of experience was applied not only to the expression of emotions, but also to objects, to animals, to the climate, in fact to all subjects of communication. To describe the danger of an approaching bear it was necessary to enact and emulate the essential nature of the animal with the body and the voice, to growl and grunt in deep, booming and thunderous tones accompanied by bodily movements which mimicked the rearing and careening of the approaching beast.

In the absence of words, the body and the voice had to assume a thousand different shapes in the course of describing a single day's events. The people of pre-verbal cultures therefore had to be great performers, sculpturing and orchestrating their bodies and their voices like singing acrobats, representing a child, an animal, performing fire and rain, expressing triumph and defeat. It is from these essential and primal vocal utterances that the act of singing originates.

In the early 1920s, while Jung and Freud were developing the techniques which underpin the practice of modern psychotherapy, Otto Jesperson published a book on the origin and development of language in the human species which has remained a classic text on the subject ever since. In it he says:

> Men sang out their feelings long before they were able to speak their thoughts. But of course we must not imagine that 'singing' means exactly the same thing here as in a modern concert hall. When we say that speech originated in song, what we mean is merely that our comparatively monotonous spoken language and our highly developed vocal music are differentiations of primitive utterances, which had more in them of the latter than of the former. These utterances were at first, like the singing of birds and the roaring of many animals and the crying and crooning of babies, exclamative, not communicative – that is, they come forth from an inner craving of the individual.
>
> They little suspected that in singing as nature prompted them they were paving the way for a language capable of rendering minute shades of thought; just as they could not suspect that out of their coarse pictures of men and animals there should one day grow an art enabling men of distant countries to speak to one another.[1]

Otto Jesperson had been influenced by a famous essay on the origin of music by Herbert Spencer which proposed that the function of 'singing' in these pre-verbal cultures was to release emotional energy, giving vent to and dispersing the psychological excitation generated by the vital experiences of life; that is to say, it was equivalent to what Freud described as 'abreactive catharsis', as we shall see in the next chapter. Jesperson endorsed Spencer's notion that 'singing, like any other sort of play, is due to an overflow of energy', which is discharged through 'vocal vivacity' and by which 'exploits, deeds and experiences of every kind' are turned into sounds which provide the raw material out of which the earliest songs were born.[2]

These vocal sounds expressed aspects of the human condition which were then and remain to this day universally recognisable. Ernst Kurth in the famous text *Musikpsychologie* also suggests that it was the primal vocal expressions of pre-verbal peoples that became incorporated into folksong: 'In investigating the *thematic* roots of folksong, one soon comes upon *psychological* roots as well; among all races there appear certain recurrent, simple idioms that are really nothing but ultimate symbols of their vital consciousness: calls, chimes, cradle rhythms, work rhythms, shouts, hunting-calls.'[3]

These acoustic symbols of 'vital consciousness', which, we speculate, were expressed through the spontaneous vocal sounds of early peoples, can be compared to the pre-verbal musical babblings of the infant. It is as though each newborn child in a matter of months traces the development of human beings played out over thousands of years. These sounds uttered by pre-verbal peoples had in common with pre-verbal infantile music a generic universality; they gave voice to a level of human experience which constitutes a collective consciousness, a trans-cultural level of feeling. They did not 'describe' or 'represent' phenomena but 'exposed' and expressed an immediate response to experience; they were, in Jesperson's words, 'exclamative rather than communicative'.

Unlike the subsequent development of culture-specific languages which have generated a communication barrier between different peoples, these trans-cultural and paralinguistic expressions of affect continue to infiltrate the oral code of humankind. In a study of the different kinds of non-verbal symbols which people use to enhance spoken language, the psychologists J. Ruesch and W. Kees state:

> Emotional expression appears most spectacularly when verbal communication fails altogether. The inability to use words occurs when people are overwhelmed by anger, anxiety, fear, shame. In spite of the incoherent nature of the things they say on such occasions, or the inability to speak at all, others can still understand the implications of their actions, human cries of fear and the kind of trembling associated with anxiety are correctly interpreted anywhere in the world, and the appearance of tears is universally regarded as a sign of tension release attributed to states of pleasure, pain, or grief. Hence the chief function of emotional expression is that of a universal and international emergency language.[4]

In pre-verbal cultures vocal sounds which were first uttered as the spontaneous exclamation of emotional states were latterly employed to paint in sound all physical properties of the environment, such as water, earth, heat, cold, night, day, sun or moon. Information about the environment and its contents was communicated through an expressive and apprehensible embodiment of the essence of their being; the act of early singing thereby preserved a close sympathetic relationship between humankind and nature. For, the sensible qualities of the environs were understood experientially and it was not possible to communicate 'about' things without first experiencing and secondly embodying their rudimentary nature through sound and movement.

In many early cultures where the notion of animism prevailed, every object and being was believed to be endowed with a soul or spirit; and the fundamental essence of something, which was transcribed into sound and movement for the purpose of communication, was believed to contain this spirit. Therefore when people sang of the bear, they became one with the animal's soul. In the same way, through their song they partook of the sun and the moon, the earth and the river.

The singing dance of pre-verbal communication then had three functions: it served to enable people to exchange knowledge about the environment and their feelings towards it; it acted as a ritual celebration of a connection with the elements through a process of becoming; and it served as a channel for the release of accumulated affective excitement.

With the development of words, this sympathetic relationship with the world gradually disappeared, not least because the sung tones of affect and experience became appropriated by a spoken code of linguistics. The acoustic composition of words became more and more abstracted from the essence of that which they sought to express, so that eventually it was not necessary to experience and embody something in order to make it the subject of communication. With the increasing abstraction of words it became possible to communicate the danger of an approaching bear by simply shouting 'bear', the meaning of which remained unaltered even when uttered with an emotional detachment, a vocal monotone and a physical stasis. Similarly, with the word 'storm', or its equivalent, the leaping and twisting of the body with hands sweeping from above the head to the floor, accompanied by great roaring breaths and guttural belches was replaced by a single syllable.

In the course of this development it became unnecessary for people to experience the essence of a subject in order to express and so identify it. People did not need to experience and embody the essence of fear or triumph, a bear or a horse, the river or the night in order to communicate about them, for the words which had come to stand in their place were understood abstractly. Humankind had ceased to express through sound and begun to describe with words.

The effects of this abstract use of language were threefold. First, the sympathetic relationship with the essence of natural elements which had hitherto been enjoyed was eroded. Second, men and women grew distant from the experience of their own emotions. Third, the tonal range of acoustic qualities and rhythms which Jesperson, Spencer, Kurth and a host of other scholars have described as the earliest form of singing was replaced by a comparatively monotonal system of words.

The development from the phono-physical voice-dance to verbal linguistics underpins a cultural move from a spontaneous and experiential process of communication based on expressing fundamental essences and affects, to a system of communication based on a fixed code of abstract signification; from emotive expression to cognitive communication. And this evolution in the history of humankind is repeated in microcosm through the birth, growth and development of each new child.

## The Vocal Dance of Infancy

It is the sound of the voice which marks the birth of every newborn child. The life and soul of the baby depends upon its capacity to breathe and the voice consists of nothing but this breath made audible by the puffs of air rhythmically released by the vibration of the vocal cords. Within moments of the baby being born, the mucous clears from its throat and it cries. This cry of birth is the first mark which a human being makes upon the world; it is universally the first affirmation of life, the sign by which we recognise that the child breathes and therefore lives.

At fourteen days old, a baby's vocal cords are only about 3mm. long and the lungs are so small that it has to breathe at a rate of around 90 cycles per minute in order to inspire sufficient oxygen to remain alive. But despite the size of its tiny body, the baby is able to make an incredible volume of sound, sometimes for periods of such duration that scientists continue to marvel that damage resulting from misuse of the laryngeal apparatus in neonates is almost unheard of.

For the first three months the baby cries only as an expression of hunger and distress, the melody of which rises and falls like a siren. To midwives and paediatricians world-wide, each of these newborn cries is much like any other; however, within weeks a mother will be able to distinguish her child's cry from that of many others without face-to-face contact. The mother has an innate aptitude, an in-built ability to detect the idiosyncratic cadences, the unique quality of rhythm and melody which her baby alone possesses. In addition to these tonal cries, the baby also makes what are called vegetative sounds: coughs, dribbles, hiccups, lip-smacking, burps and wheezes which result from physiological processes.

At around three months a new quality of crying emerges which also has a rising and falling melody but which usually has a slightly higher pitch range than the melody of distress. This is identified as the emergence of the first pleasure cry, and from this period on, the mother is able to differentiate between cries of hunger and cries of tiredness, between cries of physical discomfort and those of irritability, between cries of distress and those of pleasure. In short, the mother has the capacity to perceive in the child's melodic arrangement of pitch a language which is as sophisticated as the baby's needs.

The emerging pleasure sounds contain acoustic properties which act as the precursor for the vowels that will later be used in words; and the differentiation between the melody of distress and that of pleasure is the baby's first step towards the acquisition of speech.[5] However, whereas the verbal infant will later organise such sounds according to the rules of the dictionary, the baby, not yet familiar with such a scheme, arranges them according to an intuitive, creative and innate sense of pitch, melody and rhythm in a fashion akin to the composition of music. This inborn musical aptitude of a baby was the subject of research conducted in the early 1960s in which the melodic patterns of pitch sung by a number of babies were plotted and their compositions published by Folkways Records.[6] It is possible to hear in this infantile music-making a number of basic refrains, as though we might all have been born with the ability to sing variations of certain archetypal songs.

The results of ongoing subsequent research in this area point to a meaningful relationship between the breadth and complexity of a baby's melodious and musical crying and its proficiency in the later acquisition of speech. It seems that a limited pitch range in pre-verbal singing often occurs in children who turn out to be 'late developers' in the proficient employment of speech.[7] There are also a number of impending developmental and congenital conditions, such as Down's syndrome and chromosome 5 deficiency, which are characterised by and may be detected in the specific melodic nature of early crying. Most surprising is the evidence to suggest that the cry of a baby at risk from sudden infant death syndrome (SIDS), or 'cot death', has certain acoustic characteristics, such as radical shifts of pitch, which may be recognisable enough to assist in preventing the occurrence of cot death.[8]

This instinctive musical arrangement of spontaneous vocal sounds is known as 'cooing'. But between the ages of about three and six months a new kind of sound issues forth, called 'babbling'. Babbling is identified as the emergence of sounds which form the raw material for consonants. The first to occur are those known as 'back consonants' in which the air flow from the larynx is interrupted at the rear of the oral cavity, such as in the formation of 'k' and 'g'. This is followed by the production of what are called 'labial consonants' in which the air flow is interrupted at the front of the mouth, such as in the formation of 'b' and 'm'. The ultimate achievement of the babbling stage is the ability to combine these new staccato sounds, which are akin to consonants, with the earlier musical sounds, which sound like vowels. This gives rise to a stage in the child's communicative development which rewards parents, researchers, linguists and paediatricians with the utmost pleasure and fascination. The child talks in its own language in which attentive listeners can hear, or so they think, words from their own language, words from foreign languages, and words which are pure ingenious invention. This babbling continues until around twelve months, by which time the vocal cords have developed from their original 3 mm. to around 5.5 mm. These continue to grow and by the time the child is fifteen years old they are about 9.5 mm. Simultaneously, the original rapid rate of breathing slows down as the lungs grow in size.

Up to this point the acoustic utterances of the baby – the crying, cooing and babbling – emerge purely instinctively and not as a result of any instruction from the mother or care-giver. Deaf babies cry, coo and babble just as hearing babies do.[9] The vocalisation is phylogenetically inherited in the same way as the instinct to suckle at the breast; it is one of the biological patterns of behaviour which the human species universally possesses, and despite the unique quality of each baby's voice, there is a similarity to the crying, cooing and babbling of all babies that is recognisable worldwide.

So too the perceptive faculty of the mother, which enables her to recognise the content of these cries, is a preprogrammed instinct. The mother does not need to take a course in a foreign language to comprehend the emotion or need communicated by her baby's crying; she acquires the aptitude for such an understanding as an integral aspect of her genetic predisposition. It is part of motherhood.

So we may say that between mother and baby there exists a phylogenetic and symbiotic communication in which the mother associates the various qualities of the baby's crying, cooing and babbling with certain needs, ideas and references. It is by way of her positive response to them that the baby receives affirmation of the communicative efficacy of the sounds which it makes, and the babbling eventually leads to mock conversations with the mother or care-giver which further serve to comfort and arouse the baby.

The child absorbs a pleasure from these audible emissions, a pleasure that it will continue to seek, a pleasure that is entirely oral. The mouth becomes the seat of sensory stimulation on two counts – it is the locus of contact with the nourishing breast and the centre of operation in the production of sound. But the mouth is not only one of the first centres of pleasure; it is also the original means by which a sense of power or control is achieved. The infant learns quickly that its needs are met in consequence to sound-making and the positive response to its crying is the first experience an infant has of command and influence.

## The Rules of the Game

In the early part of the babbling stage the infant combines the consonants and vowels to make its own language according only to the music of emotion and instinct, and the smallest units of this 'jumble talk' which are usable for speech are known as 'phonemes'.

Phonemes are the acoustic differences in sound formations 'which are employed within a language to distinguish different words.'[10] For example, the sounds 'p' and 'b' are classified as different phonemes because words which are differentiated only by substituting these sounds will be decoded to signify different meanings, as in pop/bop, pig/big, fop/fob. However, phonemes are not identical to the written letters of the alphabet, as many phonemes require more than one letter to signify their sound; for example, the sound 'oy' as in the word 'boy' and the sound 'ow' as in 'cow' are both phonemes.

When listening to a baby combine these phonemes in the pre-verbal stage, we are aware of its emotional state not from 'what' is uttered but by the 'way in which' it is uttered. Likewise, the infant responds not to the linguistic content of a parent's voice but to its pitch and quality. Human communication with animals operates by this principle; a dog will respond to being scolded in French, German or in gibberish, and the same may be said of the baby.

However, a child's success as a potential adult with full communicative faculty depends upon his or her ability to bring vocal sound-making into line with a specific man-made order. This order is structured according to laws by which the phonemes are combined to formulate words which society understands as the language particular to its culture. These words are acquired painstakingly, repetitiously, until all signs of the instinctive and emotive sound of the voice are subdued and incorporated into a linguistic code which the child must acquire in order to assert his or her rights within the social and linguistic context. The ability to use this code of language efficiently in differing social contexts has been called 'communicative competence';[11] and a prerequisite for this competence is the successful acquisition of an ability to combine phonemes into larger structures.

Although phonemes are the smallest units of sound formations which constitute language, they have to be further combined into larger units to disclose a linguistically meaningful message. The smallest units of sound formations capable of conveying meaning are called 'morphemes'. For example, take the following sentence:

The foxes turned and, feeling frightened, ran for cover.

Some of these words can be broken down to form smaller units which still convey meaning: 'foxes' can be split into fox/es; 'feeling' can be divided into feel/ing; and 'frightened' into fright/en/ed. These sounds are the smallest units, the substitution of which would change their significance. For example, 'fox' tells us the name of the animal, while 'es' informs us that there was more than one; 'turn' tells us the nature of the action performed and 'ed' informs us that it occurred in the past. While 'fox', 'feel' and 'fright' can convey meaning in isolation, 'ing', 'en' and 'ed' require attachment. Morphemes that are also words are referred to as 'free morphemes' and those which require attachment are called 'bound morphemes'.

This transition from a universal musical tonality of babbling to the acquisition of the language specific to the child's culture is achieved by a process of education. The care-giver, in responding to the child, repeats and encourages those phonemes and combinations thereof which have a place in the words of her language and ignores or discourages those babbled sounds which her particular language does not utilise. In behavioural psychology, when a pleasant environmental response results from a particular action or expression, it is said to exert a 'reinforcement', while when a negative response or undesirable occurrence ensues, it is said to exert a 'punishment'. If the same action or expression is repeatedly punished, it will eventually diminish, and this is referred to as 'extinction'.[12] It is from the process of reinforcement and punishment by the care-giver towards the child's sound-making that the first words appear, from which the child pieces together the spoken language of his or her culture and during which the unacceptable or unusable sounds become extinct.

The rules of this acquired verbal communication change from one context to another, from country to country, and some sounds are accepted in one place and not in another. In German, for example, many words end with 'unf', a sound which is not accepted in English. The study of the fundamental sounds upon which the language of different cultures is built is called 'segmental phonology'. The arrangement of these phonological sounds according to certain rules gives rise to words and the study of the language which arises out of the grammatical arrangement of these words is called 'linguistics'.

The audible utterances of the adult human voice are, therefore, composed of an intricate web of elements which enables messages of extreme complexity to be encoded, and it is one of the great mysteries of human existence that so many listeners are able to decode such messages and understand what the sender intended. One of the elements which contribute to the complexity of this web is intonation; that is, the stress with which phonemes, morphemes and words are pronounced. Without intonation our voices would be colourless and literally monotonous; that is, 'mono-tonal', of one tone only. But, not only does intonation give melodic variation to our speech, it contributes to the message encoded. For example, compare the following two sentences of identical linguistic content but uttered with different intonations:

> Susan kissed her mother and then Philip kissed her.
> Susan kissed her mother and then Philip kissed *her*.

The message encoded by the first sentence informs the listener that Philip kissed Susan's mother, but by shifting the pattern of intonation so as to stress the word 'her', the second sentence implies that Philip kissed Susan. The alteration of stress is achieved by what a musician would call pitch variation. If you speak the sentences aloud in a deliberately slowed pace, you will notice that in the first sentence the word 'her' will automatically be uttered on a single pitch identical to that of the preceding word, 'kissed'. However, in the second sentence you will raise the pitch at the beginning of the word 'her' and slide downwards on a scale. This musical variation of linguistic content is called 'prosody' and the way such melodic intonations influence the message which language encodes is known as 'prosodic phonology'.[13]

Prosody is a musical phenomenon and differs from phonology in that it is a characteristic which a baby is born with. Healthy neonates will compose melodic structures of rising and descending pitch using the full vocal range available to them from the moment they are born.[14] It is the application of these musical possibilities to phonemes, morphemes and words in order to encode specific meaning that is acquired through reinforcement, and it is the process of increasing proficiency in the use of words that we associate with the notion of progress, development and increasing intelligence.

# The Child's Progress or the Suffocation of Artistic Instinct

It is impossible to consider the development of a child's psychological, expressive and behavioural faculties, of which language acquisition is foremost, without reference to Jean Piaget. No other researcher has contributed more to our supposed understanding of the way children acquire the capacity to transact in those currencies which are not instinctive and present from birth, which of course includes speech. Neither has any other researcher caused so much damage.

There is such an abundance of literature both by and about Piaget that an attempt to condense it with any degree of eloquence here would be pointless and merely imitate that which has been achieved by others more admiring of Piaget's contribution than myself. Rather, I will give an overview of his general attitude with a boldness that may rightly cause me to be accused of belittling generalisation, but which, even so, is unlikely to make a dent in the profound but disguised influence his work has had on the over-emphasis upon logical activities which contemporary education places on the process of teaching children.

Piaget's model of a full-facultied adult at an optimal stage of development is a mechanistic and scientific one. In his opinion, the qualities which differentiate the later and so-called 'higher' stages of infant growth from those accompanying the earlier years pertain to the child's ability to construct and combine abstract symbols and comprehend their relationship to the phenomena therein represented. Language is one of these forms of abstract symbols, counting is another. Piaget's view of the child's development is one which perceives a goal-directed movement towards ever-increasing sophistication in the cognitive assimilation of logical ideas and relations.

In the early stages of life a child is unable to conceive that an object exists when it is out of sight or hearing or when it cannot be touched, tasted or smelt. Her knowledge derives from the senses. However, the child gradually realises that objects continue to exist and exert an influence upon the world even when she cannot experience their presence sensibly; and it is this dawning awareness which facilitates the linguistic process of naming things. By giving objects names they acquire a permanence and the child is then able to make connections between these linguistic symbols without ever having to come into sensory contact with the objects which they signify. The names become abstracted from the things.

One of the extreme examples of such abstract cognition is pure mathematics, where the numbers bear no relationship to objects or experience and yet can be mastered to guarantee a continuum of logic. For example, imagine that a book is held 500 mm. from the ground and then dropped. In mathematical terms, for the book to reach the floor it must first fall half the distance, bringing it 250 mm. from its destination; then it must fall half that distance, bringing it 125 mm. from the ground; and so on, *ad infinitum*:

$$500 \times \frac{1}{2} = 250 \times \frac{1}{2} = 125 \times \frac{1}{2} = 62.5 \times \frac{1}{2} =$$
$$31.25 \times \frac{1}{2} = 15.625 \times \frac{1}{2} = 7.8125 \times \frac{1}{2} = 3.90625 \times \frac{1}{2} =$$
$$1.953125 \times \frac{1}{2} = 0.9765625 \times \frac{1}{2} = 0.48828125 \times \frac{1}{2} = 0.244140625$$

According to the formal operation of abstract mathematical symbols, the book would never reach the floor but would spend for ever travelling smaller and smaller distances. But of course anyone who has ever dropped a book knows that it does reach the earth and that the infinitesimal and infinite series of figures which the above calculations engender do not accord with that person's actual experience of space.

For Piaget, however, 'development', 'progress' and 'intelligence' mean a move away from such sensory experience towards proficiency in the organisation of data and ideas without experiential contact with the phenomena which they are supposed to represent. The concepts of adulthood and abstraction become equated, as do those of childhood and sensory experience. Piaget therefore grossly underestimates the significance which earlier means of experiencing the world continue to exert in a positive fashion later in life. The two main examples of adult functioning which operate according to the sensory view of the world that Piaget associates with childhood are the artistic process and certain forms of perception manifested in the behaviour of those who are verbally, physically or mentally handicapped. The benefits inherent in such functioning are not recognised by Piaget.

The most comprehensive critique and criticism of this overly logical aspect of Piaget's schema comes from Howard Gardner, who points out that Piaget has 'paid little heed to adult forms of cognition removed from the logic of science: there is scant consideration of the thought processes used by artists, writers, musicians, athletes, equally little information about processes of intuition, creativity or novel thinking'.[15] Gardner points out that an adult's ability to comprehend a phenomenon does not depend on the degree to which that person cognitively understands the systematic logic of the underlying structures; neither is such abstract proficiency necessary to partake creatively in a process with seemingly logical parameters, such as music.[16] A composer or a music buff may have as highly developed faculties relevant to the production and perception of music as an expert in score notation; but the former's approach is intuitive, creative and non-logical.

The implications of Gardner's thesis for children's education reminds us how little attention has been paid to the significance of this non-cognitive apprehension and perception in schools throughout the UK, Europe and the USA. This is as apparent in music as it is in any other subject, where the emphasis, with regard to future development and the accessibility of higher education and training, has been placed more on the individual's cerebral understanding of the logical operations that supposedly underpin music and preserve the virtuosity of its execution than on his or her artistic perception of the extra-logical aspects of the human condition which music was in the first instance created to express. Fortunately this situation is slowly being improved as a result of contemporary research, much of which emanates from Project Zero – of which Gardner is part – an interdisciplinary programme based at Harvard University, the aim of which is to investigate the non-logical process of artistic creativity and development, particularly in children.[17]

A key figure in this research is Jeanne Bamberger, who drew the distinction between the 'formal' and 'intuitive' understanding of music and set up experiments with young children to ascertain the degree to which cognition of the formal structures inherent in music enhanced or depleted the instinctive ability to appreciate it intuitively or to create it. She discovered that the more proficient children became in musical notation the less able they were to sense and describe the mood of a piece or to recreate their impressions through improvisation. Bamberger calls this the 'wipe-out effect'[18] and her plea is for an increased respect for natural, non-formal, playful and spontaneous music-making in the classroom and for less emphasis to be placed on the formal system of abstract notation which a Piaget-orientated attitude would regard as 'advanced'.

This non-formal approach to the appreciation and creation of music does not entail teaching, for children are naturally predisposed to intuitive creativity. Research contemporaneous with Bamberger's, such as that carried out by Helmut Moog,[19] Jay Dowling[20] and Lyle Davidson,[21] has shown a widespread innate tendency among very young infants to create music through the organisation of repetitive pitch patterns. Instruction in the reading and reproduction of musical notation may therefore be seen as much as a process of extinguishing a natural skill as the acquisition of a new one. The good news is that, according to a recently published statement by J. C. Berryman and others, the picture is changing in British schools at least:

> The recommendations for music in the National Curriculum now acknowledge that different skills, and thus assessment criteria, are required in different forms of music. Metric-type notation is indeed indispensable in Western 'classical' music, but it is much less important for the teaching and assessment of jazz and rock music, for example, where performances, improvisation and aural skills may be more important than being able to write a piece down. There is now official support for the inclusion of 'intuitive' alongside 'formal' musical activity: creative music making may already be overcoming the 'wipe out' effect in some school classrooms.[22]

Piaget's equating of progressive development with the acquisition of proficiency in the cognitive encoding and decoding of abstract symbols is thus a misapprehension. Communication via messages that are non-cognitive, non-linguistic, non-segmental, non-phonemic but tonal, melodic, intuitive and spontaneous is as much a sign of proficiency, but it demonstrates the artistic capacity of humankind as opposed to the scientific.

Despite the work of those such as Gardner and Bamberger, the most widespread popular attitudes still hold cognitive abstraction and scientific logic in far higher esteem than operations based on intuition and sensory experience. Consequently the process of transition from intuitive and spontaneous expression of affect to cognitive encoding of fixed linguistic symbols of meaning in the development of the infant is viewed as a progression from a primitive position to a more sophisticated one. Furthermore, this process of so-called advancement is mirrored in the way in which communication in the human species evolved from primal tonal utterances to verbal language and is unfortunately and unjustifiably as synonymous with the notion of progress in the human race as in the individual.

Rather than perceiving the relationship between these two different forms of expression in terms of teleological progress from one to the other, we would create a truer and less prejudicial picture of the human condition by considering them as two equally important aspects of our expressive potential.

The prejudice inherent in a so-called progressive and developmental attitude to the relationship between these two forms of expression becomes particularly striking when working with people whose physical or mental condition renders sophisticated cognitive processes inaccessible. Those termed 'handicapped' or 'mentally impaired', people who cannot speak or count but who continually express a vocal dance of sounds based on their experience of the world, are not communicating in a language which is less advanced or more primitive than 'normal' verbal discourse; they are speaking in a language which is based on a different formulation. We must recognise that the glorification of logical operations and the process of equating them with worth and proficiency represents a particularly damaging contribution to the general prejudice with which non-verbal people are viewed.

One of the most influential and significant contributions to a non-developmental and non-prejudicial understanding of the relationship between the primeval musical utterances of the human voice and the subsequent development of verbal language in the human species has come from the research of an American philosopher, Susanne Langer.

## The Feeling and the Form

Langer divides the process of human communication into two modes – discursive and non-discursive. Discursive communication consists of the exchange of shared symbols composed of fixed units with permanently established meaning. The words listed by the dictionary and spoken according to organised rules of pronunciation are, according to Langer, the most commonly used of such symbols. However, she points out that the realm of human experience is wider than that which this language is capable of representing: 'I do believe that in this physical, space-time world of our experience there are things which do not fit the grammatical scheme of expression. But they are not necessarily blind, inconceivable, mystical affairs; they are simply matters which require to be conceived through some symbolistic schema other than discursive language.'[23]

Langer refers to the units of this other system of communication as non-discursive symbols, the aspect of human communication which are the vital expression of an individual's subjective experience and which can only be understood by way of an intuitive interpretation. The non-verbal sounds of the human voice – sighs, grunts, gasps, the subtle variations of pitch, quality and volume and the idiosyncratic application of prosody – all these are, she proposes, non-discursive symbols.

For Langer the use of non-discursive symbols is of paramount philosophical and psychological importance, because it gives expression to a dimension of human experience for which discursive symbols are inadequate. Furthermore, she asserts that historically it has been the special role of the artist to deal primarily in non-discursive symbols. The arrangement of line, colour and shape upon a canvas and the spontaneous gyrations of the dancing body both constitute examples of non-discursive communication. Even the composition of verbal poetry is non-discursive:

> Artistic symbols are untranslatable; their sense is bound to the particular form which it has taken. It is always *implicit*, and cannot be explicated by any interpretation. This is true even of poetry, for though the *material* of poetry is verbal, its import is not the literal assertion made in the words, but *the way the assertion is made*, and this involves the sound, the tempo, the aura of association of the words, the long or short sequence of idea, the wealth or poverty of transient imagery that contains them, the sudden arrest of fantasy by pure fact, or of familiar fact by sudden fantasy, the suspense of literal meaning by a sustained ambiguity resolved in a long-awaited key word, and the unifying, all-embracing artifice of rhythm.[24]

In Langer's view, the oldest and most primal example of non-discursive artistic expression is music, which she portrays as 'a tonal analogue of emotive life',[25] an expression of 'the greatness and brevity and eternal passing of everything vitally felt',[26] and she traces the origins of music as we now conceive it to the pre-verbal vocal utterances of early humankind:

> Work rhythms, dance measures, choric utterance, these are some of the influences that formed music out of the sounds that are natural to man, that he utters at work, or in festival excitement, or in imitation

of the world's sounds – the cuckoo's cry, the owl's hoot, the beat of hooves, feet, drums, or hammers.

Such noises are incipient 'themes', musical models which artistic imagination may seize upon to form tonal ideas. But they do not themselves enter into music, as a rule; they are transformed into characteristic motifs; intervals, rhythms, melodies, all the actual ingredients of song are not *supplied* but merely *inspired* by sounds heard in nature.[27]

Music, according to Langer, therefore originates in what she called 'tonal' expression, the most obvious material of which she believes to have been the human voice; and this tonal expression is preserved by the work of artists, among whom are the singers of every culture. From Langer's perspective, Piaget's view appears entirely one-sided, lending support to Gardner's critique which highlights the former's undervaluation of artistic or non-discursive activity.

But the singing which Langer identifies as being emblematic of non-discursive artistic activity in early cultures is a far cry from the style of singing which dominates the Western classical tradition, which is perpetuated through the entirely logical, discursive, formal and abstract system of notation and which Bamberger identifies as potentially stifling to artistic spontaneity. The most supreme example of this singing culture is opera.

# An Operatic Paradox –
# An Aesthetic Contradiction

Every week, at Covent Garden in London, at Sydney Opera House and in the great halls of Venice, Rome, Paris and Berlin, people pay large sums of money to see and to hear the opera. For some it is a once-in-a-life-time experience serving to satisfy their curiosity; perhaps because opera has always seemed to be the pursuit of the educated or the rich, or perhaps because it has just never really appealed to their taste. For others it is a regular part of a social calendar, a luxuriant ritual warranting full evening dress and the consumption of fine wines and sumptuous cuisine. For others still it is an educational experience, a way of furthering an understanding of our artistic culture, past and present.

Regardless of the reasons for attendance, the opera remains the grandest and most highly elevated artistic event in the Western mind. It is at once the most admired, the most intimidating, the most exhilarating and the most beguiling of art forms. And central to the opera is the incredible dominance of the sounds made by the human voice.

People enjoy the opera because it is beautiful, and integral to this beauty in the minds of the audience is the virtuosity of the singer's voice. There is little in our culture that is held to be a more complete representation of beauty than the pristine soaring tones of the soprano or the rich velvet sound of the bass, enhanced by the supportive harmony of the orchestra. By contrast, if you take a close look at the stories which opera tells, you will find that many of them contain aspects which are, according to popular social mores, dark and torrid, ugly and despicable. If you peruse the narratives of the famous operas, you will find, on the whole, stories of murder, deception, incest, lust and promiscuity. The culture of which these operas are a part regards music as the antithesis of noise and the emblematic emissary of beauty: if it is musical, it is beautiful; if it is noisy, it is ugly. Our culture consequently produces an aesthetic in which to express something musically is to beautify it. Therefore, when you go to the opera, what you are most likely to see are stories in which all those things which our culture regards as ugly are dressed up in the most beautiful regalia imaginable – music and song. Opera thus provides an artistic form which involves the beautification of that which its social context defines as ugly.

This fundamental paradox within the operatic form has been precisely investigated by Catherine Clement with particular reference to the fate of the female characters as written in many libretti. She reminds us that, while we are assuaged, massaged and seduced by the beauty of the music, elevated to a degree of emotional sensitivity and elation which arrests all faculty of political assessment, the unpleasant story of an innocent woman being strangled by a jealous man is unfolding before our very eyes.[28]

This situation occurs partly because in opera the voice follows a discursive formal system which describes emotion through the precisely encoded and formally dictated symbolic units of pitch, diction, melody, word and rhythm and is not used to expose emotion through non-discursive and spontaneous primal utterance, such as that emitted by the infant and expressed in the emotive songs which we believe to have accompanied the actions of early peoples.

So how then did humankind come to derive such a complex, discursive and logical system as opera from such a non-logical, non-discursive and intuitive process of tonal utterance?

# From Medicine to Music: The Genesis of Formal Singing in Europe

Taken from its pedestal and disrobed of the regalia of astounding sets and costumes, thundering overtures and scholarly interpretations, an opera is usually an old story, often taken from an ancient myth, a fable or a legendary tale, told to music. And it was first performed not in the great architectural palaces which we call 'opera houses', but on street corners, in the market places and then eventually in colossal outdoor theatres.

The historic genesis of the Western operatic tradition is commonly traced to ancient Greece. Here, lone players are said to have wandered the countryside with a lyre, stopping wherever there was an audience and recounting the tales of the great myths, which everybody knew. They sang the story of Oedipus, who unwittingly killed his father and married his mother. They told of the arduous labours of Hercules, who slaughtered the raging Nemean Lion and killed Hydra, the nine-headed monster of Argos. They sang of Medusa's ferocious stare which turned men into stone and they sang of the great battle fought at Troy.

These tales required the wandering performer to play all of the characters, giving each one a distinctive vocal quality and set of characteristics while retaining a neutral voice when acting as the narrator. As he strummed the lyre, he would screech like Medusa, bellow as Oedipus put out his own eyes, yell the great battle cry as Achilles stormed into Troy, hiss and spit the poisonous venom of the Hydra and roar the lion's death cry as he fell beneath Heracles' club. His voice leapt and turned, twisted and writhed in sounds of beauty and ugliness, of fear and euphoric ecstasy.

Though European history books encourage a view which locates the origins of song culture in the Mediterranean, singing and story-telling was an integral part both of the earlier Egyptian cultures from which the Greeks absorbed many of their artistic and religious practices and of those cultures further afield.

However, it was in Greece that, according to popular history, these solo renditions developed into small ensemble performances which are identified as the earliest form of Western theatre. Playwrights wrote the mythical stories in dialogue form, and small groups of lone players came together and acted one or two characters each. In the process of transition from solo recitals in story and music to actual musical and dramatic productions, a new ingredient was added: this was the mask, which gave these mythical personages their requisite larger-than-life appearance. So now the players had a mask for each character, and the vocal dance of word and song emerged through a hole cut into the actor's mask at the mouth.

The etymology of our term 'personality' is inextricably linked to this use of the human voice and originates in these marked performances. The term 'personality' comes from the Latin *per sona*, which means 'the sound passes through', and was first used to describe the mouthpiece of the mask worn by actors. It then came to denote the character or person which the actor portrayed. Eventually the word came to mean any person, and finally 'personality' as we now understand it.

These new masked theatre productions became one of the most significant contributions which the Greeks made to Europe's future cultural and artistic development. They precipitated the genesis of Greek tragedy, the great writings of Aeschylus, Sophocles and Euripides, whose plays were attended by thousands upon thousands of Greek citizens. It was these performances that inspired Plato and Aristotle to devise their philosophy of art and the nature of human emotions.

Aristotle proposed the theory that the audiences who bear witness to these tragedies experience the fate of the central character intensely as though it were their own. In particular, he hypothesised that the onlookers feel immense pity for the character's predicament and extreme fear in imagining that such a fate might befall them. According to Aristotle, such active investment of belief in the theatre of tragedy gave rise to a means by which the audience could purge themselves of the affects of pity and fear and thereby experience a genuine psychological relief which he called 'catharsis'. It was from these ideas concocted to describe the psychological effect of theatre that Freud drew the term 'cathartic method' which he used to describe his 'talking cure', which I shall describe in the following chapter. With particular reference to Sophocles' play *Oedipus Rex*, Aristotle said that the cathartic effect could only be understood if one imagined that every person carries a little bit of Oedipus inside himself. It was from this play and this idea that Freud drew the notion of the 'Oedipus complex'.[29]

Unlike the original lone player's impromptu renditions, the performances of the great tragedies such as *Oedipus Rex* did not take place anywhere at any time, but were presented as an integral part of huge regular public celebrations. At these public events the caskets of wine from the latest grape crop, which had been fermenting undisturbed for some months, were brought out into the light of day and a festival of drinking and worship, of dancing and abandonment was played out under the Mediterranean sun in honour and worship of the god Dionysus, the patron of wine and of theatre. The celebration of this god's powers was hereby engendered in revelries and parades during which the testing of the new season's wine would form the aperitif to a festival of performances for which playwrights and actors spent a long time preparing, writing and rehearsing new plays based on old myths. These plays were performed by a small group of actors who portrayed the main characters and by a group of performers known as the chorus, who sang, yelled, spoke and chanted in a powerful and exuberant mixture of prayer and narration, serving to work the actors and the audience into a climactic state.

Many of the texts from these plays still exist, as do many vivid descriptions of the productions recorded by the ancient philosophers, historians and politicians who attended them. From these extant writings we know that the actors and chorus recited their dialogue not in a fashion analogous with daily speech, but with special intonations which were accentuated by the music of a lyre or an aulos, a flute-like instrument. The bodily movements used by the performers were also stylised, forming a choreographed gestural dance which contributed to the overall arousing effect upon the audience. To the modern ear this acoustic aspect of Greek theatre would probably sound chaotic and lacking in all melody. There was no concept of musical harmony and the utterances of the voice, pipes and strings served the purpose, not only of articulating the formal discursive logic of a musical composition, but of enhancing the text with exhilarating emotive sounds.

The theatre and the opera, as we know it in the West, originated with these masked performances of ancient Greece. The characters which populated these dramas were not everyday personalities, but giant figures whose roles embodied the universal elements and primal passions of the human condition. The most important tool which the actors and chorus used to convey these feelings and stir the passions of an audience was the human voice, which we may imagine to have been pushed to the very limits of its expressivity. The use of voice and singing in these performances in no way compares with the clear diction and polite elocution to which audiences have become accustomed in the modern theatre, or to the specialised refinement of the operatic voice. W. B. Stanford, one of the most articulate and enlightening Greek scholars, describes how in Greek drama

> every play has its nexus of inarticulate sounds of grief or fear or joy or triumph and other emotions – sobs, groans, screams, gasps, laughs and ululations . . . the most frequent and most expressive noises of Greek tragedy are articulate though not quite verbal . . . they are the most primitive of all human sounds, more like animal cries than speech. They are of supreme importance for the emotional effects of Greek tragedy, setting up physical and emotional vibrations that no articulate words could. Yet editors often ignore them and translators are commonly satisfied with a perfunctory 'oh', 'ah', or 'alas'.[30]

The use of the voice in Greek theatre was clearly acrobatic and extensive, serving to communicate emotions of extreme magnitude, the effect of which was to arouse the passions of the audience to a high degree of excitation in order that they may experience a catharsis. Indeed the term 'audience' comes from *audio*, meaning 'to hear'.

In ancient Greece, then, theatre was closely related to therapy by way of its cathartic effect which relied upon an extensive use of vocal communication, both discursive and non-discursive. Furthermore, in Greek culture generally there was far less separation between the performing arts and the medical sciences than existed subsequently in the development of European thought. To the Greeks, the art of theatre was by its very nature medicinal, and they held music in the same regard.

In Greek mythology, music and medicine were literally sister and brother. The Muses were divine characters who invented music and reigned over its human use, and Aesculapius was the inventor of medicine and able even to raise people from the dead. Both the Muses and Aesculapius were fathered by Apollo and their powers were equally revered as being capable of affecting the health of mortals. Apollo was thus regarded as the father of medicine and of music, and it was another of Apollo's sons, Orpheus, who came to be regarded as the keeper of the mysteries of song and its healing powers.[31]

In the myth of Orpheus the underworld of Hades represents the deep, dark waters of our unconscious. Just as Orpheus, in his attempt to retrieve his beloved Eurydice, charms the ferocious Cerberus, assuages the ferryman and tames with his song the raging furore that he finds there, so voice and song can be a means to contact, console and cure the ferocious dark parts of our unconscious.

Singing has always been a means to contact the depths of the soul. The song is the home of our memories, for songs more than anything become associated with certain events. Even those suffering from advanced senile dementia, normally completely indifferent to their surroundings, will light up a little when they hear a song from the era of their youth. The song is our reminiscence and the voice leaves an indelible echo in the corridors of the soul. We seek the world in a song and it can change our mood in a moment; the wrong song at the wrong time can bring us from laughter to tears.

To the ancient Greeks the fundamental principles of music – rhythm, melody and proportion of high and low, soft and loud – all these had their equivalent in the human soul or psyche. The right music could therefore bring the soul into order and integration while the wrong sounds could throw the whole person into confusion, madness and disarray. It is told that Pythagoras, a genius of mathematics and the first to explain the role of time in music, once witnessed an event that verified this effect of music upon the soul. While sitting at his window working on some calculations, Pythagoras saw a Sicilian youth who was so enraged by the fact that his mistress was entertaining another lover that he intended to burn her house down. His anger and intent were further fuelled by the playing of a nearby flute which seemed to intensify his frenzy by way of its melody and key. When, however, Pythagoras ordered the flute player to change the music, the youth was immediately calmed and returned home cured of his fit.

Later, in Roman times, Cicero proclaimed that every emotion had a corresponding vocal sound and he compared the tones of the voice to the strings of the lyre, both of which he believed could be turned to represent perfectly all the changes in human mood and temperament. Later still, during the Renaissance, the notion of a psychology of the voice was further developed into principles for the composition of vocal music. Renaissance composers took the four elements of earth, water, air and fire, originally depicted by the Greek philosopher Hippocrates, and equated them with different vocal tones. Earth was bass, water was tenor, air was alto and fire was soprano. Similarly, each of the Hippocratic elements was thought to correspond to four humours in the body – blood, phlegm, yellow bile and black bile – the balance between which was crucial for the healthy functioning of the body. Vocal music was composed in such a way as to create a harmonious and proportionate combination of the four vocal registers and so induce an analogous equilibrium in the corresponding humours of the body. Because the mental health of the psyche was thought to depend upon the balance of the bodily humours, vocal music was believed to play a role in preserving the peace and congruence of the soul and in bringing physical and psychic elements into a state of mutual stability. But by the end of the Renaissance all signs of an accepted functional relationship between music and medicine had been laid to rest. Hence the practice of medicine in ancient Greece, and its resurgence in Renaissance culture, still represents the last true homage to the curative power of the voice in the West.

We know that the Greeks did not create combinations of voice and instruments which a modern ear would describe as 'in concord'. Although such combinations as we might call harmonious may have occurred spontaneously in the course of playing, it would not have been possible to plan them or fix them from one performance to the next because the system of writing music down was not sophisticated enough. The Greeks simply used the letters of their own alphabet to indicate notes on their scale, with some letters turned around to denote changes in the quality of the sound. When the Romans infiltrated and overpowered Greek culture, they simply exchanged the signs of Greek notation for their own alphabet but did not significantly extend the Greek system.

The Romans inherited from the Greeks the use of music and drama as a form of mass public entertainment, which assumed an important role in pre-Christian Roman life. However, with the coming of Christianity, these great pagan tales of raging gods and supreme heroes, whose deeds were emulated in action with mask and song to the awe and wonder of the adoring masses, disappeared. Worship and admiration for the ways of the deity took on a more solemn form.

An important part of the solemnity which is associated with early Christian worship is the way in which holy Scripture was uttered in such sorrowful and non-elaborate tones by Church leaders and worshippers alike. This was a far cry from the spectacular vocal renditions which the Greeks gave to their religious stories and which inspired the theatre of Greek and Roman culture.

It was the pre-Christian Romans who invented the organ, the first of which was built around 200 BC. This was a contraption about 10 ft high and 4.5 ft wide, operated by means of a weight of water; later models were air-blown by hand. Although the Christian Church did not choose to inherit the revelries and masked dramas from its pre-Christian antecedents, it did retain the organ, and by about AD 350 the first schools were established in Europe to train singers to give voice to the words of God in concordance with the authoritative solemnity of the organ. By this time the organs had become gigantic affairs and required two or three players, called 'organ beaters', to thump the huge keys with gloved hands while a group of 'blowers' pumped the bellows.

As a result of these musical experiments with voice and organ, which were supported by no system of notation capable of restraining the impromptu expression of feeling, the once-solemn chants became more elaborate and often quite vigorous and the Church authorities believed this to be incompatible with the reverence due to God. As a result, the Church made precise rules dictating the kinds of vocal sounds and combinations thereof which could and could not be used. The most famous of such rulings is that of Pope Gregory the Great (540–604), whose strict stipulations led to the creation of the Gregorian chant, still in use.

During the so-called Dark Ages which followed the collapse of the Roman Empire in Western Europe during the sixth century, lone players continued to roam the lands singing and telling their own stories with the aid of music. These singing tale-tellers were to become a significant part of European song culture, the most well known of which are perhaps the troubadours, singing poets who flourished in Southern France throughout the twelfth, thirteenth and fourteenth centuries and whose wandering lives full of passion and adventure made them the typical romantic figures of their age. But the troubadours are only one example of the many kinds of singers and poets who wandered alone and in groups throughout Europe, combining story, text and music to entertain in the courts, in the taverns and on the streets.

In ancient Greece celebration was intimately connected with the artistic and spiritual adoration of the gods; for example, wine, hymns, prayer, theatre, song and dance were all part of the worship of Dionysus. However, during the Dark Ages the use of the voice became divided into two: the uninitiated masses indulged in rambling songs of love, lust and wild adventure while the Church continued to develop its solemn and structured chants which told of Christ and the Apostles.

Around the sixth century AD the crude system of alphabetical notation which had originated with the Greeks was superseded in the Roman world by a system of points, hooks, curves and lines placed above the words to be sung. These signs, called 'neumes', became formalised so that to a trained singer each had its own meaning. By this means it was possible to recall melodies already committed to memory, but it still did not enable previously unseen songs to be learnt, as the notation did not indicate pitch. It was not until around the end of the ninth and beginning of the tenth century that the pitch of musical notes began to be fixed by notation.

The first step towards this was attained when a person whose name and origin remain unidentified drew a red line horizontally across the page. Any sign placed on this line indicated the note F, while a sign placed immediately above or below it indicated G and E respectively. Soon another line was added, in yellow, and any note placed on this line indicated C, while D and B were notated by signs above and below it respectively. However, there was still a long way to go before the God-fearing men of the cloth were satisfied that the resulting sound was in tune with their Master's wishes, and in the year 1020 a learned Benedictine monk called Guido of Arezzo wrote: 'In the church service it often sounds not as if we were praising God but rather as if we were engaging in quarrelling amongst ourselves.'[32]

Guido set out to remedy this lack of harmony among worshipping vocalists. First, he added two black lines to the existing red and yellow ones and these indicated the exact notes which the performers were to sing in more than one octave. Second, to help his pupils' memories, he taught them to remember certain syllables from a Latin hymn, each line of which began on an ascending degree of the scale C, D, E, F, A:

> UT queant laxis
> REsonare fibris
> MIra gestorum
> FAmuli tuorum
> SOLve polluti
> LAbi reatum

Ut has since been changed to doh, and this gives rise to the well-known tonic scale still in use: doh-ray-me-fah-soh-la-te-doh. Guido's success in creating the four-line stave and fixing a named scale of notes has led him to be known as the father of music as we now know it.

At around the ninth century the Christian Church began to introduce music and drama into its services, in which Easter Passions and Christmas Nativities that contained spoken text and sung choruses became a part of Christian ceremony throughout Europe. As with the Greek plays, these ecclesiastical performances served the spiritual function of worship. However, these church dramas were very different from their Greek antecedents. There were no masks, no roaring lions or incestuous sons and, most significantly, none of the animal cries and primitive sobs, groans, screams, gasps, laughs and ululations which had emanated from the stage upon which Greek tragedy had been performed. Religious culture and popular culture had been severed from each other.

The formal structuring of music, which was developed primarily at the hands of the Church, began to make demands upon vocalisation which altered the way the voice was used. In Greek tragedy, although the vocal utterances of performers were organised by rhythm, pronunciation and prosodic stress, such formal ingredients were born out of the desire to enhance the affective aspects inherent in the words of the myth, play or narrative. In Christian service, however, the voice now served to articulate the written score which was attached to the words arbitrarily and in a manner completely dislocated from the emotive impulse generated by the utterance of the word.

However, in Italy towards the end of the sixteenth century there lived an influential man of music, Giovanni de' Bardi, the Count of Vernio, who invited to his house the most celebrated and learned men of music and letters, where they gathered to form a society of fellows whose shared aim was to rediscover the way in which the ancient Greeks had used voice, movement, music and drama in their theatre.

It was from the meetings of this exclusive musical society – the *Camerata*

– which took place over a period of thirty years in sixteenth and seventeenth-century Florence, that opera as people know it today was born. When Count Bardi moved to Rome in 1592, the meeting place of the *Camerata* changed to the house of the younger Jacopo Corsi (1561–1604), who kept his house open like a public academy for all those interested in the liberal arts. It was here in 1598 that what is considered to be the first true opera was performed.

The opera was called *Dafne*, with music composed by Jacopo Peri (1561–1633) and the text or libretto by the poet Ottavio Rinuccini. We know that it told the story of a Greek myth in which the god Apollo slays the great Pythian dragon, but unfortunately only a few segments of this score remain. The manuscript of Peri's second opera, however, has survived in full and tells the myth of Orpheus and of his beloved Eurydice, after whom the opera is named.

Peri was convinced that the ancient Greeks had used a form of vocal expression more musical than that of ordinary speech but less melodious than song to produce an 'intermediate form'. He too wanted to 'imitate speech in song' and use 'elegances and graces that cannot be notated', and in his preface to *Eurydice* he states that he was aiming for something between 'the slow and suspended movements of song and the swift and rapid movements of speech'.[33]

But, alas, those members of the *Camerata* who sought to achieve a renaissance of the primal vocal expression which they believed to have been at the heart of ancient Greek performance had, by their own admission, failed. Many of the forthcoming composers of Italy sought to make music itself the carrier of emotion and not merely an accompaniment to heighten the emotive vocal power of the text. The new opera-makers were seeking to combine musical instruments and voices in a total harmony and therefore a fresh demand was placed upon the performer, one that would make him a singer first and a vehicle for the expression of emotion and experience second.

These new demands required a new kind of teaching that would train singers to retain some of the ability to communicate a primacy of emotional experience while at the same time remaining formally responsive to the specifically notated music which brought instrumentalists and vocalists together into a harmonious whole.

Among the members of the *Camerata* was the great vocal soloist Giulio Caccini (c.1545–1618), who became the academy's authority on solo-singing technique. Caccini was also inspired by his belief that the ancient Greeks had possessed a natural ability to express human emotions through the voice and he combined this with his development of fixed notated musical composition. The aim of his teaching was to nurture singers to bring full expression to the portrayal of human emotions while retaining musical harmony with the supporting instruments. It was in response to this need that the school of composers and singers known as 'bel canto' arose.

Bel canto is an Italian term which literally means 'beautiful song'. Today the term is often employed very loosely without attention to its historical meaning. Singing teachers use bel canto to depict 'good breath control', a 'beautiful timbre' or 'an eloquence of diction' in singing long phrases. The only common feature in the grand variety of idiosyncratic definitions seems to be a certain relationship with beauty: a bel canto voice is a 'beautiful voice'. In fact bel canto was the particular art of singing and vocal training which flourished in Italy throughout the seventeenth and eighteenth centuries in response to the need for emotional authenticity combined with musical precision and virtuosity. The special art of the bel canto singers consisted in their ability to communicate a genuine expression of human emotion by singing precisely notated musical phrases with a wide range of qualities or timbres, spanning a vocal range of three octaves without losing refinement or eloquence of verbal diction.

Lucie Manen in her book on the history and practice of this art makes the crucial point that the extensive range of timbres possessed by the bel canto singers was not a cosmetic trick of virtuosity to make the series of emotions depicted in opera more interesting. Rather, the range of timbres was born out of the spectrum of human emotions: 'For it is only from the primeval sounds and exclamations, with which men express their inner feelings and reactions to impressions from the world around them – joy, surprise, grief, passion, annoyance, anger, hatred, etc. – that the colourful timbres of Bel Canto can emanate.'[34]

But the emphasis on flexibility of vocal characteristics or timbres was not to last long in the development of opera, because composers began to demand singers specialising in one particular quality of sound. Operas were written which demanded one voice to be high as a nightingale and another low as a bear, both following precise musical phrases; and from this development came operatic specialisations that included the familiar soprano, mezzo, contralto, tenor, baritone and bass.

While the bel canto singers were intent on extending the different emotive qualities and phonic images of each note, later singers have sought to perfect a single quality of voice and have been loath to try and extend its range. Furthermore, the increasing complexity of musical composition has led to a process of training operatic singers which has become more influenced by the technical demands of the music and less connected with the primal and fundamental role of the voice as the expression of emotion and experience. There are of course some exceptions to the composer's demand for strict adherence to the score and concentration on the production of a beautiful sound, such as Verdi's instruction that, during the famous madness scene in his opera *Macbeth*, the singer playing Lady Macbeth should not sing but 'gasp, whisper and sob'. But these remain exceptions buried amid an array of rules.

In Western European history the more the expressive function of the human voice became an adjunct of music and the more in turn music became subject to the rules of aesthetics, the demands of the Church and the craving for all things bright and beautiful, so the more the voice lost its fundamental capacity to give expression to the full range of psychological experience that it had once possessed when performing upon the great Greek stage. As a result, the voice became stripped of its fundamental therapeutic value. In addition, the more medicine was subsumed into the mechanistic framework of so-called scientific progress, the more music became dissociated from curative and remedial processes and relegated to the pleasurable arts. Consequently the voice ceased to be a healer and instead became an entertaining purveyor of beauty.

Yet both music and song have been used as a healing agent by different cultures across the world since the earliest times; and while music and song may have been disavowed of their curative function in the West, this is fortunately not the case the world over.

## Rituals of Vocal Healing Beyond the Bounds of Europe

In many indigenous cultures that have been relatively untouched by the ways of Western medicine, the use of vocal sounds to heal the sick is often the closely guarded practice of a select member of the community – a medicine man, a magician, a sorcerer, a witch-doctor or a shaman.

Shamanism is still practised in widely different parts of the world, including Siberia and Central Asia,[35] the Malay peninsula,[36] Alaska[37] and Central America.[38] Despite the broad geographical area over which such activities are distributed, there are none the less significant similarities between the various healing rituals, and one element that they all have in common is the crucial role of the human voice in the process of healing.

In cultures where the medicinal services of shamans or other chosen individuals have been or still are employed, the process of healing is intimately connected with a belief in a spiritual cause for physical illness, and the treatment issued by the healer is aimed not at allaying the physical symptom but at ridding the body and soul of the spirits which are thought to be its cause. This process is born of a mutual belief, held by both healer and patient, in the spiritual and emotional genesis of physical disease.

Central to the act of spiritual exorcism by which the shaman flushes from the sick the causative evil is the process of catharsis. The patient discharges pestilent and violating spirits and emotions and is thereby purified; and these bottled-up fragments of emotion often emerge in the form of terrifying vocal noises which the patient emits while in a state of semi-consciousness. A vestige of this process can be perceived in the glossolalia or 'speaking in tongues' which occurs among certain evangelical and pentecostal Christian sects.

This spiritual approach to curing disease brings a religious dimension to the healing process, in which the healer is not the objective and detached representative of science, but an active participant in the liaison between the earthly life of the patient and the spiritual world. The shaman must sometimes take the evil spirits from the patient into his own body and later coax them out through a self-exorcism. The shaman dances deliriously, uttering piercing cries or chanting a maniacal and indecipherable spirit language. Often such rituals are aided by an onlooking audience who enforce the atmosphere of climatic purgation by chanting, yelling, sobbing and screaming.

But not all shamanic healing rituals are non-verbal. K. Rasmussan[39] provides a report of a case that occurred in the 1940s among the Eskimos and which consisted of a process of verbal confession very similar to Freud's talking cure, which we shall look at in the next chapter. A woman had become physically ill but told the shaman that she believed her sickness was due to a failure to 'fulfil her duties' and a continual participation in 'bad deeds'. The shaman asked her to confess these deeds, and after each admission he asked for yet another until eventually her confession was considered complete. She then recovered.

Another case of the curative power of shamanic confession is reported in an anthropologist's observations made in 1946 while visiting the Guatemalan Indians.[40] The patient was a 63-year-old woman who had become consumed, first by anxiety, then by depression and as a result had withdrawn from all social contact. She also suffered from diarrhoea, stomach pains and loss of appetite. The shaman began his healing process by confirming local suspicion that she was suffering from 'magical fright', after which he urged the woman to confess. The woman subsequently gave vent to a flood of emotion and told the shaman her life story, culminating in a description of a recent experience which had caused her emotional pain and physical suffering. After this intimate confiding, the patient was noticeably more relaxed and the shaman made an appointment to see her again in four days. He said that he knew what had caused her physical affliction and promised that at the arranged appointment he would be able to cure her.

At the healing ceremony he led a small group of people through darkness to the spot where he believed the event which precipitated the illness had occurred. Here he addressed the spirits, after which he walked with the patient into a field, shared with her a drink of curative liquid and then spewed it all over her naked body and face. Next he massaged her naked body with eggs and sent her to bed where she was told to rest underneath blankets. By the following day the woman had recovered.

Here, as in the previous case, one of the key elements is the opportunity for cathartic confession, which plays a part in many magical healing processes among indigenous cultures. For example, several different American Indian tribal healing ceremonies share the therapeutic strategy of talking about guilt and worries to a willing listener.[41] The culture of the American

Indians also has a long history of using voice and song as an integral part of their healing rituals. In the many of the northern tribes, for example, part of the cure for illness involves finding the person who knows the right song appropriate to a particular disease. These medicine songs come to certain 'chosen ones' in special prophetic dreams which warn of the havoc that will be wreaked by the arrival of a particular disease. Often the singing of these songs is accompanied by the ritual chanting of the whole family to the rhythmic beat of a rattle held by the medicine man.[42] Only by guarding the memory of the song can the dreamer protect the tribe from impending destruction, and these songs are therefore preserved by being passed down orally through the generations.

Anthropologists report the medicinal use of music, song and voice in many other indigenous peoples, including the Aborigines of Australia, the tribes of Papua New Guinea and the nomadic peoples of the Sahara and the Sudan.[43] In all of these instances the human voice plays a central role in giving direct expression to the very depths of the soul through an unbridled utterance of chant, scream, laugh, yell and complex emotional cacophony.

# The Ancient Foundations of Modern Therapy

My purpose in describing these rituals of vocal healing and mass catharsis among the ancient Greeks and non-Western indigenous peoples is to show how the principles underlying these practices are those which provided the bedrock upon which modern psychotherapy is founded.

We speak of therapy very easily these days and the differing approaches to psychological healing are multitudinous. This is a time of boom for mental medicine. However, it is essential for any understanding of the human voice and its therapeutic potential that we trace the development of the notion of psychotherapy back to its genesis in the early work of Sigmund Freud and C. G. Jung, while in turn remembering that the principles they propounded can be traced further to ancient and universal practices.

# CHAPTER TWO

# Psychotherapy and the Medicinal Wonder of Words

## Sigmund Freud and the 'Talking Cure'

The most common complaint among Freud's early patients in the late nineteenth century consisted of bodily pains for which there appeared to be no physiological explanation. These included headaches, paralysed limbs, stomach upsets, respiratory problems and disturbances of speech, sight and hearing. Freud proposed to have discovered that the cause of these 'phantom diseases' usually consisted of a psychological trauma which the patient had experienced in the past, in some cases many years prior to the occurrence of the physical problem which had brought the patient to the doctor. Indeed, quite frequently it was a distressing childhood event, the emotional effects of which continued to disturb the patient long after it had apparently been forgotten.

Freud referred to these patients as 'hysterics': those in whom the emotional reaction or affect provoked by a specific psychological trauma had been converted into a physical symptom which persisted for many years afterwards. The hysteric seemed genuinely unable to recollect the precipitating event and had no idea of the causal connection between it and the bodily dysfunction.

Freud identified two distinct processes by which psychological trauma became converted into physical symptoms. The first process occurred when a person experienced a particular mental trauma while suffering from a genuine physiological disease. Although the person recovered from the disease, the physical symptoms recurred whenever he or she was reminded of the traumatic event which originally accompanied it. Let us take, for example, someone suffering from the severe stomach pains caused by appendicitis who simultaneously suffers the trauma of losing a close relative, which naturally arouses a strong affect of grief. If this person has what Freud called a hysterical disposition, he or she may continue to experience the stomach pains whenever grief is aroused by new situations involving a bereavement, even long after the appendix has been removed. In such an example, a physical symptom originally generated by organic causes is later revived as an expression of a psychological affect, simply because by chance they originally occurred simultaneously.

The second process involved the patient's unwitting translation of a verbal phrase from its metaphorical into its literal meaning. For example, a traumatic event which morally disgusts and abhors the patient may pre-

49

cipitate sporadic fits of vomiting, the linguistic term 'to be sick' being translated from its metaphorical description of psychological disgust into the literal experience of vomiting. A man who is being continually pressurised by his colleague to agree to a transaction that he feels is dubious may begin to suffer from pins and needles in his arm, because his colleague is metaphorically 'twisting his arm' over the deal. A 'slap in the face' describes both a severe facial neuralgia and the effect of a swiping insult; 'feeling choked' describes both respiratory constriction about the larynx and the affect of deep sadness. By converting such linguistic metaphors into a literal somatic experience, the hysteric could genuinely feel severe back pain when people 'got his back up', experience agonising shooting pains in the arm when colleagues 'twisted his arm' over an issue at work, or be caused to vomit when morally disgusted. Hysterics were therefore those people who possessed a particular susceptibility to the power of suggestion or imagination.

Through careful analysis of the patient's speech, Freud noticed that many linguistic phrases which patients used to describe physical symptoms at the same time denoted emotional responses; this provided the key to the precipitating trauma.

Freud believed that in both processes the persistence of the bodily symptom was caused by the patient's insufficient active emotional reaction to the original event or scene, which had consequently caused the emotions to become 'strangulated' or 'bottled up'. He compared the psyche to an electrical system which becomes charged with a certain amount of energy when it is affected by an event. For example, a patient who is insulted becomes excited in such a way as to increase the amount of energy in the nervous system. In healthy situations this increase in energy is immediately expended by the individual's verbal or physical response, such as a bout of abusive swearing or a histrionic waving of fists. Freud described such active responses as 'motor activity' because they are stimulated by the neurological impulses of the motor neurons which stem from the central nervous system; the function of such activity is to bring the energy level of the psyche back to a state of balance or neutrality. If, however, for reasons of social prohibition or personal inhibition, the individual 'swallows' the insult, refrains from responding and retains the heightened level of energy, it becomes bottled up and seeks expression by converging upon a weak spot localised in a part of the body. Freud termed the ideal expenditure of increased energy in response to the original event 'abreaction' and suggested that the physical symptoms of hysteria were the result of the emotional affect having been insufficiently abreacted.

Freud proposed to have discovered a method of curing the somatic disease by assisting the patient to remember the original upsetting experience which had accompanied the genesis of the physical symptom. This involved a thorough psycho-archaeological excavation of the patient's past in search of a single precipitating trauma which, when located, caused the symptom to vanish for ever.

However, the somatic cure was not achieved through recollection without affect; the patient had to revive and re-enact the same intensity of emotional response to the memory of the event as was evoked by its original occurrence. The principles of this method are contained in Freud's famous words:

> For we found, to our great surprise at first, that *each individual hysterical symptom immediately and permanently disappeared when we had succeeded in bringing clearly to light the memory of the event by which it was provoked and in arousing its accompanying affect, and when the patient had described that event in the greatest possible detail and had put the affect into words.* Recollection without affect almost invariably produces no result. The psychical process which originally took place must be repeated as vividly as possible.[1]

In encouraging the patients not only to 're-member' the past verbally – that is, to put back together the original event – but also to imbue the text of this memory with the full emotional excitation which had been denied at the time of its first occurrence, Freud gave the patient a second chance to 'complete his reaction'[2] and in so doing release both the stored affect and the somatic symptom which had hitherto served to contain it. Freud described this process of giving vent to stored-up feeling as 'catharsis', a word which, as we have seen, he took from the effect achieved by ancient Greek theatre.

Thus Freud proposed that the hysterical phenomenon 'comes to an end as soon as the patient has spoken about it'.[3] Even if the original abreaction would have normally involved a muscular or physical reaction – such as a punch or other display of aggression – the full abreaction could be achieved the second time round through words alone; so, for Freud, 'words are substitutes for deeds'.[4]

However, because the verbal memory of the precipitating trauma had to be experienced in full emotional depth, the patient was encouraged not to remember in a cool, detached and reflective way, but to speak as though he or she were experiencing it all over again. If the patient simply spoke the words which described the remembered event with no emotional recollection, the cure did not work. It was, therefore, not the words alone that performed the cure, but the voice which, through its tonal quality, expressed all the emotions associated with the memory, ranging from bitter grief and rage to intimidated fear.

We experience this fundamental tenet of psychoanalysis every time we repeat to ourselves the things we wished we had said in an argument. While involved in a quarrel with someone, we often remain calm and objective, asserting only a fraction of the aggression we feel. Then later, when we are alone, we rant and rave to ourselves as though we were back again at the scene, and afterwards we feel relieved. In such a situation, just as in Freud's consulting room, it is not the words themselves that become a substitute for deeds, but the voice which utters them in a tone and timbre equivalent to the emotional intensity of the affect.

In many cases of abreaction the tone and timbre of the voice is actually more important than the words, as for example when bottled-up tension and frustrations are released through yelling, screaming, laughing or crying. Freud referred to such non-verbal processes as providing an important opportunity for 'letting off steam'. But, for him, non-verbal sound-making was not sufficient to facilitate genuine and complete cathartic abreaction; words were essential to remembering and describing the specific historical event which had caused the physical problem.

## The Language of Dreams

Freud's preoccupation with language and the significance of words, which had originated in his analysis of psychosomatic disorders, continued to colour his beliefs during his subsequent work regarding the nature of dreams.

In 1900 he published *The Interpretation of Dreams*, rescuing the dream from the clutches of superstitious and amateur dabbling and bringing to it a new respectability. For Freud realised that studying dreams presented a rare opportunity to perceive the elements of a person's unconscious unrestrained by the censoring devices of consciousness. In fact, he applied the same framework of linguistic analysis to dreams as he had done to the hysterical symptoms which resulted from converting semantic phrases from their metaphorical to their literal meaning. Freud said that, after his work on hysterical symptoms, 'it was then only a short step to treating the dream itself as a symptom and to applying to dreams the method of interpretation that had been worked out for symptoms'.[5]

According to Freud, thought is a linguistic activity reliant upon words, while the dream is primarily concerned with 'representability in visual images';[6] thus he proposed that the process of dreaming consists of the 'transformation of thoughts into pictures'.[7] This process of transformation from thoughts, which operate through language, to dream images, which operate through pictures, was described by Freud as a form of 'displacement': 'The direction taken by the displacement usually results in a colourless and abstract expression in the dream-thought, being exchanged for a pictorial and concrete one.'[8]

The interpretation of dreams in the psychoanalytic consultation therefore involved a process of translation which sought to decode the visual dream image by reconverting it back into the linguistic thought which had originally created it. Consequently the analysis of the pictorial dream image divulged by the patient was much less important than the analysis of the words with which the patient described it. For example, within Freud's framework of analysis, the dream image of a tennis racket may imply a

patient's preoccupation with a 'shady deal', an important financial transaction being processed at work which makes the patient feel uneasy and
suspicious. The analysis of the dream involves translating the pictorial
image of a racket into a linguistic code, which in turn points to its meaning.
In the psychoanalytic consultation the focus of the interpretation centres
on the word 'racket' as a signifier for immoral transactions. The dream has
transformed this into its other meaning of 'an object for sport' in order to
give it visual representation.

This interpretative decoding and unravelling of linguistic transformations, or displacements, also demanded that attention be paid to the multiplicity of simultaneous potential meanings contained within a single linguistic phrase; for many single words signify a number of different things.
A racket, for example, may also signify 'a terrible noise' and could therefore lead the psychoanalytic process to an entirely different conclusion regarding the patient's mental preoccupations. Faced with this multiplicity,
Freud proposed that the 'correct interpretation can only be arrived at on
each occasion from the context'[9] and he turned his attention to the
patient's specific personal history, letting it determine the personal associations evoked by certain words.

In the same way that Freud had sought the genesis of hysterical symptoms in the autobiographical history of the individual patient, so too the
contents of dreams were perceived as an expression of the patient's unique
and idiosyncratic experience of the world. Thus Freud maintained that the
significance of dream images depended upon the varying personal circumstances which had informed each patient's psychological disposition. In
other words, two patients may have exactly the same dream, but the significance of the images contained therein will be entirely different as a result of
differing life-experiences. For Freud, therefore, dreams were ultimately
composed of the residue of life's events, and he further proposed that they
presented to the dreamer the fulfilment of wishes which had not been
achieved during waking hours. So the appearance of a tennis racket in another person's dream may signify that the patient is preoccupied with the
unbearable noise or racket generated by a local nightclub which has recently opened near his or her home. Winning the game of tennis and hurl-
ing the racket away in triumphant celebration would, for Freud, be the fulfilment of the wish to beat or defeat the nightclub owner and get rid of the
noise coming from the discothèque.

However, Freud's theory regarding the individual determination of
dreams was called into question when he discovered that the meaning of
some dreams involved the use of linguistic metaphors of which the patient
could not possible have had knowledge in waking life. Most people would
know the various definitions of the word 'racket', but often Freud believed
that he had discovered images which originated in word-meanings which
could not possibly be known to the patient; and on occasions this involved
a translation from a foreign language which the patient could not speak.

For example, he pointed out that 'the commonest expression in German for male sexual activity is "to bird"' and that 'the male organ is actually called "the bird" in Italian'. Freud thus proposed that when people dream of being able to fly it is 'only a disguise for another wish' which is 'nothing else than a longing to be capable of sexual performance'.[10] Freud further added the fact that small children are told that babies are delivered by a stork and that the ancients portrayed the phallus with wings, as further evidence to connect the dream image of a bird with sex. He believed that it was irrelevant whether or not the dreamer was aware of these word-meanings or ideas in waking life and that the significance of the bird was trans-cultural, independent of language or tradition.

## Sex with Everything

Despite his belief that personal circumstances were mostly responsible for shaping mental outlook, Freud could not avoid postulating that each individual inherits a certain body of psychological information, a process known as 'phylogenesis'. This led him to propose that humankind possesses what he called an 'archaic heritage':

> Dreams make an unrestricted use of linguistic symbols, the meaning of which is for the most part unknown to the dreamer . . . They probably originate from the earlier phases in the development of speech . . . Furthermore, dreams bring to light material which cannot have originated either from the dreamer's adult life or from his forgotten childhood. We are obliged to regard it as part of the *archaic heritage* which a child brings with him into the world, before any experience of his own, influenced by the experiences of his ancestors. We find the counterpart of his phylogenetic material in the earliest human legends and in surviving customs. Thus dreams constitute a source of human pre-history which is not to be despised.[11]

However, Freud remained uncomfortable with the concept of an archaic heritage: it threatened his stringent individualistic stance and it encouraged psychoanalysts to entertain immeasurable hypotheses regarding inherited patterns, which Freud was keen to avoid.

In order to link together the notion of an undeniable inherited psychological predisposition on the one hand and the belief in the primary importance of personal context on the other, Freud proposed that a universality of dream images occurred only within the field of sexuality. In seeking to validate this hypothesis, Freud traced the significance of trans-personal dream images to a strictly sexual origin, even to the point of considering that all words may have their genesis in a sexual signification. Indeed, in a footnote which he added to his essay 'The Dream Work' in 1925, Freud supports the theory of Hans Sperber, who was of the opinion that originally all words 'referred to sexual things but afterwards lost their sexual meaning through being applied to other things and activities which were compared with the sexual ones'.[12] Consequently Freud went to great lengths to argue that just about every dream image has a sexual origin and that, more often than not, the words used to describe it have a sexual connotation also. The following passage is an enlightening example of Freud's commitment to such an idea:

> A little time ago I heard that a psychologist whose views are some-what different from ours had remarked to one of us that, when all was said and done, we did undoubtedly exaggerate the hidden sexual significance of dreams: his own commonest dream was of going upstairs, and surely there could not be anything sexual in *that*. We were put on the alert by this objection, and began to turn our atten-tion to the appearance of steps, staircases and ladders in dreams, and were soon in a position to show that staircases (and analogous things) were unquestionably symbols of copulation. It is not hard to discover the basis of the comparison: we come to the top of a series of rhythmical movements and with increasing breathlessness and then, with a few leaps, we get to the bottom again. Thus the rhyth-mical pattern of copulation is reproduced in going upstairs. Nor must we omit to bring to the evidence of linguistic usage. It shows us that 'mounting' [German '*steigen*'] is used as a direct equivalent for the sexual act. We speak of a man as a '*Steiger*' [a 'mounter'] and of '*nachsteigen*' ['to run after'; literally, 'to climb after']. In French the steps on a staircase are called '*marches*' and '*un vieux marcheur*' has the same meaning as our '*ein alter Steiger*' ['an old rake'].[13]

Central to Freud's strictly sexual vision of phylogenesis was his belief in the inheritance of an innate identical disposition in every child which, for boys, consisted of an unacknowledged desire to kill the father and con-summate his love for the mother. Freud took the ancient Greek myth of Oedipus (preserved by the tragic play of Sophocles), who in ignorance kills his father and marries his mother, as a literary allegory for this internal psychological disposition which no man can escape and which every man must overcome. He termed this innate disposition the 'Oedipus complex' and maintained that it was central to the phylogenetic inheritance of in-formation from previous generations.

Freud proposed that young boys become so deeply stimulated by the nourishing and affectionate attentions of their mother that they nurture a deeply buried desire to consummate their filial love through sexual activity. They are, however, at the same time prevented from expressing or realising this by an established and externally enforced moral code which marks in-cestuous desires as taboo. Simultaneously, boys have equally ambiguous relationships with their fathers, who, although the object of their sons' love and respect, are at the same time loathed and despised by them for their un-fettered sexual intimacy with the mother. The deeply buried wish for consummation with the mother is therefore accompanied by an equally buried wish to murder the father and thereby remove the competition.

These desires, buried though they may be, none the less provoke in the child much anxiety, confusion and energetic disturbance; and in order to escape the subsequent discomfort, the desires are buried even deeper, to the point of being apparently forgotten. However, refraining from incest and patricide causes an accumulation of psychic energy. Just as Freud's early patients had suffered physical and psychological impairment as a result of retaining the affective energy associated with certain events, so too the affective energy associated with the Oedipus complex tended to manifest itself in a host of mental and physical disturbances. These included headache, backache, impotence, phobias, anxieties, obsessional repetition of certain activities, sadistic impulses and excessive orderliness and cleanliness.

In this next stage of his work, Freud became less interested in reviving the now seemingly minor idiosyncratic traumas of the individual and more in tracing a patient's psychological suffering to certain universal sexual traumas suffered by everyone. In limiting the concept of a trans-personal aspect of psychological functioning to innate patterns of psycho-sexual development, Freud retained his belief in the primary importance of personal history. The key to decoding the patient's psyche lay in discovering the unique way in which the fundamental inherited material had been manipulated by personal circumstances and the way in which the accumulated energy expressed itself.

Freud created for himself an ensnaring dichotomy between the undeniable occurrence of inherited and trans-personal elements in the psyche on the one hand, and his firm belief in the primary importance of individual experience on the other. This dichotomy was never fully resolved and it formed the single most important principle which separated the intellectual foundations of Freud's thinking from those of Jung.

At the end of his life and work Freud discouraged psychoanalysts from further considering the process of phylogenesis as a primary determining factor in the psychological constitution of the individual. He remarked: 'It is not easy for us to carry over the concepts of individual psychology into group psychology; and I do not think we gain anything by introducing the concept of a "collective unconscious".'[14] The reference to the collective unconscious was, of course, a direct attack on the work of Jung, to whom psychological inheritance was the primary determining aspect of a person's psychological make-up. For Jung the Oedipus complex was only one of many psychological structures which gain allegorical expression through the myths of ancient traditions, and many of these bear little relation to sexuality.

As a young man, Jung was deeply influenced by Freud and went on to become a devoted pupil. One of the most striking similarities between Freud's early work and the first professional investigations carried out by Jung was a mutual concern with verbal language.

# C. G. Jung and a Cacophony of Voices

In 1904 Jung conducted some remarkable experiments with words which led to the discovery of the 'complex'. Jung took a group of healthy adults and read to each one in turn a list of 400 words. After hearing each word, the subject was asked to respond with the first word which came into his or her head; this response and the time it took were recorded.

Sometimes the responses to certain words were simple and predictable, as in:

> window – pane
> house – roof
> green – grass

However, some of the responses seemed at first rather unusual, such as:

> window – cat
> house – lost
> green – fire

Closer examination of the patient's personal circumstances revealed that certain words produced seemingly odd reactions because they were connected to an emotionally charged preoccupation which the subject had, but of which he or she was unaware. Let us imagine an example. On the way home from work one night you pass a newspaper stand where you stop for a moment and purchase the *Evening News*. There is a song being played on the newspaper-seller's radio called *Green Street Green*, which you notice because you heard it earlier at lunch time. On the commuter train you browse through the paper, where your attention is caught by the story of a cat which survived a fall from a fifteen-storey window. You leave the train at the appropriate station and begin the usual five-minute walk home. As you turn the corner, to your horror the area adjacent to your house is surrounded by fire engines and a police car. Your house is ablaze. The fire officer approaches and you immediately enquire about your cat; to your relief she is still alive. You are, however, overcome with a feeling of terror at the loss of your house.

Later you take part in the word-association experiments. To the word 'window' you respond with 'cat', because you associate a window with the story in the newspaper which in turn reminds you of the fact that you nearly lost your cat in the fire. To the word 'house' you respond with 'lost', because you have indeed lost your house in the blaze. To the word 'green' you respond with 'fire', because you associate 'green' with the song you heard at the newspaper stand on the day of the fire. These seemingly odd associations are of course perfectly understandable in the light of the fact that you have had your house burnt down. Any word which relates to something you did or heard at the time of the fire is bound to remind you of losing your house and revive a feeling of terror.

A year later, after you have reclaimed your losses on your insurance and set up a new home, you feel you have recovered from the experience. However, one afternoon, while in a café with a friend, you find yourself feeling irritable, uneasy and anxious, almost terrified. You have to leave. Later on, in a new environment, you feel fine again. You did not realise it but the jukebox at the café was playing the song *Green Street Green* which brought back the memory of your fire although you were not conscious of this happening. Therefore, we might say that you have a fire complex, a network of half-forgotten mental images, which are held together by a common emotion or affect – in this case, that of the terror associated with the fire – which, though you are not aware of it, can continue to affect you for a long time.

It is in the quality of the human voice that the affect or the emotional tone of the complex is expressed rather than in the actual words that a person utters. As you sit in the café, you may say the simple words 'I would like to go to another café', but it is in what we call the 'timbre' of the voice that we recognise something serious and a little uneasy.

In each person there are many complexes which arise and dissolve as part of the natural process of shifting preoccupations. A pregnant woman will be preoccupied with preparing for her child and perhaps anxious that all will go well. We would expect her therefore to have a child complex, cemented together by an emotional tone of anxiety. She will react to things accordingly; anything that reminds her of her pregnancy will cause a slight rush of trepidation, even though she may not always be aware of the thing that stimulates it. Later, when her child is born and all her anxiety relieved, her attention may become absorbed in the bereavement for her dying father. Thus the dominating child complex subsides and is replaced by a father complex. In the former the emotional tone is anxiety, in the latter it is grief.

Of course we are all under the influence of many complexes simultaneously; it is from them that we draw our moods, our feelings and our reactions. Because the complexes are unconscious, we are often not aware where these moods come from, as in the case of the subject in the café. A bad mood gets hold of us and there is nothing we can do about it. We can no more control our moods than we can control what is on the jukebox before we go into the café.

Disturbing memories remain unconscious for good reason; they enable us to forget. Many of the complexes, arising as they do from traumatic circumstances, are too painful to be allowed to remain in our scrutiny, and a human being has a remarkable ability to put out of sight that which he or she cannot bear to see.

Complexes, then, are not a disease. They are not a sign of disorder or disturbance; on the contrary, they are the very means by which we feel. As Jung said, 'There is no one who has no complexes, just as there is no one who is without emotions.'[15] Indeed, we might say that complexes *are* emotions.

# Ego *in the* Middle

Though we have many complexes, there is one particular network of images which is, at least in the healthy individual, dominant and central. This is called the ego.

Every day you receive thousands of different stimuli from the outside world which are processed and organised by the ego. Let us take a simple example. While lying on the beach during your holiday, you can feel a cool breeze on the back of your neck, the sun on your face and the fine sand beneath you. You can hear the rushing of the waves and, in the hypnotic morass of dull voices in the background, you can pick out the sound of your children further down on the shore. At the same time you can read a book, contemplate the story and think about what you will have for lunch. Because you are on holiday, this network or complex of images is held together by the emotional theme of happiness. However, when you return from lunch later, you discover someone has stolen your bag. You become enraged and it puts you in such a bad mood that all of the previous happiness subsides. As there is nothing you can do, you carry on reading and sunbathing but you cannot get rid of the feeling of anger. However, you can remember what had happened in the story and you manage to absorb some pleasure from finishing the novel.

In this short scene you are literally bombarded with stimuli. Furthermore, you experience an extreme swing of mood from one of happiness to one of anger. How do you maintain through all of this any sense of order? How do you distinguish between the fantasy world of the novel and the reality of the beach? And how do you manage to maintain a feeling of being yourself throughout the change in mood? There must be something at work in us which not only pulls all these stimuli together, but also remains constant regardless of our moods, something that carries on telling us that we are who we are, like a reliable friend, a steadfast and trustworthy person who we know will always be there, who will always be the same and from whom we obtain a sense of constancy and stability. Without this organising centre we would not be able to put the wind and the sun and noise and the words of our book all together into a whole picture. Without this inner friend at our centre we would have no constant identity and consequently our mood changes would make us feel like a completely different person. This central control is the ego.

The ego is not one thing, but a complex of sense impressions and images, networks of ideas which we associate with the emotional tone of our own body. For Jung the ego is to a large extent a conglomeration of the information which we receive through sight, hearing, taste, touch and smell.[16] It is by way of the ego's association with the body that 'I' feel bunged up when by body is bronchially congested, or that 'I' feel aggravated when my skin is irritated. In Jung's words, 'One's own personality is therefore the firmest and strongest complex, and (good health permitting) it weathers all psychological storms ... the ego-complex, by reason of its direct connection with bodily sensations, is the most stable and the richest in associations.'[17] Although ego consciousness is affected by the state of the body, the unconscious remains free of bodily influences, otherwise a person in a wheelchair could not possibly dream of running. Furthermore, if the unconscious were brought too close to the ego, the slightest somatic illness would turn us insane.

# The Influence of the Complexes upon the Ego

The ego is influenced by the other complexes. Indeed, the complexes constantly guide us in what we do, making us leave cafés or utter seemingly inappropriate words. The complexes are unconscious and yet they actively cause us to behave in different ways. This gives them the appearance of independent beings, acting of their own accord. Hence Jung described the complexes as the 'little people', 'mini-personalities' and 'splinter psyches', for they possess a certain autonomy, or a life of their own.

This appearance of autonomy is due to the affect or emotional tone that underpins the complex. Emotion is such a strong influence compared to the reason that motivates the ego that any group of images which are united by a powerful affect will always have their way. The emotion of terror at our house being burnt down is much stronger than the reason which tells us it is all in the past. It is this very strength that causes us to bury the emotion, but it goes on living a life of its own. According to Jung:

> Researches have shown that this independence is based upon an intense emotional tone, that is upon the value of the affective elements of the complex, because the 'affect' occupies in the constitution of the psyche a very independent place, and may easily break through the self-control and self-intention of the individual ... For this property of the complex I have introduced the term *autonomy*. I conceive the complex to be a collection of imaginings, which, in consequence of this autonomy, is relatively independent of the central control of the consciousness, and at any moment liable to bend or cross the intentions of the individual.[18]

Sometimes, if there are two or more complexes at work at the same time, the ego may become confused, feeling pulled first this way and then that. In a healthy individual the ego is so strong that it can take account of these voices and have the final say. But if the ego becomes weakened, it gets lost, becoming only one voice among many. In such cases the psyche splits up into a multitude of voices all clamouring for domination. This is precisely what happens in schizophrenia, where, as Jung says, 'the psychic totality falls apart and "splits up" into complexes, and the ego-complex ceases to play the important role among these. It is just one among several complexes which are all equally important, or perhaps even more important than the ego.'[19]

Because the ego is affirmed and maintained primarily through its association with the body, such a swallowing of the ego by the other complexes gives rise to a so-called 'mind–body split', where the body becomes the seat of sensations which come from the complexes as well as from the outside world. This is also what happens in schizophrenia.

If our subject who lost his house becomes schizophrenic, his body may genuinely feel burnt when he touches a cat and the sound of the song *Green Street Green* on the radio may bring him out in a cold sweat of terror. In addition, everything green becomes unbearable, so much so that he calls anything green 'the fire' and will not touch it for fear of getting burnt. In these circumstances the voice of the fire complex is stronger than that of the ego and to the outside world these imaginations are so illogical that we cannot hope to penetrate their meaning; the green fire remains an absurdity to us. This resulting experience of the domination or submersion of the ego by one or more of the complexes is called a 'dissociation of personality'.

# The Voices of the Dead Speak Through

For his medical thesis Jung studied the extraordinary case of a girl aged fifteen and a half who acted as a medium for the voices of the dead. Jung attended her regular seances, where he witnessed these dead people expressing themselves through the girl's voice. Each time the girl evoked a different character, the quality or timbre of her voice would completely change. On occasions this involved major transformations in dialect and language, moving from German to French or Italian. Furthermore, though the girl displayed only a faint knowledge of High German in her normal life, in her trance she spoke the language faultlessly. The following passage comes from Jung's notes on her seances, in which he refers to the girl as 'SW':

> SW sat on the sofa, leant back, shut her eyes, swaying lightly and regularly. She gradually became cataleptic. The catalepsy disappeared after about two minutes, whereupon she lay there apparently sleeping quietly, muscles quite relaxed. Suddenly she began talking in a low voice: 'No, you take the red, I'll take the white. You can take the green, and you the blue. Are you ready? Let's go.' (Pause of several minutes, during which her face assumed a corpse-like pallor. Her hands felt cold and were quite bloodless.) Suddenly she called out in a loud solemn voice: 'Albert, Albert, don't you believe

your father? I tell you there are many mistakes in N's teaching. Think about it.' Pause. The pallor decreased. 'He's very frightened, he couldn't speak any more.' (These words in her usual conversational tone.) Pause. 'He will certainly think about it.' She went on speaking in the same conversational tone but in a strange idiom that sounded like French and Italian mixed, recalling now one and then the other. She spoke fluently, rapidly, and with charm. It was possible to make out a few words, but not to memorise them, because the language was so strange. From time to time certain words recurred, like *wena, wenes, wenai, wene*, etc. The absolute naturalness of the performance was amazing . . .

The next day at the same time there was another attack. After SW had dropped off, Ulrich von Gerbstein suddenly announced himself. He proved to be an amusing gossip, speaking fluent High German with a North German accent . . . His eloquence was astonishing, since SW had only a very scant knowledge of High German, whereas this new personality, who called himself Ulrich von Gerbstein, spoke an almost faultless German abounding in amiable phrases and charming compliments . . . [20]

One had the impression that a mature woman was being acted with considerable dramatic talent.[21]

Jung later understood that these characters were different aspects of the girl's own personality, ramifications of her autonomous complexes; SW was undergoing a dissociation of her personality and it was through her voice that the complexes took on an identity which could be communicated to those observing.

Later, Jung noticed how schizophrenics often talked to themselves in voices with very different qualities and he noted that in severe cases of psychotic disturbance the words of the voices degenerated into a pure muddle with no linguistic meaning:

A catatonic used to sing verbigeratively, for hours on end, a religious song with the refrain 'Hallelujah'. Then she started verbigerating 'Hallelujah' for hours, which gradually degenerated into 'Hallo', 'Oha', and finally she verbigerated 'ha-ha-ha' accompanied by convulsive laughter . . .

Sentences that were originally simple become more and more complicated with neologisms, are verbigerated loudly or softly, and gradually become more and more muddled, until finally they turn into an incomprehensible jumble that probably sounds like the stupid chattering about which so many schizophrenics complain.[22]

Jung concluded that in schizophrenia 'eventually all words can be replaced by a "hm-hm-hm"' which is 'uttered in a stereotyped manner'.[23]

What remained was the tone in both its senses: the emotional tone of the complex, which was expressed through the audible tone of the voice.

The schizophrenic does not hear the jumbled word fragments in monotone, but in pitches and qualities expressive of the affect of the complex. One is aggressive, spiteful and provocative, the other luring, sly and seductive; another is Italian, confident and full of bravado, the other English, polite and reserved. The voices of the schizophrenic each have characteristics expressed vocally through an acoustic tone, whether there are words present or not. Thus in vocal terms we might describe the concept of 'tone' as the affective nucleus of a complex as expressed through the acoustic quality of the voice.

In schizophrenia the degeneration of a 'word salad' into a purely vocal, non-verbal composition has a parallel in bodily movements. The schizophrenic patient will, in the early stages of the disorder, repeat movements which have their genesis in some domestic gestural act, such as smoking a cigarette or combing the hair. Eventually, however, these movements become more and more abstracted until it is impossible for a newcomer to recognise where they originated. Jung gives an example:

> In the year 1900 a patient used to comb his hair a few hours every day in a stereotyped manner, in order to remove the 'plaster that had been rubbed into it during the night'. In the following years the comb got further and further away from his head; in 1903 he beat and scratched his chest with it, and now he has reached the inguinal region.[24]

# Archetypes

Though the complexes are often the result of personal memories, usually of a distressing nature, there are other networks of images which have not been formulated through experience but have been inherited as so-called instincts. These may be described as patterns of behaviour, ways of reacting to things that can be detected in all human beings. Such instincts are readily observed in animals. For example, we know that hen chicks are killed and eaten by hawks but not by gulls. If you take a group of chicks and enclose them in a cage before they have had any contact with the world, then draw a stuffed gull along a wire above them, the chicks will not react. If you take a stuffed hawk and draw it backwards across the cage, they still will not react. But if you draw it forwards, the chicks begin digging and scratching, cooing and clucking in an attempt to get away. In this tiny creature there is therefore an inherited instinct of fear and flight that is attached to a certain image of form and motion.[25] If such an animal can possess such complicated hereditary information, imagine what the human being inherits!

These inherited instincts are like complexes in that they cause us to react in a certain way. They lie beneath the personal unconscious in a stratum of the psyche called the 'collective unconscious'. They are known as 'archetypes' and cause us to behave in particular ways at certain times.

Let us take an example. In every person there lies a certain appetite or instinct for childlike mischief. This appetite may be expressed as a playful desire for frivolity or, by playing devil's advocate in a conversation, it may manifest itself as an evil desire to mock or ridicule someone's success. It might cause us to contemplate stealing something for the sheer thrill of it or to torment someone by hiding their belongings. At such times we might say that the 'trickster archetype' is dominating our behaviour. However, Jung looked not only at the way these archetypes gain expression through our behaviour, but also through the images contained in dreams, fairy-tales, myths, legends, poetry and painting.

In literature we see the trickster archetype reflected in characters such as Dicken's Artful Dodger, who dances quick-footed between the crowds, picking the pockets of the local gentry; in Rumpelstiltskin, who plays a wicked trick in posing the riddle of his name; in Puck, in Shakespeare's *A Midsummer Night's Dream*, who pours love juice into the wrong eyes and causes the havoc of infatuation; in the Greek god Eros, who mischievously causes people to fall into love by infecting them with his poisonous arrows; or in the character of the Penguin in the Batman story. All cultures have their examples of the childlike mischief-maker, for the archetype of the trickster illustrates a universal and primordial instinct within us.

Another important archetype is the 'mother', the central figure to the art, culture and mythology of all peoples and always characterised by certain qualities. The mother is the great nourisher, nurturing our growth with the milk of human kindness; she provides warmth and comfort reminiscent of the womb which kept us safe from life's dangers. She is the protector and life-giver.

However, all archetypes have a positive and a negative side. Just as the trickster is not only the harmless pick-pocket, but also the wicked conniver, causing death in the trail of his traps, so too the mother has a dark side. While we would all love a taste of that ultimate dependence upon the mother – a return to the womb – so too we fear our independence being engulfed by the mother's ways, for part of the mother's dark side is her inability to let her children go. She is the suffocator, the giantess who swallows her children whole, thwarting their independence and thus their very life.

The representation of the archetypes often takes the form not of a character, but of an object or an animal. The trickster may appear as a magpie or a fox. The mother, in her bright aspect, may appear as a safe haven, a cave where the evil men on our trail will not find us, or as a cool pool of water in which we swim, kept buoyant by the nourishing minerals. In her dark aspect the mother may appear as the dragon that will swallow us up, or the great hole in the earth that we fall into just before we wake up with a jump.

All these archetypes reveal themselves in our behaviour at different times; we are like actors playing out the roles allotted to us according to their whim.

Thus Jung discovered two levels to the unconscious psyche; the first he called the 'personal unconscious' and the second the 'collective unconscious'. In the personal unconscious reside all the complexes of images grouped according to our personal experience; while the collective unconscious houses the patterns that we have inherited:

> I define the unconscious as the totality of all psychic phenomena that lack the quality of consciousness . . . From this it follows that the unconscious is the receptacle of all lost memories and of all contents that are still too weak to become conscious . . . Besides these we must include all more or less intentional repressions of painful thoughts and feelings. I call the sum of all these contents the 'personal unconscious' . . .
>
> But, over and above that, we also find in the unconscious qualities that are not individually acquired but are inherited, e.g., instincts as impulses to carry out actions from necessity, without conscious motivation. In this 'deeper' stratum we also find the *a priori*, inborn forms of 'intuition', namely the *archetypes* of perception and apprehension, which are the necessary *a priori* determinants of all psychic processes. Just as his instincts compel man to a specifically human mode of existence, so the archetypes force his ways of perception and apprehension into specifically human patterns. The instincts and the archetypes together form the 'collective unconscious'. I call it 'collective' because, unlike the personal unconscious, it is not made up of individual and more or less unique contents but of those which are universal and of regular occurrence. Instinct is an essentially collective, i.e., universal and regularly occurring phenomenon which has nothing to do with individuality. Archetypes have this quality in common with the instincts and are likewise a collective phenomenon.[26]

The constant appearance and influence of both the personal complexes and the collective archetypes led Jung to propose that each of us is not one, but many, and that we all have many voices which need to have their say. Jung believed that the original state of the psyche is 'one in which the psychic processes are very loosely knit and by no means form a self-orientated unity'.[27]

Jung believed that daily life consists of a continuous dialogue between the many voices of the psyche and that this dialogue is absolutely crucial to a healthy and balanced life. Only through 'talking out' the different possibilities, needs, moods, complexes and archetypal influences that a person has can he or she decide for the best.

# The One and the Many

In psychotic disturbance Jung observed merely an exaggerated form of the dialogue, necessary for healthy living, between different voices in the psyche. But, whereas for most people this dialogue is chaired by the dominating strength of the ego, in schizophrenia each of the voices acquires such an increased intensity that the ego becomes swamped and the psyche ends up drowned out by a chorus of voices, each wanting to assert a different mode of behaviour.

However, for the healthy person with a strongly affirmed ego Jung proclaimed the importance of maintaining a dialogue between the many voices. To this end, Jung proclaimed that 'one should nurture the art of conversing with oneself' and encouraged people to develop the ability to give each of their complexes a voice:

> We know that practically every one has not only the peculiarity, but also the faculty, of holding a conversation with himself. Whenever we are in a predicament we ask ourselves (or who else?) 'What shall I do?' either aloud or beneath our breath, and we (or who else?) supply the answer ... The psyche not being a unity but a contradictory multiplicity of complexes, the dissociation required for our dialectics with the anima is not so terribly difficult. The art of it consists only in allowing our invisible partner to make herself heard, in putting the mechanism of expression momentarily at her disposal, without being overcome by the distaste one naturally feels at playing such an apparently ludicrous game with oneself, or by doubts as to the genuineness of the voice of one's interlocutor.[28]

For Jung psychotherapy was simply an extension of this process, with the added advantage of having the objective ear of the therapist to listen in on the dialogue. Anything which permitted a balanced conversation and interplay between the different voices was in itself therapeutic. This could take the form of a verbal conversation, or it could involve translating the voices into characters and painting them in oil or water-colour. It could involve writing a play where different personalities, each one representing a different voice from within the author's psyche, argue for what they want.

# A Mythical Language of Dreams

Jung believed that the psyche retains many ideas, images and linguistic symbols which originate from humankind's earliest days, through a genealogical inheritance. The Oedipus complex was, for Jung, only one of a vast spectrum of image-matrices comprising emotions, instincts, ideas and characters to which the human psyche or imagination plays host. All the characters and narratives which formulate religious mythology reflect the structure of and thus provide an allegorical metaphor for internal psychological processes, as it is from them that they emanate. In 're-placing' the Oedipus complex as an equal among an extensive pantheon of other myths and figurative manifestations in folklore, Jung removed the sexual emphasis that Freud had given psychoanalysis.

Freud's psychoanalysis reconstructed a specific autobiographical narrative in which he contextualised the images central to the patient's psychological constitution, tracing the origin of the symptom and the cause of the neuroses to a specific event or events in this narrative of the patient's past. Jung, on the other hand, rather than contextualising the images in the patient's narrative, conducted extensive cross-references between individual dreams and fantasies, observing how their structure was represented in different guises in different individuals and cultures. He revealed how the roots and significance of symptoms and dream images originate not in the sociological circumstances which influence the development of individual consciousness but in unconscious universal structures, a system of genetic blueprints or archetypes,[29] which are continually reinvented through the personages which appear in myths: 'In the dream, as in the products of psychoses, there are numberless interconnections to which one can find parallels only in mythological associations of ideas (or perhaps in certain poetic creations which are often characterised by a borrowing, not always conscious, from myths).'[30]

Instead of tracing the significance of a dream to the idiosyncratic stories of the patient's daily life, Jung traced them to the larger stories of the myths, to ascertain to which archetypal pattern the dream belonged: 'Thus there are not only typical dreams but typical motifs in the dreams. These may . . . be situations or figures.'[31] As a further challenge to Freud's emphasis on individual experience, Jung focused less on the significance of linguistic description than Freud had done. For Jung words were less important than the analysis of the dream contents as pictorial symbols. Language was the necessary means by which analyst and patient communicate, a transcription of the actual material, which for Jung was always symbolic.

According to Jung, a dream of flying was not an indication of a particular sexual problem, but took place in the context of universal myths where flight symbolised freedom, spirituality, heavenly ascension, escape and a host of other non-sexual significations. Jung's method of dream analysis amplified the patient's image of flight to encompass all the other motifs which often occur alongside flight in mythical stories, and he was thereby able to relate age-old wisdom from relevant myths to the life of the patient.

In tracing their dreams to myths, Jung consequently raised his patients' attention above a preoccupation with their own problems and dilemmas and enabled them to see that they were not alone in their suffering, but that they were temporarily hosting the eternal problems of humanity:

If a man reckons the unconscious as part of his personality, then one must admit that he is in fact raging against himself. But, in so far as the symbolism thrown up by his suffering is archetypal and collective, it can be taken as a sign that he is no longer suffering from himself, but rather from the spirit of the age. He is suffering from an objective, impersonal cause, from his collective unconscious which he has in common with all men.[32]

Jung therefore developed an ever-deepening respect for the ability of ancient myth to offer a timeless, figurative and allegorical reflection of a person's inner psychic life. What for Freud had been a single-minded preoccupation with the one myth of Oedipus and its psychological parallel as made manifest by the Oedipus complex, became for Jung an inexhaustible investigation of the insights provided by a wealth of mythical narratives from the world over.

## The Stone Left Unturned

Jung's almost religious adherence to the potency of myth and the ceaseless vitality of the collective unconscious extinguished the deep personal and professional unanimity which he had originally enjoyed with Freud. The famous split between the two of the most brilliant and perspicacious men of the twentieth century is still to be seen today, reflected in two schools of psychotherapeutic practice. But despite their differences and despite their mutual brilliance, both Freud and Jung left the same fundamental stone unturned.

From Freud we have learnt to what degree psychological health is dependent upon an ability to articulate feeling. We have come to understand that the repression of our affective reaction to individual traumas suffered in childhood or in adult life causes mental suffering which can in turn produce physical symptoms. We have learnt that there are certain universal instincts of a sexual nature which society requires us to repress and which also lead to psychological impairment. Repression leads to bottled-up energy, which in turn leads to pain.

Freud's legacy to those suffering from such syndromes was his discovery of the power of verbal discourse to bring to light causative trauma, and his further realisation of the ability for emotionalised dialogue to release repressed feelings. Freud's insistence on the essential role of verbal language in this curative process remains a visible inheritance of the classic schools of psychoanalysis, where the method of communication between patient and therapist continues to be purely verbal.

Although Freud was clearly aware that the non-verbal acts of sound-making, such as screaming, shouting and yelling, were also cathartic, he did not pursue in any detail the means by which the therapeutic method might employ non-verbal articulation.

Jung perhaps cannot be accused of ignoring other means of expression besides the verbal; in fact, some would argue that his most significant contribution to modern culture was to highlight the way in which literature, painting, sculpture and other artistic media may be shown to constitute formal manifestations of psychological contents. He was also a genuine pioneer in showing that the apparently senseless and chaotic expressions of schizophrenics contain symbols comparable with those in ancient myth. He therefore elevated the physical movements, cacophonous vocal utterances, obsessive diaries and eccentric paintings of psychotic patients to the level of art.

However, despite the importance Jung continually placed on the therapeutic value of artistic forms of psychological expression such as writing and painting, and despite the fact that Jung was fully aware of the significance of the voice in revealing psychological images, particularly in the vocal degeneration of schizophrenics, nowhere in his writings does he elaborate any further upon the significance of vocal sound-making as an expression of psychic contents in a therapeutic context. Jung did not speak of the therapeutic and curative value of voice and song, remaining as distant as Freud from investigating the way in which vocal tone and timbre gives shape to psychic images of a personal and archetypal origin.

That this stone remained unturned is perhaps particularly surprising in the light of the fact that both Freud and Jung were influenced by the religious, curative and artistic practices of those very cultures to whom nonverbal vocal sound-making was a central feature. The writings of both men draw consistently on the principles which governed the behaviour and expressive faculties of those who are variously described as 'primitives', 'savages', 'tribal peoples' and 'the ancients'. Without reference to the myths and rituals of those from an earlier time, much of the terminology and conceptual references used by Freud and Jung would never have come into modern psychotherapeutic use. Central to the culture of these earlier peoples was a medicinal, therapeutic, curative and expressive use of sound and song which preceded verbal language by an inestimable span of years, and ran parallel to it for many more, yet this was never considered to be significant enough to be incorporated into the practical strategy and theoretical methodology of Freud's and Jung's respective approaches to psychotherapy which remained modelled upon the talking cure.

However, there were those who, though admiring the principles founded by Jung and Freud, none the less felt that the strategy of static verbal discourse left too much to be desired. There consequently arose a revolution, or a series of revolutions, in the field of psychotherapy, led by individual researchers who each sought to drive the therapeutic process off the couch. It is within this revolution that we begin to find the non-verbal utterances of the human voice playing their part upon the psychotherapeutic stage.

CHAPTER THREE

# The Pioneering Foundations of a Singing Cure

## Wilhelm Reich and the Mind Within the Muscle

It was a pupil of Sigmund Freud by the name of Wilhelm Reich who became particularly interested in the conversion of so-called psychic energy into physical as well as psychological expression.

Reich, however, proposed that bottled-up psychic energy is expressed not only in specific physical malfunctions and extreme psychological states, such as muscular paralysis, depression or anxiety, but also in the general psychological outlook of the individual. He saw a person's character as comprising certain identifiable attitudes, such as cynicism, bitterness and envy. He believed that the process of repressing the demands of the instincts in the face of moral requirements led to the erection of strong emotional guards which served to keep the two apart and which subsequently become a regular feature of the person's character. These guards were for Reich the mainstay of what Freud called 'resistance'. The stronger and more firmly established a certain emotional attitude, the more firmly was the person able to resist giving in to the demands of the underlying instincts. Emotional guards also served to protect the individual from the threatening attacks and demands of the outside world. Reich said that it is as if the personality has 'put on an armour, a rigid shell on which the knocks from the outer world as well as the inner demands rebound'.[1] Thus, for Reich, the first aim of therapy was to break through the resilient habitual attitudes which seemed to form the nucleus of a person's character. However, the innovation achieved by Reich's insight lies not here but in the next stage of his thinking.

Reich proposed that the elaborate armour of strongly defended emotional barriers created by the patient manifests itself in his or her posture and physical carriage – what he described as 'chronically fixed muscular attitudes'.[2] In order to bind and stem the flow of suppressed psychic energy, a person tends to develop a high degree of tensile rigidity in his or her muscle tone or, in Reich's words, 'muscular armour'; this preserves a 'pent-up' and intransigent psychological outlook engendered and unconsciously adopted in the person's past. So, for Reich, muscular armour and 'character armour' are 'functionally identical'[3] and reveal themselves through a host of psycho-physical expressions, such as 'the manner of talk-

70

ing, of the gait, facial expression and typical attitudes such as smiling, deriding, haughtiness, over-correctness'.[4]

The character armour develops 'as the chronic result of the conflict between instinctual demands and the frustrating outer world', and 'the continuing actual conflicts between instinct and outer world give it its strength and continued reason for existence';[5] the character armour therefore becomes fixed and preserved by the muscular armour of the body. Thus one of the primary functions of character armour and muscular armour is that of 'absorbing dammed-up energy'.[6]

Reich, like Freud, saw the quality of these instinctual demands and their constituting energy as essentially sexual in nature; and he termed this energy 'orgone', a word which he derived from 'organism', 'organic' and 'orgasm'. Reich also shared with Freud the belief that the resistances which a patient concocts as a means of debarring the instincts must be broken down. However, there marks the end of Reich's unanimity with Freud.

Because Reich believed that the manifestations of this dynamic were psycho-physical, he maintained that a successful therapeutic process would have to be psycho-physical also. For this reason Reich attacked the purely verbal strategy of Freud's work. According to Reich, the nature of a patient's repression, problems and resistances could not be ascertained or dissolved by the words which he or she spoke; rather, the therapist had to examine the movements of the body, and by manipulation of and direct contact with the muscles, cause the pent-up energy to be released. Reich stated that 'orgone therapy is distinguished from all other modes of influencing the organism by the fact that the patient is asked to express himself biologically while word language is eliminated to a far-reaching degree'.[7] But what did Reich mean by expressing oneself biologically?

## Respiration and Repression

Reich believed that one of the methods employed by a neurotic individual to keep his character armour and muscular armour in place was a restricted pattern of breathing. By maintaining a shallow intake of breath or an overly quick rate of respiratory cycles, the patient was able to retain and restrain the affective constructs. Reich therefore abandoned the couch and static verbal dialogue and worked directly on the patient's body. Applying pressure to abdomen, chest and other areas which housed important organs, he encouraged his patients not to talk, but to focus on 'letting go' of their feelings through breathing.

By dismantling restricted patterns of inspiration and expiration and encouraging long, deep, free breaths, Reich caused emotions to be freed in the form of sobs, tears, screams and sighs, which left the patient feeling purged, cleansed and disengaged from the previously unpliant condition to which he had become accustomed.

But it was not the process of breathing enhancement itself, but the resulting movements of the body which Reich attended to in his analysis. He believed the human body had an in-built tendency to express itself through free-flowing, unbound undulating physical movements, the ultimate expression of which occurred during orgasm. However, Reich maintained that what most people experience as orgasm is but a tiny vestige, a minuscule moment of climatic release completely divorced from a total bodily experience. He observed that when a free and unbound respiratory cycle was achieved, it was always accompanied by undulating movements of the body, which Reich called the 'orgasm reflex'. This orgasm reflex was not equivalent to the genital climax of copulation or masturbation, but was the total bodily experience of climactic release of which genital orgasm should ideally be only a part.

Reich's overly publicised and misinterpreted preoccupation with sexuality in its most biological and physically expressive form made him a scapegoat for the American conservative authorities under whom he conducted his research. His unpopularity was further enhanced by the results of his later work, among which was his claim to have built a machine which, if you sat in it for a certain amount of time, increased your free flow of sexual energy and cured all degrees of impotence. This claim, together with his constant obsession with the sexual nature of fundamental human instinct and energy, made him the subject of continued scrutiny and persecution by the American authorities, and many of his written works were destroyed.

Despite the eccentricity which characterised and, according to some, depleted the integrity of Reich's later work, one fact remains undeniable. It was Wilhelm Reich who initiated the breakthrough in Western psychotherapy from a purely verbal analysis to direct work with the body, central to which was the concentration on the process of respiration by which, it was recognised, a patient kept instincts repressed. Furthermore, because the freeing of their breathing from restriction caused many of his patients to let out vocal sounds as an expression of feelings which had been pent up for a long time, Reich may also be credited with having made a significant, if unwitting, contribution to the significance of the voice in psychotherapy.

## Alexander Lowen and Bioenergetics

It was one of Reich's pupils who developed the principles of working with the body into a more systematised and practicable process, thereby highlighting further the importance of the human voice in therapeutic methods. This was Alexander Lowen.

Lowen was Reich's pupil from 1940 to 1952 and inherited from him a dissatisfaction with the underachievement of the verbal therapy initiated by Freud. He believed that though 'much valuable information was gained through these inquiries . . . they left untouched the most important domain of personality – namely, its base in bodily processes'.[8] He stated that 'the weakness of psychoanalytic technique is that it ignores the body in its attempt to help the patient work through his emotional conflicts. Since it fails to provide any significant body experience, the ideas that emerge in the course of treatment remain impotent to produce any major changes in personality.'[9]

Lowen was deeply influenced by Reich's discovery of the unity of psychological and bodily experience and went on to extend the principles by which a person's emotional preoccupations may be read from his somatic condition. He believed that 'the functional identity of psychic character and body structure, or muscular attitude, is the key to understanding personality', for he proposed that it enables us to 'read the character from the body and to explain a body attitude by its psychic representations and vice versa'.[10] Lowen saw the damming-up and impediment of the body's innate physical malleability and capacity for expression not as a problem unique to neurotics or to those suffering from severe trauma, but as the curse of Western society. He proposed that the inhabitants of the modern world have betrayed the body, that 'all our personal difficulties stem from this betrayal' and that 'most of our social problems have a similar origin'.[11] Gathering impetus from Reich's research, Lowen developed further the principles and practices by which people could be released from these psycho-physical restraints and so rediscover an unbound and unencumbered capacity for emotional and physical expression. Lowen called these principles 'bioenergetics', the aim of which was 'to remove the barriers or blocks to self-expression' and thereby 'to help a person become more spontaneous and more self-expressive'.[12]

Also inherited from Reich was Lowen's understanding that the respiratory act can be one of the primary barriers to self-expression, the primary means by which instincts and feelings are repressed and therefore also the means by which the blocks and instincts can be released. As a result, central to the therapeutic method of bioenergetics was concentration on enhancing the patient's freedom of respiration. But Lowen took his research one stage further than Reich.

# From Breath to Voice

Lowen believed that the quality of vocal sounds which patients released as an involuntary response to the therapeutic process conveyed important information about their character and psychological predicament. Lowen listened therefore not only to the gasps, cries and sighs which were emitted during the physical manipulation of a patient's body, but also to the timbres inherent in the patient's speaking voice, the patterns of 'inflection, tone, rhythm and gesture, which in large part are spontaneous and unique to the speaker'[13] and which often have 'greater impact than the words he utters'.[14]

Lowen therefore introduced into the psychotherapeutic process the idea that the quality of a voice mirrors the nature of the underlying emotions. From his belief that freeing the body resulted in a freeing of the psyche, it was simply a logical extension to propose that the freeing of the voice resulted in the same psychological liberation.

> There is no question in my mind that a rich voice is a rich manner of self-expression and denotes a rich inner life. I believe this is something we all sense about a person, and this sensing is valid, even if unsupported by objective studies. What do we mean by a rich voice? The essential factor is the presence of undertones and overtones that give it a fullness of sound. Another factor is range of expression. A person who speaks in a monotone has a very limited range of expression, and we tend to equate this with a limited personality. A voice can be flat, without depth or resonance, it can be low as if lacking energy, and it can be thin and bodiless. Each of these qualities bears some relationship to the personality of the individual . . .[15]
>
> If a person is to recover his full potential for self-expression, it is important he gain the full use of his voice in all its registers and in all its nuances of feeling. The blockage of any feeling will affect its expression vocally.[16]

Therefore Lowen's techniques of physically manoeuvring the patient's body and enhancing the breathing process through methodical exercises encouraged not only the release of the undulating movements of the orgasm reflex, but also the emission of vocal sounds, which in turn freed pent-up emotions and contributed to the overall process of catharsis.

## Scream and Leave it at That

Of all the various involuntary sounds which Lowen's patients emitted, the most powerful emotionally was the scream, which Lowen described as 'an explosion within the personality that momentarily shatters the rigidity created by chronic muscular tension'[17] and which has a 'powerful cathartic effect on the personality'.[18] Lowen also claimed that other vocal emissions like 'crying and deep sobs produce a similar effect by softening and melting body rigidities'.[19]

> Because the voice is so closely tied to feeling, freeing it involves the mobilization of suppressed feelings and their expression in sound. There are different sounds for different feelings. Fear and terror are expressed in a scream, anger in a loud, sharp tone, sadness in a deep, sobbing voice, pleasure and love in soft, cooing sounds. It can be said

generally that a high-pitched voice indicates a blocking of the deep notes that express sadness; a low-pitched, chesty voice indicates a denial of the feeling of fear and an inhibition against its expression in a scream.[20]

As with his work on the body, Lowen was here in the realm of catharsis. He made no attempt to shape the vocal sounds to give form to specific inner psychological images, concentrating instead on the release of generalised emotional accumulations.

Lowen's primary focus was not on the voice, but on the body. Although he realised the psychological significance of vocal emissions which occurred as a by-product of physical movement, he did not develop a methodological approach to the voice in its own right. Consequently we cannot really credit Lowen with pioneering the therapeutic function of singing. However, Lowen did record an episode which reveals that he had encountered the positive psychological benefits of singing:

> About two years ago I became acquainted with a singing teacher who was familiar with bioenergetic concepts and understood the role of the voice in self-expression. Earlier I mentioned the feeling that my mother had cut my throat. This created some difficulty for me in speaking, in crying, but especially in singing. I have always wanted to sing but rarely did. I was afraid my voice would crack and I would start to cry. No one sang in my family when I was a child. So I decided to take some singing lessons from this teacher to see what it would do. She assured me that she understood my problem and that since it was a private lesson, I could just go ahead and cry if I felt like doing so.
>
> I went for one lesson with considerable excitement. She started me making a sound, any free and spontaneous sound. Then I sang a word, 'diabolo', which allowed me to open my throat and vocalize fully. I let myself go. I moved around and hammed it up. My voice became freer. At one point I made a sound that came out so effortlessly, so fully that it seemed I was the sound, the sound was me. It reverberated through my whole being. My body was in a constant state of vibration.
>
> To my surprise I didn't feel like crying once. I just opened up and let it out. I knew then that I could sing, for some of the sounds had a beautiful, musical quality. As I left the session, I had a sense of joyfulness such as I have known on only a few occasions. Of course, I continued the lessons.[21]

Though we know that Lowen continued his singing lessons, we must assume that he did not investigate further the means by which the act of singing could contribute to the animation of psychotherapy, because no record of such investigation occurs in his writings. What we do know from his writings is that his fundamental belief that emotional disturbance is audible in the tone of the human voice was inherited from the work of a man called Paul Moses, whom it is clear that Lowen respected.

## Paul Moses and the Voice of Neurosis

Paul J. Moses was a clinical professor in charge of the speech and voice section of the Division of Otolaryngology at the Stanford University School of Medicine in San Francisco. It was here in 1940 that he conducted an experiment in which he analysed the personality of an adolescent boy, whom he had never met, from a recording of the boy's voice.[22] The boy had previously been analysed by a psychiatrist and had been subjected to a psychological examination known as the Rorschach test. Based on what he perceived in the patterns of rhythm, pitch, melody and timbre of the boy's voice, Moses gave an analysis of the character and psychological constitution of the boy which was found to agree on many points with the Rorschach findings and the psychiatrist's own report.[23]

Moses believed, like many before him, that oral communication is composed of speech and voice. While speech denotes what we say, voice denotes the way we say it. In addition, he adamantly maintained that it was possible to detect in the voice alone any underlying emotional and psychological disturbance. He believed that 'vocal dynamics truthfully reflect psychodynamics' and that 'each emotion has its vocal expression'.[24]

Moses was deeply influenced by both Freud and Jung. From Freud he learnt that traumatic events which occur during childhood can come back to haunt the adult in the form of physical sufferings; and disturbances in the quality of the human voice were for Moses manifestations of such traumas. From Jung he learnt that there is a deeply buried layer of images in the human psyche which belongs to a collective unconscious. These images were, for Moses, also evident in the sound of a person's voice:

> Voice is an indicator of different phases in a person's life. It is free from static qualities. Vocal changes accompany the development of the individual, but in addition, voice contains archaic properties originating in the cradle of mankind. One can go as far as to say that vocal expression is a record of the history of mankind as well as a record of the individual.[25]

Moses proposed that the child's vocal development, from his first cry to the acquisition of speech, retraces the development of the species, that emotional disturbance in adult life can cause him to 'return symbolically to a phase that gave greater security' and that the regression will be expressed through the vocal characteristics which accompanied that stage.[26] Just as Jung had perceived in the paintings of psychotics images which mirror those contained in ancient myths, so Moses believed that the paralinguistic utterances of schizophrenics mirror the acoustic remains of an earlier time.

Moses was a laryngologist and as such was involved in the treatment of the voice problems of which his patients complained. However, just as Freud had discovered no organic or physiological cause for the broad range of somatic sufferings experienced by his early patients, so too Moses discovered that the larynx of many of his patients was completely healthy. Moses therefore assumed Freud's role of searching for the underlying psychological cause for physical disorder, in these cases disorders which affected the voice. He sought to encourage an interdisciplinary approach to treating voice disorders, in which psychodynamics played a central role. He believed that the 'ideal speech and voice specialist should be a combination of otolaryngologist, psychiatrist, psychologist, speech trainer, singing master, and experimental phonetician'.[27] Moses felt that it was important to recognise that it is often 'emotional disturbance' which causes misuse of the vocal instrument and in turn causes the symptoms with which the patient comes to the laryngologist.

Moses argued that a certain amount of psychotherapeutic knowledge is necessary in order to deal with the high number of cases of vocal dysfunctions for which there appear to be no physiological cause: 'It is in such cases that the laryngologist must step into the realm of psychiatry and psychotherapy because it would be a technical impossibility to consult the psychiatrist for each of this group of patients.'[28] Moses believed that treatment of the voice had to run in tandem with treatment of the psyche, and his prime aim was therefore to introduce the precepts of psychotherapy into vocal analysis.

Among the case studies which Moses recorded, he gives an example of a man with a persistently high voice:

> If one remembers that in our culture high and low voices are identified with young and old, female and male, and that the adult range and register are acquired during adolescence, one gets an inkling of the psychological roots of this phenomenon. Psychiatrists term the underlying emotional problem 'unsuccessful identification' with the parent of the same sex (which usually takes place during adolescence); the 'mother complex', 'sister imitation', or hatred of the father. Whatever the terminology, persistent falsetto voice expresses marked neurotic conflicts (though it does not necessarily imply homosexuality). The fact that the patient comes to a physician for help shows that he suffered much by ridicule, social disapproval, and discontent with self. This raises hopes for a favourable prognosis.
>
> Whether the case merits the attention of a psychiatrist or can be handled by the psychologically oriented laryngologist will depend on the degree and complexity of the underlying emotional pathology. Either way, psychotherapy alone will not lower the voice, just as

voice therapy alone will not reveal and cure the causing factors. Since it is possible to lower a persistent falsetto voice to the natural speaking level within one session – usually to the great surprise of the patient – the laryngologist should endeavour to achieve this. This usually increases the patient's confidence both in the physician and in his own ability to change, and makes him more ready to accept the psychological as well as the technical aspects of therapy.[29]

## The Voice in Psychoanalysis

Paul Moses was not the first to make such psychological interpretations of vocal quality. In 1943 a psychoanalyst of the Freudian school by the name of Morris Brody noted that 'disturbances of the voice and of voice production occur not infrequently as an outward manifestation of emotional conflict, in short, as a symptom of neurosis',[30] and he recorded a number of case studies of patients who were neurologically normal, free from the physiologic voice changes of puberty and yet manifested vocal disturbance. One of these was a 24-year-old male with a self-admitted strong dependence on his mother, who had always 'babied' him. Brody detected in the timbre of this patient's voice a 'break which sounded almost like a sob' which, according to Brody, 'attested to his yearning to remain a child'; the analyst concluded that the 'bass voice was repressed in an effort to retain his mother's love'.[31]

In this case the man used his voice as an expression of his wish to identify with a child, and indeed the voice is used frequently as a means of identifying vocally with someone. Children at play adapt their voices to assume, for example, a hard, deepened and domineering tone, which they identify with a teacher, and then 'act out' a game of schools. The most frequent of these vocal identifications is the mimicking of the parents, in which very often the mother is portrayed with a meek and mild tone of gentility and serenity and the father, meanwhile, is given a booming, gruff and aggressive voice.

Our parents continue to influence the way we think and act even when we become adults and believe ourselves to have acquired an independence from the ways of our family. If there has been an obvious fundamental tension between the views of our father and those of our mother, we may well go back and forth like a pendulum when trying to make decisions, adopting first the attitude of one and then that of the other parent. One of the cases recorded by Morris Brody reveals how a patient expressed his identification with his father through his voice.

The patient was a man in his late thirties who had been raised a Catholic by a cruel and violent father and who later renounced his religion. This patient was very weak and timid physically though he very much wanted to be strong like his father. Unable to compete with the father physically, he had strived to become intellectually superior to him. In addition, he did what many boys do in order to disguise their competitive relationship with their father; he displaced his competition on to something and someone else, in this case the Church or, more specifically, the priest. The patient was thus consumed with what Brody describes as 'ideas of a grandiose ecclesiastical nature' and became completely celibate. However, bubbling away under this attempt to outdo his father was the patient's preoccupation with sexual ideas about women. Brody notes:

> When expressing sexual ideas the patient's voice assumed a low chanting tone as if he were praying. This tone of voice acted as a means of avoiding punishment. At other times his voice seemed to carry all the incantations and inflections of the clergy as if he were not really expressing his sexual ideas but were delivering a sermon on sexuality. In this way he tried to undo the feelings of wickedness about his ideas and to deny his rivalry with his father. By means of these defence mechanisms in the tone of the voice, assisted by his identification with the priest, he was able to talk like his father (the father used profanity freely) and thus to compete with him. It is noteworthy that when the patient's attention was drawn to his change of voice and he felt that he was expected to speak normally, he was then unable to bring himself to talk about sexual matters.[32]

Based on cases from his own consulting practice, Brody concluded that 'to hear the voice solely for what it has to say and to overlook the voice itself deprives the analyst of an important avenue leading to emotional conflict'.[33] Further to Brody's comments, Harry Stack Sullivan, an influential Freudian analyst, stated that the psychoanalytic interview 'is a situation of primarily vocal communication – not verbal communication alone',[34] and since then many psychotherapists and psychiatrists have paid special attention to the voice as well as to the speech of a patient.

For example, in 1960 a group of researchers made a tape recording of the first five minutes of an interview between a psychiatrist and a patient and then made a written transcription of absolutely all the vocal sounds emitted by the patient. This included the actual words spoken, the way they were uttered and all other emissions, such as a quick gasp of breath or a contemplative 'mmm'. Words were denoted with standard phonetic and linguistic signs, while paralinguistic activities – shifts of rhythm, tempo, inflection and other noises – were given special signs.[35] The discrepancy between the conclusions reached about the patient's predicament based only on the usual written case notes and those based on the transcription of all the paralinguistic information highlighted how vital it is to take into consideration an assessment of all audible noises made by a patient in order to come to a satisfactory analysis of his or her conscious and unconscious ideas. An analysis of a patient's speech alone is not enough.

We may all be familiar with the fact that the same sentence can be said a number of different ways, each time acquiring a different meaning. But it is easy to forget that in the mouth of a seriously mentally ill patient such twists of meaning given to words by the subtle turning of the voice are of crucial significance in understanding their fears, phobias and preoccupations.

# Paul Moses and the Concept of a Singing Cure

Despite earlier references, such as those above, it was Paul Moses who really rooted the notion of a vocal psychology in the theoretical principles established by psychoanalysis. In particular, Moses recognised that analysts of the Freudian school believed that the most significant trauma suffered universally by children is being weaned off the breast, and that many psychological difficulties suffered in adult life can be put down to the fact that the patient has never fully recovered from having been separated from the once reliable source of nourishment and comfort. But Moses proposed that there was another more shattering trauma which could have equally severe repercussions in later life.

He believed that the action of phonation at birth and the subsequent pre-verbal noises of a child are extremely pleasurable and liberating to it. The child derives sensual oral pleasure from the process of suckling at the breast which becomes associated with the vegetative sounds of sucking to such a degree that the process of vocal sound-making becomes an important source of pleasure, whether accompanied by feeding or not. This pleasure is unhampered by any external restriction and the sounds are composed according only to the baby's own whims, feelings, responses and as a result of involuntary physiological operations. However, Moses proposed that the acquisition of speech is, by comparison, a traumatic experience which interferes with this free-functioning of vocal expressivity. To learn language the child is required to bring his or her feelings and instincts, moods and affects, which have hitherto been 'sung' in a fashion reminiscent of pre-verbal peoples, under the jurisdiction of words.[36] This involves the child in a game of punishment and reward which he or she finds terribly traumatic.

According to Moses, therefore, patients who have found this transformation from being non-verbal to verbal particularly traumatic are subconsciously yearning for an opportunity to once again give free reign to their feelings and instincts via the spontaneous emissions of non-verbal vocal sounds. The success of any vocal and psychological therapy therefore depended on giving the patient an opportunity to give voice once more to the psychological dimensions for which no words are appropriate.

In his search for a means to give patients such an opportunity, Moses concluded that singing was the only activity which answered their needs. It was in this connection that he wrote the words which mark the transposition of Freud's cathartic method of verbal therapy on to the act of singing:

> In archaic days, when sounds, and not abstract constructions of grammar, were the interpreter of human thoughts and emotions, the complete range of voice was used more freely. Like the infant who lets his vocal powers range to their fullest extent, primitive peoples at the dawn of society used their voices to their heart's content to express their feelings and reactions. Sensual sound phenomena also preceded syntax. As we ceased to communicate in gestures; imitative sounds, cries of sorrow and jubilation, and acquired, instead, words, our vocal range began to shrink to the point where speech melody is now merely a weazened emotional scale on which articulation plays its piece. Only when our controls get out of hand, when we become excited or intoxicated, do we become savages again. We forget our civilised range limitations and the primeval cry can be heard again. Range is the language of emotions, as against articulation, the language of ideas.
>
> Singing is something of a compromise, a willed recall of an echo of the pure satisfaction of primitive vocalisation. It is an auto-erotic activity, releasing the tensions built up by our repressions.[37]

Unfortunately, it was not until towards the end of his life that Moses discovered, in theory, that singing was an aid to psychotherapeutic development; so he had little opportunity to explore the use of singing with patients. However, in 1959 he came to London as a delegate at the London World Voice Conference, which brought together doctors, psychologists and other voice specialists to share ideas regarding all aspects of the human voice. One of the presentations given at this conference consisted of a lecture by a singing teacher called Alfred Wolfsohn and a practical demonstration by one of his pupils.

Moses, who by this time was an internationally renowned figure, respected in many fields for his work on the psychodynamics of the voice and yet still in search of the practical representation of his ideas on singing, saw in this demonstration the confirmation in practice of all that he had formulated in theory. Later, Moses wrote a testimony to Wolfsohn, which read:

> I consider Mr Wolfsohn one of the greatest experts in problems of the human voice in the world.
>
> His achievements do not only cover the teaching of singing but go far beyond this: they encompass entirely new areas of expression and communication. Mr Wolfsohn has been able to prove his theories through practical results of his teaching: to me and to many other scientists in the field of vocal expression there is no doubt that it will be absolutely necessary that his work continues since most valuable discoveries have been made by him and should be expected from him

if he is able to go on. His work should be known to singers and to singing teachers, but just as much to laryngologists, psychiatrists and psychologists. In my own teaching I quote Mr Wolfsohn's discoveries constantly and do as much from an anthropological point of view.[38]

The presentation which Alfred Wolfsohn gave with his students at this conference was the result of his life's work, a life which yielded some astounding discoveries about the psychology and expressivity of the human voice. Yet, strangely, the story of Alfred Wolfsohn's research remains one rarely told.

## Alfred Wolfsohn and a War Neurosis

Alfred Wolfsohn was born in Berlin of Jewish descent in 1896 and at the outbreak of World War I he was called to serve as a medic in the front-line trenches. During this time, Wolfsohn became both horrified and fascinated by the incredible sounds which the adverse conditions and suffering prompted from the voices of wounded and dying soldiers. He heard screams, groans and cacophonous pleas which were pitched higher and lower than he would ever have thought physically possible. He heard voices which were so intense with fear and which carried for such a distance that, had he not been faced with the sight of the appalling conditions which elicited the voices, he would not have believed them to come from the mouths of men. He recorded his experiences thus:

> We are now in a foreign country. Here in this foreign country are trenches, trenches are everywhere. I am living in these trenches. Every now and then the darkness of the night is lit up by Very lights, strange stars made by man. Shells burst right and left.
>
> I throw myself on the ground, my hands are clawing the earth. Often, someone next to me is hit. Each time I am astonished that I have been spared!
>
> Once I sink down in a trench, I sink into the mud. My comrades, like phantoms in the darkness, pass me by and do not help me. I am stuck in the morass and I am alone. Everything depends on my army boots; they have become my greatest enemies, for they hinder me in every movement. I rip open the sides of my boots with my bayonet and begin to crawl on all fours.
>
> Barrage all around me. The guns from which it is coming are manned by four or five Frenchmen. I don't know where they come from, I don't know who they are. They don't even know they could easily kill me. They have to take a certain stretch of earth under fire. It's no good shouting: 'Jean-Baptiste – Maurice – Pierre – I have done you no wrong, what do you want from me?' I keep crawling.

The hours pass. The firing is getting stronger and my peril greater. I pray to God but He doesn't hear me. From somewhere I hear a voice shouting: 'Comrade! Comrade!' I close my eyes shaking with terror, thinking: how can a human voice utter such a sound, a voice in extremis!

Grenades whistle, a voice implores, I curse God, I hear his scornful laughter in an infinite space, the earth is ripped open, the sky a fiendish back-drop, a realm between being alive, only just, and dying.

What continues are the automatic movements of my body. This is all and the unceasing question: WHY? FOR WHAT?[39]

It was these incredible vocal utterances, this 'voice in extremis', that plagued and obsessed Alfred Wolfsohn. But there was one particular voice, the echo of which remained with him for many years afterwards, causing him to suffer from a deep and all-consuming sense of guilt. Wolfsohn records the incident in this way:

The year was 1917, we were entrenched somewhere at the front, we did not know where, under heavy bombardment. At long last came the relay. Heavy rain had turned the trenches into swamps of mud and in a short while I became trapped in it. I called for my comrades for help but no one heard and soon I was quite alone. Hour after hour, inch by inch I crawled back. After a while I heard a voice nearby moaning incessantly: 'help, help, help'. I fought a terrible struggle with myself: should I try to crawl to him or not. I did not do it. After an agony of more than twenty hours I reached a reserve dugout. I do not remember what happened after that except that I learnt later that I had been hit and buried by a grenade and that I awoke the next morning in the cellar of a house in St Quentin, amongst a heap of corpses.[40]

Wolfsohn had been confronted with a terrible dilemma. If he had gone back to help his comrade, he surely would have stood a high chance of being killed himself. But in remaining he had to live with the knowledge that he had let a man die. It was the guilt arising from this knowledge that caused him a severe emotional disturbance. However, like thousands of others, Wolfsohn returned from the war to have his state of mental disturbance classified as 'war neurosis' or 'shell-shock'. Wolfsohn resented these terms, not only because he felt that they deprecated and minimised the severe experiences which he and his comrades had suffered, but also because they took no account of his specific trauma.

During the year following the war his illness worsened and he became plagued by aural hallucinations of the extreme vocal sounds which he had heard in the trenches. His inner world was bombarded with sounds which recalled the cacophony of the front line, and at the centre of this hallucinated landscape of sound were the pleading screams and groans of the dying.

Wolfsohn became convinced that his illness arose from an intense feeling of guilt at having denied help to his dying comrade, and the voices continued to sound in his mind despite prolonged psychiatric treatment. In the end, he felt that there was no choice but to search for his cure in himself. This search led Wolfsohn to an idea that was not only the beginning of his recovery, but which gave rise to a radical practical investigation into the boundaries of vocal expression.

## Cure Thyself

While in hospital during the year succeeding the war, Wolfsohn had read some of Freud's writings and had made acquaintance with those who were informed about the development of psychoanalysis. For Wolfsohn the most appropriate aspect of this new science, as he understood it at the time, was the concept of the release of unabreacted energy and the consequent relief of somatic symptoms. Indeed, Wolfsohn had been forced to 'bottle up' enormous quantities of emotional excitation in the trenches and his psyche was surely saturated with the affect of terror and of guilt, which he had never been able to express. His job and his very survival had depended on the ability to 'buckle down' and get on with the task of tending to the wounded as best he could. Wolfsohn thus wondered whether his aural hallucinations were an expression of this accumulated energy and considered how he might give himself a second chance to 'complete his reaction' and 'let off steam', as Freud had put it.

Through constant and painful contemplation of his own mental state, Wolfsohn became convinced that if he could actually sing the sounds that haunted his mind, he would be able to stop them. He wanted to perform nothing less than an oral exorcism, getting his own voice to emulate the extreme sounds that he had heard and thus perform a cathartic release of the bottled-up emotions of terror and guilt associated with them.

Wolfsohn began by taking lessons with a number of singing teachers who had varying responses to his intense emotional need. Some of them allowed Wolfsohn to pursue sounds of an extreme and intense nature, others simply confined him to musical exercises. None of them were adequately equipped to deal with the strength of his mission and the overwhelming burden of his mental state. Wolfsohn sensed that there must be another way of training the voice which would release the potential range he knew to exist. Since he also wanted to find a way of utilising such vocal liberation to positive ends, he therefore terminated the lessons and began a process of individual investigation.

Wolfsohn began to work upon himself, training his voice to go a little higher and a little lower each day, fuelled by the belief that 'there exists a universal human voice of much broader circumference than has hitherto been imagined'.[41] In extending the range of his voice and holding in mind the extreme emotive sounds he had heard in the trenches, Wolfsohn placed himself back in the war and re-enacted much of his experience. He put himself in the shoes of the suffering and when he yelled out, he yelled for them.

Through this process Wolfsohn discovered that his voice was capable of a range of tonal qualities far in excess of anything even he had imagined, and he heard himself make sounds both higher and lower than the extreme ends of the grand piano, which he used as a measure. He also realised that his voice could express an extensive collage of emotions, moods and characters which embraced not only the sounds of bitter suffering and agony, but those of the utmost joy and pleasure.

As a result of this process, not only did Wolfsohn recover from his illness, but he believed that he had developed his voice to a range in excess of eight octaves! It was now his intention to teach this method to others.

## Jewish Singing Teacher Survives Nazis

Having been denied the opportunity of a professional training by the untimely occurrence of World War I, Wolfsohn found it difficult to establish a context for his work. His lack of professional status also made him highly vulnerable in the face of the growing anti-semitic attitude of those around him, for Jews who were not ensconced in a state-recognised profession were the first target for harassment in the early 1930s.

An important Jewish figure at that time was Kurt Singer, who worked to ensure the preservation and continuance of Jewish cultural activities and who was deeply involved in the politics of the arts and its funding strategies. He had been successful in attracting money from abroad, especially from America, and was regarded highly by Göring despite the latter's fundamental stance against the Jewish race. Göring thus turned a blind eye to the fact that Singer was giving shelter to many Jews under the pretence of them being employed in the Opera as singers or musicians, many of whom even mimed playing in the mass orchestra.

Like many others, Wolfsohn went to Singer for help, though at this time there was no work available. However, Singer put Wolfsohn in touch with Paula Salomon-Lindberg, a renowned Jewish opera singer and teacher. In 1933 Salomon-Lindberg gave Wolfsohn a job teaching singing to some of her younger students and this enabled him to pass on to others the results of his own investigations.

Between 1936 and 1938, during his time spent at the home of Paula Salomon-Lindberg and her husband, Professor Albert Lindberg, Wolfsohn wrote a manuscript for a book entitled 'Orpheus or The Way to a Mask'. In this manuscript, which has never been published, he weaves together his autobiography with his views on life, music, painting, birth, death and the overcoming of suffering.

One of the female students who attended the classes in these early years had been a patient of Jungian psychotherapy prior to working vocally with Wolfsohn. She records:

> During the treatment of a cardiac neurosis in Jungian analysis, I was made to practise meditation. I was urged to concentrate on my inner breathing. As up to then I had lived exclusively in the outside world, this journey inside myself was an extraordinarily impressive experience for me. I saw visions coming from another world and experienced the depth in which these visions had their origin. I realised that by the concentration of breathing in a centre lying somewhere below the solar plexus, a language of pictures was evoked – a language arising from contact with the subconscious, which alone made possible psychic development. When I started to sing, once again there began the concentration on that mysterious centre. When I was asked to train my consciousness on the source of sound, I felt the origin of the sung note to be in that selfsame place. As time went on, I realised more and more that the road taken in the development of my voice was similar to that taken in following the psychology of Jung ... In this work [with Wolfsohn] of developing the human voice the singer penetrates deeper and deeper into the depths of his body and so arrives at the new, unknown sound of his voice, to which he listens as to a strange voice.[42]

Around fifteen years later, Wolfsohn acknowledged the importance of his encounter with this student in contributing to his belief that his approach to working with the human voice 'ran parallel to the basic principles of psychotherapy'.[43]

In addition to teaching singing and writing, Wolfsohn worked as a home tutor and counsellor to a growing number of Jewish adolescents who found themselves outcasts in Berlin and who desperately needed someone to harness their talents and direct their minds. Among these was Charlotte, Professor Albert Lindberg's daughter by his first marriage, who, while sheltering from the Nazis in France, painted some pictures based on her memories of Wolfsohn and his work. Charlotte was later killed in a concentration camp but her work, including over seven hundred completed paintings, still survive and many of them are published in the form of a pictorial diary.[44]

## The Alfred Wolfsohn Voice Research Centre

In 1939 Wolfsohn escaped from Germany and fled to London, and when the war was over, he gathered a fresh set of students and began teaching at a small studio in the suburb of Golders Green. It was here in London, free from political pressures and now fully recovered from his psychological difficulties, that Wolfsohn achieved the practical realisation of his vision. Through methodical and in-depth work, Wolfsohn enabled his pupils to exceed what had been regarded as the boundaries of vocal expression. Marita Günther, his long-standing friend, colleague and now guardian of his estate, records her first encounter with Alfred Wolfsohn's work:

> I was 21 when I came to England in 1949. With me I had the address of Alfred Wolfsohn which my mother had given me on the way should I need help and advice. I contacted him and a meeting was arranged. He had at this time his own and first small studio, let us say a sparse cell in a suburb of London . . .
>
> This first encounter left a deep impression on me, not that I could have explained or analysed it; I was content to keep it as a personal experience which allowed me to look into a world unknown to me, and to listen to this man who had built up something in this post-war time that pointed out a way at once life-giving and life-affirming.
>
> For the first time in this studio I heard how Alfred Wolfsohn worked with his pupils . . .
>
> What had his pupils in common? They could reach heights and depths as I had never heard before, and could produce within that range different colours of sound which moved me deeply. But what appealed to me more than the virtuosity of their voice range was the witnessing of what was happening between teacher and pupil; it was the give and take on both sides. This incredible concentration and intensity emanating from both. It was the physical effort in the extreme which seemed to transform their body and facial expressions.[45]

Wolfsohn's approach to singing was indeed highly addictive, and many of those who had lessons with him in these early days after the war remained his pupils for over ten years.

Wolfsohn's intention was not to nurture the diligence and technical proficiency of the 'voice beautiful', but to utilise the potential range of the human voice as a probe and a mirror, investigating and reflecting the many aspects of the human psyche. Therefore those who took lessons with him committed themselves not only to a thorough excavation of their psyche, but to the process of acquiring the courage and the ability to express the many aspects of themselves through the voice.

## Jung and the Acoustic Archetypes

In his reading, Wolfsohn had by now moved from Freud to Jung, whose principles of complex and archetype he felt to be highly applicable to vocal expression. Though he had not forgotten the significance of Freud's principles in contributing to his own cure, Wolfsohn none the less felt he had found both a more artistic and more sophisticated vision in the writings of Jung. At the centre of this intellectual conversion was Wolfsohn's inspiration by Jung's views on dreams, which he felt offered more insight than those of Freud. Jung's notion of a collective suffering made a particularly deep impression on Wolfsohn: the sounds that he had heard and the pain he had endured were not his own, but those of humankind. Wolfsohn began to look afresh at the myths and legends in which characters underwent great difficulties, suffered great pains and endured many labours in order to be born again, transformed. He now approached his vocal investigations with a fresh outlook.

While Jung was preoccupied with the pictorial expression of archetypal motifs in dreams, Wolfsohn felt he had discovered a way of making them audible through the sounds of the human voice. He proposed that the dream is the foundation, the constituting material for all art in every form. He believed that everyone who dreams is an artist, but that to realise this universal faculty depends upon the ability to make concrete one's dreams. In his own words: 'Art is the possibility to dream and to be able to fashion one's dreams.'[46] An important part of Wolfsohn's work therefore involved a translation of visual dream images into sound, and his pupils were asked to record and recount their dreams throughout their training. Marita Günther states how 'Alfred Wolfsohn maintained that every human being has the capacity to sing, just as every body is given the ability to dream in waking and in sleeping'.[47]

Wolfsohn had become particularly interested in an archetype which Jung called the 'shadow' and which represents the 'dark side' of our personality, that which we would never wish to identify with. As Jung said: 'The shadow personifies everything that the subject refuses to acknowledge about himself.'[48] For the overtly heroic man of bravado, the shadow is a shy and vulnerable boy; for the orderly and punctilious woman of sobriety and intellect, the shadow is an intuitive and inspired poet; for the kindly and devoted husband who exercises consistent but controlled affection, the shadow is the passionate and promiscuous lover within. For each individual the shadow takes on a different shape. However, as it is an archetype, it also possesses certain fundamental elements which are the same in all people of every culture. The shadow belongs to the same pantheon of universal figures as the trickster and the mother.

One of the definitive and universal aspects of the shadow is its animalistic quality. The shadow provides a counterbalance, indeed an opposite, to the overly sophisticated and so-called 'civilised' nature of human behaviour. It is the werewolf and the child-eating mother; it is the sum total of those aspects of our psyche which preserve the residue of the evolutionary process, a time when the distinction between humanity and animality was not so great. By 'shadow' Jung meant 'the inferior personality, the lowest levels of which are indistinguishable from the instinctuality of an animal'.[49]

The psychological concept of the shadow corresponds to the aesthetic concept of ugliness. The shadow is a constellation of images which constitute the darker, torrid, perverse and 'downward-pointing' part of the personality, and to it belong all those aspects of oneself which tend to remain disguised and hidden beneath the grace and manner of the persona, or the public face.

Wolfsohn recognised that if the voice was to be employed as an expression of the true nature of the psyche in its entirety, it would have to establish a connection with the shadow. This meant that the voice had to be permitted to yell, scream, sob and give voice to the animalistic, primal, pre-verbal utterances which are part of the rightful expression of the shadow.

It was the prohibition of the shadow in the voice, which had been upheld by the tradition of vocal training inherited from the demands of opera and a misinterpretation of bel canto, that Wolfsohn's work challenged; and it was these so-called primal noises that his teaching nurtured, until a voice emerged in his pupils that was wider and more malleable than any ever heard before.

## *Against the Tradition of Beauty*

When a singer reaches the higher or lower end of his or her easily accessible singing range, the voice begins to express a change in quality or an initial inability to sing the note. It is at this point that the voice breaks down into what many singing teachers call 'noise' in contradistinction to 'music'. The continual attempt to convert these noises to clear musical notes and thereby extend the breadth of the range has always been considered a damaging process. Consequently, by tradition, singers have been confined to the process of perfecting their comfortably obtainable register. However, Wolfsohn's work involved nurturing and extending these so-called 'noises' which were released at the very places where the voice apparently breaks down. He was not concerned with a judgement of their degree of aesthetic beauty but, rather, he perceived them in psychological terms as a viable expression of aspects of the shadow side of the psyche. Marita Günther records:

> This was a far cry from singing beautifully. In the beginning it was a squeaking and a squeezing, a screaming and a peeping; and out of this developed a different kind of beauty, the beauty of the dared expression.
>
> Like out of the days of the creation, something emerged that was not only beautiful, it was authentic, and this authenticity was nurtured, polished and repeated until the ear got accustomed to it; or let us say the ability to hear underwent an equally intensive training.[50]

Wolfsohn was concerned with discovering a process by which it would be possible to reconnect the voice to its murkiest, most deeply buried images. His experiences in the trenches had left him with an indelible belief that only in confronting and overcoming the dark side of oneself is it possible to achieve true artistic expression. To concern oneself only with the 'beautiful' is to turn a blind eye and a deaf ear to the true nature of life, which is always a combination of dark and light.

As a result of this auditory excavation of the soul, Wolfsohn was able to release in his students sounds which gave authentic expression to the deepest, most elemental levels of the psyche. Marita Günther records the emergence of some of these archetypal sounds:

> Another aspect of the breaking of sound barriers was the spontaneous emergence of an extraordinary variety of animal, bird and mechanical motor sounds. These had a very special meaning for each pupil, almost a certain life experience, as if suddenly a deeper strata of a past evolutionary process had been touched upon and was being relived.[51]

Wolfsohn was keen to oppose systematically the tradition of specialisation upon which classical singing had been founded, a tradition which nurtured a voice to possess a qualitative beauty of timbre within a given range – usually around two to two and a half octaves. These so-called natural ranges had been traditionally divided and allotted according to gender – soprano, mezzo-soprano and alto for women, and tenor, baritone and bass for men.

Because so many singing teachers had believed it to be unnatural to 'force' a voice to encapsulate more than one of these registers, particularly if it meant attempting to sing in a range associated with the opposite sex, singers had always been encouraged to specialise from the very beginning of their training. But Wolfsohn was of the opposite opinion, claiming that 'what is unnatural is the tradition of specialisation in the area of the human voice and the way in which it is artificially restrained'.[52]

## The Androgynous Voice

Wolfsohn thus challenged the popular preconceptions regarding the expressive limits implied and imposed by human gender and drew support from Jung's belief in the existence of the archetypes 'anima' and 'animus'. Jung proposed that

> it is a well-known fact that sex is determined by a majority of male or female genes, as the case may be. But the minority of genes belonging to the other sex does not simply disappear. A man therefore has in him a feminine side, an unconscious feminine figure – a fact of which

he is generally quite unaware. I may take it as known that I have called this figure the 'anima', and its counterpart in a woman the 'animus'.[53]

Like all unconscious contents, the animus and anima are experienced in projection; that is, they can only be apprehended through phonic or visual images which appear to exist outside ourselves. As we know, the many forms of projection identified by Jung include the motifs of painting, the characters of literature and the images in dreams. In addition, the apparent personality traits of another person often contain aspects of the beholder's projection. For example, Jung pointed out that the qualities which a man longs for and idolises in a woman reflect more the particular quality of his own anima than the true qualities of the lover upon whom he projects them. However, the sounds of the voice too contain the fabric of our projections and may be apprehended by an attentive ear.

In the normal course of events a person is unaware of the processes by which images are projected out of the depths of the psyche into the world, hence the term 'unconscious'. However, in order to facilitate psychological maturity and to realise fully our potential creativity, Jung believed that it is important to make an attempt to integrate these images into consciousness. Only then can we become aware of the particular shape which our archetypal influences take. Jung called the process of becoming conscious of our hidden dynamics 'individuation' and he believed this to be the very goal and purpose of analytical psychology.

While Freud had regarded verbal discourse as the mainstay of the psychotherapeutic dialogue, Jung had incorporated into the analytical process other forms of psychological expression, particularly painting. In his work *The Archetypes and the Collective Unconscious*, he records a whole case study through which the paintings produced by a client over the period of her therapy are analysed as a parallel expression of her psychological development.

Wolfsohn's thoughts, then, were entirely in line with Jung's when he conceived of the idea that the anima and animus were potentially audible through the human voice. Wolfsohn believed that, in giving a voice to the other sex, the anima or animus could be projected into sound, confronted audibly and aurally and, finally, accepted and integrated into consciousness.

By contacting and expressing the other sex within, Wolfsohn's pupils were able to develop singing registers which are normally associated with the opposite gender; hence he nurtured a bass voice in women and a soprano voice in men. Marita Günther records:

We must remember that at that time one hardly spoke of the range of a voice. It was generally understood that, let us say a baritone, was singing in the middle register between tenor and bass; it was of much greater importance that a voice simply had to be beautiful. A man therefore who produces also distinctly female sounds, and a woman who goes down into a deep register, after all run the risk of venturing into the grotesque; at best something for a variety show. Although we understand, and accept quite easily from the psychological aspect, that in every female being there is also a male side – in some stronger, in some weaker – and vice versa that every man also possesses female qualities – nevertheless it was then a big step to search for these parts in oneself and to express them audibly, not as a parody or as a sensation, but as a serious attempt to find these other sides and thus to learn more about oneself.[54]

Like Jung, Wolfsohn believed that humankind once had to express the elements, the animals, feelings and experiences with sound. But Wolfsohn took this one stage further, proposing that somewhere in the depths of the psyche a sympathy with these elements remained. His approach to singing consisted of a conversion of this psychic residue into the somatic phenomenon of the human voice:

> In my attempt to discover the secret of singing nothing has compensated me more for all my searching and worrying than the discovery that that which I had one-sidedly understood as expression in its symbolic and spiritual sense had to be taken in its literal meaning.
>
> I found that the sound of the human voice gained its fullest expression exactly at the point where the singing person, having found the right balance of concentration and tension, could express it bodily.[55]

By giving voice to the images of the psyche, Wolfsohn believed that he was converting the psychic into the somatic. In reconnecting these archetypal images to the voice, his pupils gave bodily expression to what Jung had referred to as the collective unconscious.

## Scientific Validation and Recognition

Many people became suspicious, not only that Wolfsohn's approach was 'unnatural', but that he was causing damage to his pupil's vocal apparatus. In order to assuage these fears, some of the pupils had their voices subjected to scientific measurement while producing their extended range.

Among these students was a young woman called Jenny Johnson, who in 1955 had her voice examined by Professor Luchsinger of the Zurich Otolaryngological Clinic using X-ray, high-speed film and a stroboscope. This examination confirmed a range of six octaves and discovered no abnormality in the anatomical structure or physiological functioning of the larynx. Luchsinger noted, however, that while the larynx appeared to be very relaxed, a high degree of 'mental effort' was required to produce the high notes.[56]

Luchsinger's discoveries corroborated Wolfsohn's deepest belief that the range of the voice depended not on any exceptional physical virtuosity or on an unnatural or maladjusted anatomy, but on the psychological investigation of the deepest regions of the psyche. In Wolfsohn's words:

> Physical training only plays a secondary role in my work with my students; the main task is a psychological one . . . The range, strength and timbre of the voice are not determined by the size and shape of the larynx, the vocal cords or the rib cage, but solely by emotional factors . . . Nobody will dispute the fact that the human voice can lose in range, power and tone-colour as a result of particular emotional events . . . so why are there then doubts about the voice being capable in exactly the same way of taking advantage of another set of emotional circumstances?[57]

In order to demonstrate his achievements to a wider audience, Wolfsohn and Jenny Johnson gave a demonstration in Paris to the psychotherapist Eric Weiser which was then reported in the Swiss newspaper *Die Weltwoche* in an article entitled 'The Unchained Voice'. At this demonstration Jenny Johnson displayed a range in excess of eight octaves.

> Jenny Johnson, her voice recently assessed by musicians and examined by a Swiss laryngologist, is capable of between eight and nine octaves. A Gift of Nature? A world record? An abnormality? 'Absolutely not', says Jenny's teacher, the voice therapist Alfred Wolfsohn . . .
>
> Beside him stood a tall, slim young woman possessed of a strange and radiant kind of beauty. Her name was Jenny Johnson, a young English woman and one of the fourteen male and female students working with Wolfsohn at his London studio. She had come with him on a short visit to Paris to help give myself and others interested in Wolfsohn's work some idea of what they had achieved.
>
> The three of us went to the attic flat of a Parisian singer who had put her old, slightly out of tune piano at our disposal. Jenny climbed the five flights of stairs and wasn't at all out of breath when she got to the top. She was smoking a strong American cigarette and didn't have to clear her throat once before she began to sing, accompanied by her teacher. With a voice as clear as a bell, she sang the highest and lowest notes the piano could produce. The piano with its seven octaves fell silent, since Jenny Johnson's voice had a range of between eight and nine octaves. The impossibly high notes of a coloratura soprano, which can only be compared with the song of the nightingale, then rang out unaccompanied – the next minute we were treated to a full, deep male voice.

Jenny Johnson's voice . . . takes in both the male and the female ranges, allowing her, for example, to sing all the parts of the *Magic Flute*, from the coloratura soprano role of the Queen of the Night right the way down to Sarastro's bass . . .

The psychic relationship between Wolfsohn and his students cannot easily be defined using the normal psychological terms. Suggestion and psychoanalysis undoubtedly play an important role. The psychic effects are probably closest to that process termed 'relaxation through self-hypnosis', which modern psychotherapy has partly learnt from the Indian Yogi – the release of previously hidden creative energies brought about through relaxation and the consequent mastery of mind over body . . .

I tried in vain to discover in the face of the nigh sixty year old man something of the incredible strength which flowed from him to his students. Those slightly sad, resigned eyes of his hidden behind his spectacles were those of the eternal seeker or explorer. Alfred Wolfsohn's profound knowledge of the connections between body and soul is the hard-won harvest of a long and painful journey: the trenches of two world wars, wounding and years of illness, persecution in Berlin, escape to London, and later – a new beginning.[58]

It was in this article that Wolfsohn gave the most lucid description of the beliefs upon which his investigations were based:

Man has for many centuries failed to appreciate his voice; he has underestimated it and neglected it and allowed it to waste away; he has virtually strangled it, chained it up and confined it in a straitjacket; as he has so often done before, man has once again turned his sinning against nature into dogma: the dogma of tightly restricted, neatly labelled categories – male and female voices, high and low voices, children's voices and adult voices; the dogma that maintains that every human being has been assigned a particular register from birth, or at least from the moment the voice breaks, that covers no more than around two octaves; soprano, mezzo-soprano and alto for women, and tenor, baritone and bass for men. The truth is that the natural human voice, freed from all artificial restrictions, is able to embrace all these categories and registers – indeed, it is able to go much further . . .

My first concern is to free my pupils from the fear of heights and the fear of depths conditioned in their voices by tradition. The baby, not yet acquainted with these fears, screams with all his might using the whole of his body as a resonating chamber. But alongside the fear of heights and the fear of depths, each individual is variously prey to a whole host of psychic inhibitions and conflicts, anxieties and complexes the elimination of which leads to the opening out of the personality and the voice.

But none of this has anything to do with the mystical, it is a completely natural process . . . I am neither a sorcerer nor a hypnotist. I can only help my students to overcome their inner tensions and difficulties, and through this easing of tension to loosen the inhibitions which hold their personalities as well as their voices in chains.

But the bulk of the work they must do themselves.[59]

Wolfsohn wrote to Jung early in 1955, enclosing manuscripts which described his work, but on 3 May 1955 Aniela Jaffe, Jung's colleague and secretary, wrote back to say that Jung himself would not be able to take note of his investigations. This was a great blow to Wolfsohn, who now felt that he may never have his work formally appreciated in more established circles. It was only through receiving recognition from Paul Moses that Wolfsohn realised that he had not been the only one searching for a psychology of the human voice during all those years, and by the time Wolfsohn died in 1962, he had proven beyond doubt a fundamental connection between voice and psyche.

The psychotherapeutic benefits of singing and sound-making under Wolfsohn's direction are preserved in the testimony of many of his students who are still living, some of whom continue to teach the work which he pioneered. Many of these had originally gone to Wolfsohn for help with mental difficulties and they exemplify how the process of working upon the voice can be curative and reviving. Among these pupils is the well-known British rabbi, Lionel Blue:

I went to Wolfsohn because I had become very confused, completely detached from my body, from my feelings and from who I was.

I worked with Wolfsohn for over five years and I think the work was one of the single most important influences on my life. It not only brought me closer to myself, it brought me closer to God, to my family. It revived my sexuality and it revived myself.

Everything came out, ugly sounds, beautiful sounds, cracks, groans, screeches and a multitude of different characters. Some of these characters sounded male, some female, some angelic, some brutish. But it was never a process of taking part, but of putting together all the pieces into a whole, a whole that I had never experienced before – and this whole was me.[60]

Wolfsohn's contribution may be seen as drawing together the various threads of research conducted in the post-psychotherapeutic years of the twentieth century; it adds to the accumulation of evidence which points to the fundamental curative potential of vocal work.

When Wolfsohn died, the direction of his work and the leadership of the group which had grown up under him was taken over by an actor called Roy Hart, who had worked with Wolfsohn for over fifteen years. What had begun as a therapeutic investigation with elements of musical performance now became a theatrical investigation with therapeutic implications as Roy Hart began to steer the work towards presentations of experimental vocal performances. It was from this transition that the Roy Hart Theatre was born.

During the mid-1960s the Roy Hart Theatre group was visited by two of the most influential and celebrated experimental-theatre directors of their time, Peter Brook and Jerzy Grotowski.[61] They were not only impressed by what they saw, but also influenced by the group in their thinking and in their approach to vocal work. Brook wrote to the British funding authorities urging further financial support for their work,[62] and in 1979 Grotowski publicly acknowledged his debt to the work initiated by Wolfsohn and continued by Hart.[63]

## Homage to a Little-known Mad Man

No British theatre director is more renowned than Peter Brook for making such radical and innovative contributions to the definition, practice and products of performance. Like the *Camerata* of Renaissance Italy, Brook's mission to remould the theatre which his generation inherited, a theatre which he considered stale and deadly, was fuelled by a sense of something greater having gone before him. Brook absorbed from accounts of Greek theatre the image of a form of performance capable of activating the deepest and most fundamental feelings and instincts in an audience. But, for Brook, the twentieth-century British theatre was restrained from dealing with such archetypal images by an unceasing adherence to the eloquent articulation of text. By the same token, Brook perceived the opera to be deprived of its potency by an overly scrutinising attention to the artificial formal structures of music:

> Opera started fifty thousand years ago with people making noises as they came out of their caves. And out of those noises come Verdi and Puccini and Wagner. There was a noise for fear, for love, for happiness and for anger.
>
> That was one-note, atonal opera, and that's where it all began. At that point it was a natural human expression, and that turned into song. And, at some later time, that process became codified, constructed, and turned into an art . . .
>
> I would say the greatest challenge now, at this point in the twentieth century, is to replace – in the minds of performers as well as audiences – the idea that opera is artificial with the idea that opera is natural. That's really the most important thing, and I think it's possible.[64]

The means by which Brook sought to revive the natural expressive function of the human voice was to set up experimental-theatre workshops at the Royal Shakespeare Company in which he required of his actors that they communicate to an audience without the use of words.

Brook's investigations had been inspired by the writings of an earlier artistic experimenter called Antonin Artaud, an actor, poet and theorist whose extreme intellectual vision for a new form of theatre was prevented from ever being actually realised by his bouts of mental illness.

Central to Artaud's quest was the search for a non-verbal use of the voice to communicate fundamental aspects of the human condition. Not only did this quest leave an indelible impression on Peter Brook, but it also bequeathed a mission that was to be taken up by a range of experimental-theatre groups in the 1960s and 1970s who sought non-verbal ways of communicating feelings and ideas to an audience. As Jacqueline Martin says in her book *The Voice in Modern Theatre*, the range of vocal delivery styles which resulted from the investigations of these later groups, which used sounds rather than words, screams and cries rather than speech, owed much to the original impetus provided by the writings of Artaud.[65]

Artaud asked a simple but important question: 'How is it Western theatre cannot conceive of theatre under any other aspect than dialogue form?'[66] His desire was to liberate Western theatre from what he described as the 'exclusive dictatorship of words',[67] which, he believed, had arisen as a result of the dominance of the written text. Artaud's aim to release theatre from a concern with text was, however, an integral part of a more fundamental and overall objective to remove from the theatre the natural-istic presentation of human characters in a recognisable social context. He asked: 'Whoever said theatre was made to define a character, to resolve conflicts of a human emotional order, of a present-day, psychological nature such as those which monopolise current theatre?'[68]

Artaud was reacting against the great wave of realistic plays that had swept Europe during the late nineteenth and early twentieth century; plays which, unlike the legendary narratives and mythical characters presented in Greek tragedy, revealed only ordinary people in mundane situations; plays which, unlike the tremendous guttural cascades of vocal passion which thundered through the mouths of Greek masks, uttered only the language and tones of everyday speech.

Artaud criticised such a theatre for reducing what he regarded as the mysteriously unapproachable and evasive images of the human psyche into the language of conversational banality and linguistic discourse:

> Psychology persists in bringing the unknown down to a level with the known, that is to say with the everyday and pedestrian. And psy-chology has caused this abasement and fearful loss of energy which appears to me to have really reached its limit. And it seems both theatre and ourselves want nothing more to do with psychology.[69]

For Artaud the main factor which kept theatre shackled to what he described as 'psychology' was the written text and the spoken word of the actor which he proposed had perpetuated and preserved a 'purely descriptive, narrative theatre, narrating psychology'.[70] He saw that in 'Western theatre, words are solely used to express psychological conflicts peculiar to man and his position in everyday existence'.[71] He believed that this use of words had turned theatre into an arena for 'psychological conflicts', a 'battlefield for moral passions',[72] containing nothing but stories about 'money troubles', 'social climbing' and 'sexuality sugar-coated with eroticism yet shorn of mystery.'[73]

Artaud maintained that theatre had a higher function which could only be rediscovered by challenging and changing the way it employed language. His vision of this higher function of theatre was that it should 'make a break with topicality'[74] and concern itself with the presentation of the metaphysical aspects and aspirations of the human condition. He proposed that this theatre would not attempt to express in a different manner the same things that words communicate, but would instead approach those subjects for which speech is inadequate or is unable to express.

In the place of 'psychological theatre' Artaud sought a theatre which 'rediscovers the idea of figures and archetypal symbols'.[75] He proposed that this theatre should not be verbal but vocal, not histrionic but physical, a 'genuine physical language, no longer based on words but on signs formed through the combination of objects, silence, shouts and rhythms'.[76] In this new theatre 'words will be considered in an incantatory, truly magical sense' perceived 'not only for their meaning but for their sensual radiation'.[77]

Artaud sought a theatre which would be a 'powerful appeal through illustration to those powers which return the mind to the origins of its inner struggles'.[78] He thought that the theatre, in seeking to realise this, should return to 'the higher idea of poetry underlying the Myths told by the great tragedians of ancient times'.[79] And, for Artaud, integral to this return to myth was a confrontation with all that is bloody, violent, dark and torrid:

> Thus all great Myths are dark and one cannot imagine all the great Fables aside from a mood of slaughter, torture and bloodshed, telling the masses about the original division of the sexes and the slaughter of essences that came with creation.
>
> Theatre, like the plague, is made in the image of this slaughter, this essential division. It unravels conflicts, liberates powers, releases potential and if these and the powers are dark, this is not the fault of the plague or theatre, but life.[80]

# Peter Brook and the Search for a Universal Language of Sounds

It was these thoughts that fuelled Brook's determination to investigate the degree to which Artaud's pleas might be fulfilled by his actors at the Royal Shakespeare Company. Encouraged by his discoveries, Brook continued with his vocal experiments throughout the following year of 1965, when he collaborated with the writer Ted Hughes to devise a production of *Oedipus* which used chants based on those uttered by the Maoris of New Zealand and irregular breathing rhythms derived from a recording of a medicine man in a trance.[81]

Brook became so intrigued by experiments into the nature of vocal sound that he left his career as a highly successful, semi-commercial, text-bound British theatre director and went to Paris, where he founded the International Theatre Research Centre, a company of actors of different nationalities, many of whom could not converse with one another because they spoke different languages. The theme of the first year's work at the Centre was a study of the structures of sounds.[82] John Heilpern, a journalist who has documented Brook's work, describes this work as 'a search for myths and archetypes, sounds and forms that touched the power beneath the surface', endeavouring to give expression to aspects of 'the collective unconscious'.[83]

Brook later collaborated again with Ted Hughes, this time to create an entirely original language called 'Orghast' with which the group of actors devised a play of the same name that became the subject of newspaper reports world-wide. In Brook's words:

> We found that the sound fabric of language is a code, an emotional code that bears witness to the passions that forged it. For instance, it is because the ancient Greeks had the capacity to experience certain emotions intensely that their language grew into the vehicle it was. If they had other feelings, they would have developed other syllables. The arrangement of vowels in Greek produced sounds that vibrate more intensely than in modern English – and it is sufficient for an actor to speak these syllables to be lifted out of the emotional constriction of the twentieth-century city life into a fullness of passion which he never knew he possessed.
>
> With Avesta, the two-thousand-year-old language of Zoroaster, we encountered sound patterns that are hieroglyphs of spiritual experience. Zoroaster's poems, which on the printed page in English seem vague and pious platitudes, turn into tremendous statements when certain movements of larynx and breath become an inseparable part of their sense. Ted Hughes's study of this led to *Orghast* . . .

Though the actors had no common language they found the possibility of a common expression.[84]

Later still, in 1972, Brook set off with his actors to see if it was possible to communicate with people of the tribal communities of Africa through a non-verbal theatre. J. Roose-Evans, a London theatre director documenting Brook's work during this time, says in his book *Experimental Theatre* that Brook's intention was to 'create a work of theatre that could be accessible to everyone wherever it was played;'[85] and that the aim, ultimately, was to discover whether the level of the 'collective unconscious . . . can be tapped in sound'.[86]

The journey of Peter Brook and his actors in Africa is recorded in *The Conference of the Birds*, a book by John Heilpern, who went to Africa with the troupe. In one part of the book Heilpern talks of the Peulh tribe, who had become hypnotically fascinated by their own reflections in mirrors supplied by the troupe. Brook, meanwhile, was wondering how it would be possible for the two groups, who did not speak each other's language and who were from entirely different cultures, to communicate and share a common experience. Brook's first idea was for the acting troupe to sing a song, but the Peulhs were not interested, so he tried something else:

> He asked the group to make a sound they had worked on during the research in Paris. He asked for an 'ah' sound – just this one basic sound that was to be extended and developed as far as it could possibly go . . .
>
> The group began to make the sound. The Peulhs were still staring into the mirrors. I watched the actors grow hesitant, uncertain whether to continue. But the sound stretched and grew – and the Peulhs unexpectedly looked up from their mirrors for the first time. The sound took life, vibrating. The Peulhs discarded their mirrors and joined the sound. Oh, it seemed miraculous! It was as if the Peulh were pulling the sound from them. They pointed to the sky.
>
> Just as the unimaginable sound reached its height, or seemed to, no one would venture any further. Somehow it was frightening. The two sides had met and come together in one sound . . .
>
> But now the Peulh offered an exchange and sang their songs. And they told Brook something very precious. He knew at last that he was on the right road in the search for a universal language.[87]

While Peter Brook was searching for a universal language of sounds at Stratford, in Paris and in Africa, Jerzy Grotowski was researching a similar area in Poland.

# Jerzy Grotowski – Towards an Archetypal Theatre

In 1959 Jerzy Grotowski became director in Opole, Poland, of what was known as the 'Theatre of Thirteen Rows'. In this tiny theatre, in one of the poorest countries in Europe, a group of actors came together to explore new forms of theatrical expression without employing the spoken word.

In the programme notes to their production of *Akropolis*, of which the première was in October 1962, one of the members stated:

> The means of verbal expression have been considerably enlarged because all means of vocal expression are used, starting from the confused babbling of the very small child and including the most sophisticated oratorical recitation. Inarticulate groans, animal roars, tender folksongs, liturgical chants, dialects, declamation of poetry: everything is there. The sounds are interwoven in a complex score which brings back fleetingly the memory of all forms of language.[88]

Grotowski and his group of devoted actors became known in particular for their revolutionary work on the human voice. Alan Seymour, speaking of their production of *Faustus* (which opened in April 1963), noted that 'their voices reached from the smallest whisper to an astonishing, almost cavernous tone, an intoned declaiming, of a resonance and power I have not heard from actors before'.[89]

The use of non-verbal voice in these productions was part of Grotowski's investigation into the use of the actor's own psychological make-up as the substance of performance, and his work was intricately and overtly bound up with a belief in the ability of a human being to express physically and vocally aspects of the psyche, including those parts which are buried in the 'collective unconscious', without recourse to words. Grotowski said that theatre 'is a question of a gathering which is subordinated to ritual: nothing is represented or shown, but we participate in a ceremonial which releases the collective unconscious'.[90] In Grotowski's scheme of things the actor had to be able to draw from his psyche images of a personal and collective significance and give them form through the motion of the body and the sound of the voice.

Grotowski's ultimate aim was to effect in the actor change and growth, transformation and rebirth in order that the actor, in turn, could entice a similar development in the audience. Jennifer Kumiega, who has provided a most comprehensive documentation of Grotowski's work, says:

> His [Grotowski's] aim therefore, is to bring us momentarily into contact with the deepest levels within ourselves, deeper than those engaged within the order of forms, through incarnate mythic confrontation. If we succeed, through the shock of exposure, in touching

those depths, we are changed for ever. The process does not involve release: it is rather a re-awakening, or a re-birth, and in consequence potentially painful.

Whether or not one chooses to attach importance to categorizations such as 'tragedy', the significant factor to be borne in mind is Grotowski's continual submission to the real possibility of *change* within the work and performance process (for actor and spectator).[91]

It was for this reason that Grotowski chose works based on timeless myths and legends as subjects for his productions, for he believed that they 'embodied myths and images powerful and universal enough to function as archetypes, which could penetrate beneath the apparently divisive and individual structure of the Western psyche, and evoke a spontaneous, collective, internal response'.[92] In his words:

> In order that the spectator may be stimulated into self-analysis when confronted with the actor, there must be some common ground already existing in both of them, something they can either dismiss in one gesture or jointly worship. Therefore the theatre must attack what might be called the collective complexes of society, the core of the collective subconscious or perhaps super-conscious (it does not matter what we call it), the myths which are not an invention of the mind but are, so to speak, inherited through one's blood, religion, culture and climate.[93]

Grotowski said that he 'saw that myth was both a primeval situation, and a complex model with an independent existence in the psychology of social groups'.[94] Of the images and characters in a production based on Shakespeare's *Hamlet* which opened in March 1964, one of the members of the group, Ludwik Flaszen, said, 'we draw these out from the depths of the unconscious with the aim of healing'.[95]

Speaking of the form of theatre generated by experimenters like Artaud, Brook, and particularly Grotowski, Roose-Evans states:

> Such a form of theatre speaks directly to the fundamental experience of each person present, to what Jung described as the collective unconscious. It is a theatre of symbols. It will be argued, rightly, that many great dramatists also deal with symbols, from Ibsen to Shakespeare. But what Grotowski . . . [asks] of the actor is not that he play the Lady from the Sea or Hamlet, but that he confront these characters within himself and offer the result of that encounter to an audience.[96]

Grotowski, like Artaud, did not consider the text to be primary, but believed that the text 'becomes theatre only through the actors' use of it – that is to say, thanks to intonations, to the association of sounds, to the musicality of language'.[97] Grotowski thus pursued the possibility of creating 'ideograms' made up of 'sounds and gestures' which 'evoke associations in the psyche of the audience'.[98]

But, for Grotowski, there was, between the psychic image and its bodily and vocal expression, a series of inhibitions, resistances and blocks which prevent transformation from one to the other, and it was these obstacles that his acting exercises set out to remove:

> The education of an actor in our theatre is not a matter of teaching him something; we attempt to eliminate his organism's resistance to this psychic process. The result is freedom from the time-lapse between inner impulse and outer reaction. Impulse and action are concurrent: the body vanishes, burns, and the spectator sees only a series of visible impulses. Ours then is a via negativa – not a collection of skills but an eradication of blocks.[99]

This eradication of the blocks which prevent expression in an actor is comparable to Freud's attempt to remove the obstacles which prevent abreaction in a patient, and Grotowski's recognition of the psychological implications of his work led to a synthesis of theatre and therapy at the Polish theatre laboratory.

Grotowski said that the 'important thing is to use the role as trampoline, an instrument with which to study what is hidden behind our everyday mask – the innermost core of our personality – in order to sacrifice it, expose it'.[100] The acting exercises developed at the laboratory were therefore not a systematic acquisition of principles, but a process of discovering the means to removing and breaking down the personal inhibitions which prevented the physical and vocal expression of psychological material,[101] and Grotowski proposed that such a training process 'leads to a liberation from complexes in much the same way as psycho-analytic therapy'.[102]

In rediscovering the power of mythical tales told not only through language but through the expressive power of the human voice, Grotowski reclaimed the therapeutic role of theatre which had been so fundamental to Greek tragedy and upon which Freud built his original cathartic method. What Grotowski discovered was that the physical movements of the body and the non-verbal utterances of the voice have the capacity to embody and express images which occupy the deepest recesses of the collective unconscious, and which thereby have an arresting significance, or numinosity, for the audience. Such an immediate form of expression was for Grotowski comparable to the primitive voice-dance, oral gesture or primeval song and dance, and its enactment stimulated an abreactive catharsis in actor and audience alike.

## And It Spreads Like Wild Fire

The mid twentieth century witnessed the widespread application of psychotherapeutic principles by experimental-theatre practitioners. Actors began to partake of the same process of psychological investigation as the patients of Freud and Jung had done, except that the means by which they raised aspects of their unconscious to the level of conscious scrutiny was not verbal dialogue, but voice and movement. This means was also employed by those clinical practitioners with a progressive response to traditional psychotherapy and who shared with the vision of experimental theatre a belief in the significance of vocal and bodily dynamics in the expression of unconscious drives, images, instincts and affects.

The evidence provided by the anthropological, laryngological, psychological and artistic quarters clearly points to the prevalence world-wide and throughout history of divergent approaches to the therapeutic use of voice and singing, from ancient healing rituals in Guatemala to the respiratory exercises of Alexander Lowen, from the stereotypical schizophrenic chants observed by Jung to the acoustic shaping of archetypal images by Wolfsohn, from the absolving effects of Greek tragedy to the psychodynamics of vocal tone perceived by Moses. All this provides the bedrock upon which a methodological strategy of vocal work may be built, a strategy which can improve the psychological awareness and physical well-being of a broad spectrum of people.

That vocal work can contribute to a process of psycho-physical growth is further verified by the research carried out by a number of contemporary practitioners who have sought to bring the self-enhancing aspects of vocal sound to the attention of an increasingly wide range of people. Among them is Jill Purce, whose teaching is based on an aesthetic and psycho-spiritual appropriation of the vocal practices used by Mongolian monks, in particular their techniques of chanting. Another of the more celebrated contemporary teachers is Frankie Armstrong, whose work is based upon the preservation of a way of singing, known as the 'open-throat technique', which has been part of the European folk tradition for may centuries. Both Purce and Armstrong share a deep commitment and allegiance to vocal practices that originate in cultural and historical contexts which have paid more heed than our own culture to the essential role of voice in self-expression.

There are also less-renowned but equally important pockets of vocal work and experimentation that have become established in a variety of settings, not only in workshops and singing studios, in theatres and music colleges, but in hospitals and day centres, youth clubs and special-education centres. More and more people are becoming aware that the first steps in incorporating the human voice into the field of education and therapy are being taken. More and more people are becoming aware that the unsympathetic attitude which society holds towards unbridled vocalisation leaves deeply ingrained inhibitions in those practitioners who want to explore such work. In order for those tenets discovered by the research which has gone before us to be accessible and practicable on a broad scale and among a diverse spectrum of people, it is necessary to make the first steps towards documenting an integrated therapeutic vocal strategy applicable in a range of settings. This is the aim of Part Two of this book.

# PART TWO
## Introducing Voice Movement Therapy

# CHAPTER FOUR

# The Scientific Principles of Vocal Sound

## *Breathing*

The Greek word *psyche*, meaning soul, has the same root as *psychein*, meaning 'to breathe'; and the Greek word *pneuma*, meaning 'spirit', also means 'wind'. Furthermore, the Latin words *animus*, meaning 'spirit', and *anima*, meaning 'soul', come from the Greek *anemos*, which is another word for 'wind'. Similar connections also exist in Arabic and German and they remind us that in many cultures the notions of psyche, spirit and soul have been related to the idea of the movement of air.

This connection between air and soul is also contained in the fact that the human voice as the audible expression of the psyche can only be created through the emission of air from the body.

The thorax, or thoracic cavity, which constitutes the upper half of the trunk, houses the lungs, two spongy balloon-like organs which are composed of over three hundred million minuscule air sacs or alveoli. (See Figure 1.)

*Figure 1* Lungs

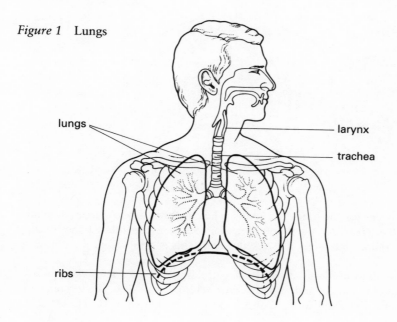

When we breathe in, the lungs inflate with air and oxygen passes through the alveoli into the blood stream. In addition, unwanted gases pass from the blood stream into the alveoli and when we breathe out the lungs deflate and air is expelled. This process of respiration is crucial to the maintenance of life. If it ceases for more than four to five minutes, death is inevitable. (See Figure 2.)

*Figure 2*   Respiration

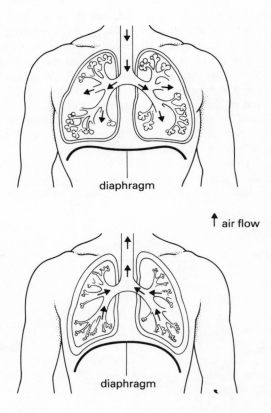

In order for the lungs to expand when we breathe in, increased volume has to be created in the thorax, for when the lungs are inflated, they occupy more space than when they are deflated. This is achieved in the following way.

The lungs are housed within a scaffolding of bones known as the rib-cage and both men and women have twelve pairs of ribs. The top ten pairs are curved in shape and are attached to the backbone or vertebrae behind and to the breast bone or sternum at the front. The lower two pairs of ribs are shorter than the others and are attached only to the vertebrae, with their other end protruding; these are known as the floating ribs. Although the top ten pairs of ribs are attached front and back, they are not fused solidly but are joined by cartilage and joints so as to be able to move. (See Figure 3.)

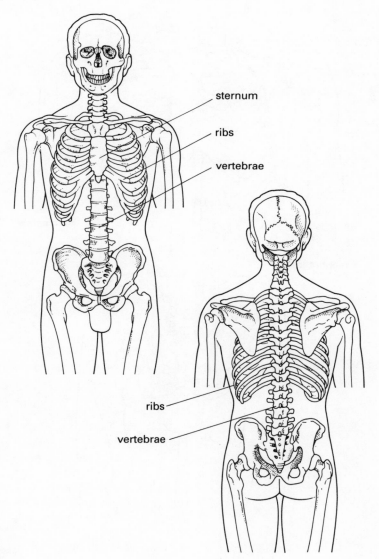

*Figure 3*   Rib-cage

*Figure 4*  Intercostal muscles

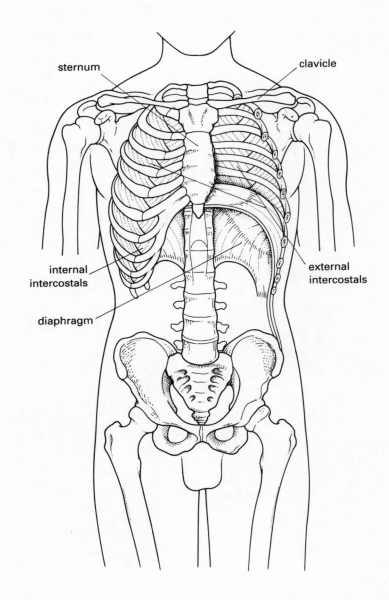

Between the ribs, inside and outside the cage which they form, there are two sets of muscles, the internal intercostal muscles and the external intercostal muscles. (See Figure 4.) The neurological instigation of a certain distribution and adjustment in tension, contraction and expansion in the intercostal muscles causes the ribs to be pulled upwards and outwards, increasing the size of the thoracic cavity. (See Figure 5.)

However, there is another activity which further increases the space in which the lungs expand. Underneath the lungs there is a long muscle called the diaphragm which is stretched out from one side of the trunk to the other, separating the thorax from the abdomen. (See Figure 6.) When the diaphragm is relaxed, it has a shape similar to an upside-down salad bowl; but when it contracts, it is pulled downwards and flattened. The floor of the rib-cage is consequently lowered, creating an increased space into which the lungs can expand. (See Figures 7 and 8.)

During inspiration the contraction of the diaphragm occurs in tandem with a series of complex adjustments in the distribution of tension among the intercostal muscles, increasing the volume of the thoracic cavity in which the lungs may expand to accommodate the inspired air. When we breathe out, an adjustment in the distribution of intercostal-muscle tension accompanies the relaxation of the diaphragm, decreasing the volume of the thoracic cavity and promoting the expulsion of air from the lungs.

*Figure 5* Thoracic expansion of the rib-cage

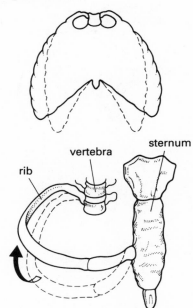

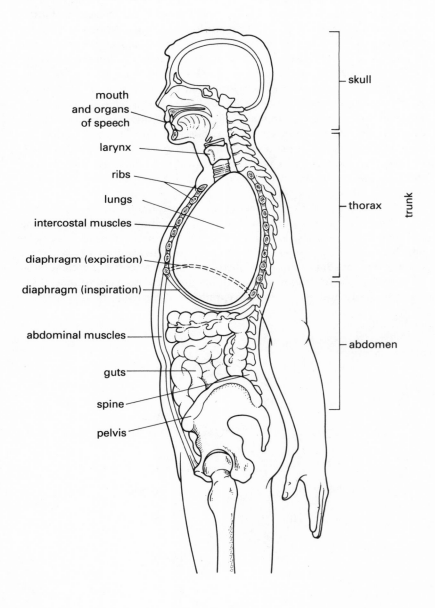

*Figure 6*   Diaphragm in relation to the trunk

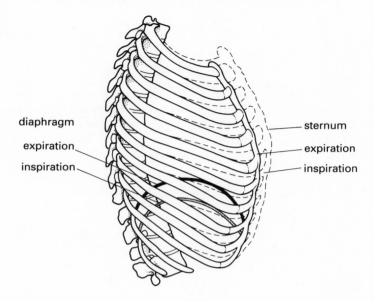

*Figure 7*   Diaphragm in relation to the ribs (a)

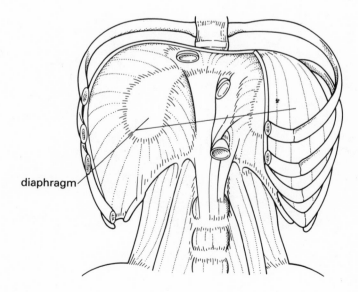

*Figure 8*   Diaphragm in relation to the ribs (b)

# The Vocal Cords

In order for air to reach the lungs, it has to pass through the mouth and down the windpipe, or trachea, which begins in the back of the throat in a cavity called the larynx and at its lower end it splits into two forks, the left and right bronchus, which enter the lungs and divide further into smaller tubes called bronchioles. (See Figures 9 and 10.)

*Figure 9*　Lungs, left and right bronchus and bronchioles

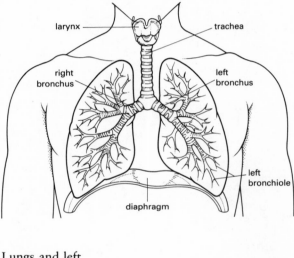

*Figure 10*　Lungs and left and right bronchus

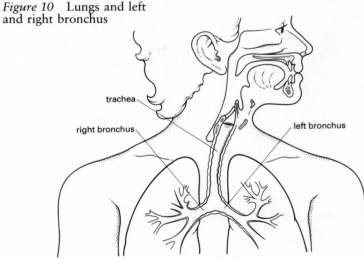

Lying stretched out across the top of the trachea in the larynx there are two folds of tissue. At the front they are attached to the Adam's apple, or thyroid cartilage, and at the back they are connected to two movable cartilages called the arytenoids. These two folds of tissue are the vocal cords and are further attached to the trachea and the surrounding inner walls of the larynx by a complex set of muscles collectively known as the laryngeal musculature. (See Figures 11–14.)

*Figure 11*   Larynx, thyroid and arytenoid cartilages and position of the vocal cords

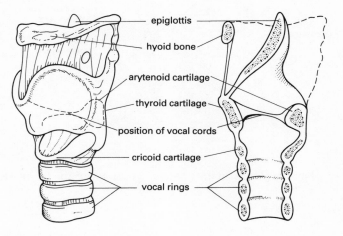

*Figure 12*   Laryngeal musculature (a)

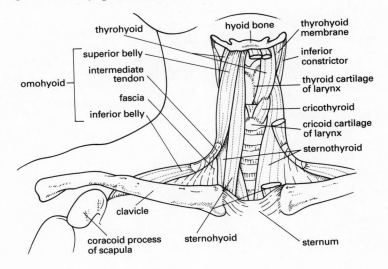

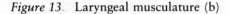

*Figure 13* Laryngeal musculature (b)

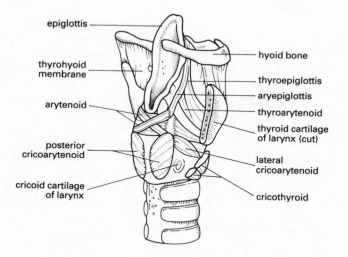

*Figure 14* Laryngeal musculature showing position of the laryngeal nerves

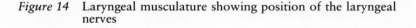

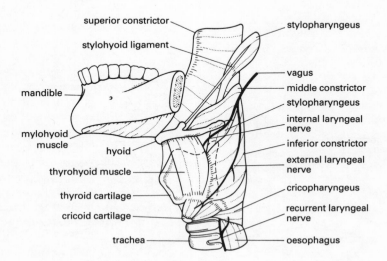

During normal breathing the vocal cords lie at rest, one each side of the trachea, like an open pair of curtains allowing air to pass freely through a window. The hole betweeen the vocal cords through which air passes is called the glottis.

Adjustments in the distribution of tension in the laryngeal musculature cause the vocal cords to close, preventing air from entering or leaving the trachea, like a thick pair of curtains drawn tightly shut across a window.

The vocal cords and the surrounding laryngeal musculature are fed by an incredibly high quantity of nerves, which means that the movements of the vocal cords can be controlled very precisely.

The sound of the human voice, such as in saying 'ah', or singing a series of notes or speaking, is not caused by a static position of the vocal cords, but is generated by their rapid and successive opening and closure hundreds of times per second, and it is to this process that people refer when they speak of the vibration of the vocal cords. The opening of the cords is called 'abduction' and the closing is called 'adduction'. The rapid abduction and adduction of the vocal cords causes the expelled air from the lungs to be released through the glottis in a series of infinitesimal puffs and it is these puffs of air emerging through the vibrating vocal cords which create the sound of the human voice. This process is called 'phonation'. (See Figures 15 and 16.)

Because the vocal cords are attached front and back to the thyroid and arytenoid cartilages, they can be stretched out by tensile adjustment in the laryngeal muscles, making them longer and thinner. When this happens, the sound of the human voice is higher in pitch. Conversely, when they are slackened off, the voice deepens.

*Figure 15*   Vocal cords and glottis

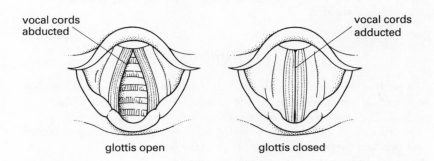

vocal cords
abducted

vocal cords
adducted

glottis open        glottis closed

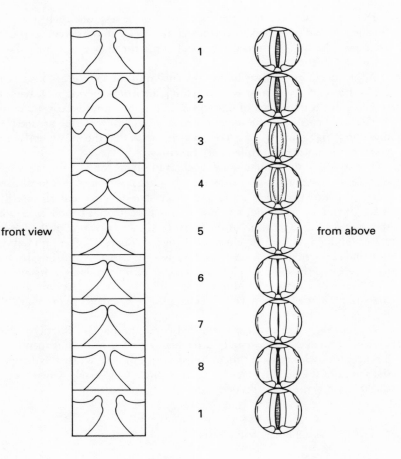

front view    1 2 3 4 5 6 7 8 1    from above

*Figure 16*   Vocal cords during one phonatory cycle of adduction and
abduction

# Frequency

The pitch of the human voice is controlled not only by the degree of tension
in the vocal cords, but also by the rapidity with which they adduct and
abduct. The faster the rate of vibration, the higher the pitch.

In order to picture this more clearly, imagine a piece of string stretched
taut between two stationary pins. If you take hold of the piece of string at
its centre and pluck it, the string will vibrate from side to side, passing
through its rest position many times before coming to rest again. (See
Figure 17.)

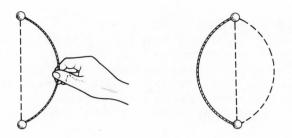

*Figure 17* Vibratory motion of a string

Now, if we made a slow-motion film of this action, we would discover that the string makes a definite number of side-to-side vibrations per second. This number represents the string's 'fundamental frequency'.

Every material object vibrates when struck by an external force such as the wind, a hammer, or when plucked by the fingers. Furthermore, every material object has its own fundamental frequency, a fixed number of times per second that it will vibrate. It is the frequency of vibration that determines the musical note or pitch that an object gives off.

Thus, when physicists speak of frequency and musicians speak of pitch, they are in fact referring to the same notion. When a physicist plucks a piece of string, he or she describes its frequency as 264 cycles per second (c.p.s.) because the centre of the string passes through its rest position from side to side 264 times every second; a musician, meanwhile, describes the resulting audible pitch as middle C.

The same holds true for the human voice. The amount of times that the vocal cords adduct and abduct per second is known as the 'frequency of vibration' or the 'frequency of phonatory cycles', and this determines the musical pitch that the voice emits. The lower the frequency, the deeper the pitch.

# Mass

If you tap a pint beer mug with a spoon, it will vibrate fewer times per second than a wine glass. Consequently a wine glass gives off a higher pitch. The reason for this is that the fundamental frequency of an object is partly determined by its mass, the amount of material of which it is made:

Greater Mass = Slower Frequency = Deeper Pitch

Twenty grams of glass, for example, will vibrate faster than 40 g. It is possible to vary the mass of a glass and therefore its frequency of vibration by adding water to it. If you line up ten identical wine glasses and add 1 ml. of water to the first, 2 ml. to the second, and so on, increasing the amount by 1 ml. per glass, the pitch given off by each glass when tapped with a spoon will be deeper the more water it contains.

The relationship between mass and frequency applies also to a piece of string stretched taut between two pins. A thick, dense string made of 10 g. of fibre will vibrate at a lesser frequency and therefore give off a lower pitch to the ear than a thin string made of only 5 g. of fibre under the same tension.

# Tension

This principle applies also to the human voice. Someone with thick, dense vocal cords will tend to produce a lower pitch than someone with thinner, lighter cords. However, the mass of the vocal cords or of a string is only one characteristic which determines its frequency; another is the tension it is under.

The same piece of 10 g. string will vibrate at a higher frequency the tighter it is stretched, a concept which is familiar to anyone who has tightened a guitar or violin string.

# Length

The length of the string also determines its frequency. A thick, short string under great tension will vibrate faster than a long, thick string under the same tension.

Now, from what we have said so far, we might well imagine that the only factor that determines the pitch of a voice is the material mass, rate of vibration, length and the degree of tension in the vocal cords. In fact, there is a further important determinant and that is the shape of the glottis or space created between the vocal cords as they vibrate.

# Glottic Shape

Let us imagine a man with a very wide pitch range – that is, a voice that can sing from very high to very low. Now let us further imagine that this man sings three notes in succession, first his highest, then one in the middle of his range, then his lowest possible note.

We have already established that the higher the voice the faster the frequency of vibration; so we might speculate that while singing his highest note, the vocal cords are vibrating 600 times per second; while singing his middle note, the cords vibrate 450 times per second, and while singing the lowest note, they vibrate only 200 times per second. We might also say that at the highest note the muscles hold the cords in great tension, at the middle

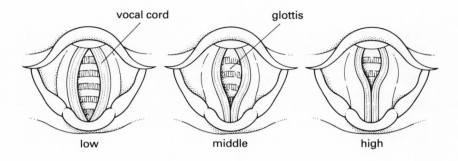

*Figure 18*  Shape of glottis during phonation in different pitch ranges

note slightly less and at the lowest note they are significantly more relaxed.

The third factor which determines the pitch is the shape of the glottic opening between the vocal cords during phonation. It is likely that, when making the low note, the vocal cords abduct to form an oval-shaped glottis; when singing the middle note, one third of the vocal cords remains closed or adducted while the other two thirds adduct and abduct; and when singing very high, only one third of the cords vibrate. The pitch of the voice is thus determined partially by the shape of the glottis. (See Figure 18.)

## The Constituting Factors

Therefore the fundamental frequency or audible musical pitch of the human voice is determined first by the frequency with which the vocal cords phonate or adduct and abduct per second, second by the mass of their constituting tissue, third by the tension which they are under as a result of the distribution of tension in the laryngeal musculature which also effects their length, and finally by the shape of the glottis or opening created between them during phonation. It follows that musical pitch is the outcome of a complex and potentially infinite combination of variables. A little less tension can be compensated for by an increase in frequency, and a decrease in frequency can be compensated for by an adjustment in glottic shape. In other words, there are many ways to create the same pitch.

## Harmonics

Unfortunately, the frequency with which an object such as a piece of string vibrates in a second is not as simple as I have so far implied.

A piece of string drawn taut between two pins does not only vibrate from side to side in one whole unit. It also vibrates in smaller segments simultaneously, and each of these little segments vibrate at their own frequency, which is higher than the string's fundamental frequency.

Let us imagine that the fundamental frequency of a piece of string under tension is 100 cycles per second, that is to say that the centre of the string passes through its rest position from side to side 100 times in a second.

Now imagine the string as two halves, each with its own centre. These two halves both vibrate at a frequency twice that of the fundamental frequency, in this case 200 c.p.s. Then imagine the string as three equal segments, each one with its own centre; each of these segments vibrates at 300 c.p.s.

This is in fact what is happening when a piece of string vibrates. While the whole string vibrates at a fundamental frequency, small segments are simultaneously vibrating at a faster rate which is determined by multiplying the number of segments by the fundamental frequency. In order to gain an accurate and complete picture of the vibratory action of a string, each of the diagrams in Figure 19 would therefore have to be placed on top of one another.

It follows that the string is not giving out only one pitch determined by its fundamental frequency, but is in fact simultaneously emitting a number of other higher pitches which are determined by the frequency of the segments. This combination of the pitch generated by the fundamental frequency and the higher pitches generated by the frequency of the segments is known as 'harmonics'. Of course, it is very difficult to hear these upper pitches or notes because they exist only in combination with the fundamental frequency, which is bolder and masks out the upper harmonics in most situations.

Material objects, then, such as glasses, pieces of string, chairs and tins, all have their own fundamental frequency which determines the audible musical pitch they give off when struck, and in addition they give off harmonics which are less audible to the human ear.

However, it is possible to accentuate certain harmonics by altering the quality of the space in which the material vibrates. An identical piece of string under exactly the same tension will sound different when stretched

*Figure 19*  Segmental vibration of a string

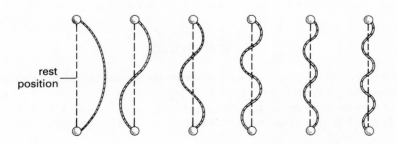

122

across a tin box to the sound given off when it is stretched across a hollow wooden guitar body. This is because not only do the material objects such as the tin box and the guitar body have a fundamental frequency of their own when struck, but they also accentuate particular harmonics in other material objects when they vibrate in close proximity to them. The name given to the object which acts upon a sound in this way is a 'resonator'.

## Timbre

It is the degree to which certain harmonics are accentuated by a resonator that partially determines the tonal quality or 'timbre' of a sound. A clarinet and a saxophone may play the same pitch, but they will sound different in timbre because the resonating tubes of the two instruments accentuate different harmonics.

Which harmonics are accentuated is determined by the mass, size, substance and shape of the resonator, the vessel in which the sound vibrates. It is possible to find a resonator which accentuates one of the harmonics to such a degree that it becomes more overt to the human ear than the fundamental frequency. This then produces a higher audible pitch with lower harmonics.

The harmonic that any resonator will most accentuate will be that closest to its own fundamental frequency. For example, imagine that a wooden box has a fundamental frequency of 300 c.p.s. when struck with the finger; that is to say that the shell vibrates from side to side 300 times per second. Now imagine that a piece of string is stretched across it so as to have a fundamental frequency of 100 c.p.s. As I have explained, this string will have an upper harmonic of 300 c.p.s. because the string is vibrating in segments, and it is this pitch that the box will accentuate.

Now imagine a tin box with a fundamental frequency of 600 c.p.s., with the same string stretched across it to have a fundamental frequency of 100 c.p.s., as before. Although the string has the same fundamental frequency, it will sound different because the tin box will accentuate its upper harmonic of 600 c.p.s., giving it a more tanging, crisp timbre. Both sounds are, however, producing the same musical pitch.

In the case of the human voice, the harmonics created by the frequency with which the vocal cords vibrate are accentuated by the parts of the body which act as resonators.

## Vocal Resonators

The resonators for the voice, those parts of the body where technological instruments have been able to discern physical vibration caused by vocal sound, include the chest and all the spaces in the larynx, the mouth, the skull and the nasal passages.

Just as a tin box, or guitar body, or table, or a room has its own fundamental frequency and a tendency to accentuate certain harmonics, so this holds true for the vocal resonators.

We have established that timbre is generated in part by the particular harmonics that are accentuated, which are in turn governed by the shape, size and substance of the resonating vessel. Because each person's larynx and resonating cavities are different in shape, muscle tension, density, mass and size, each human voice has a distinctive timbre which can usually be discerned from another voice even if both phonate on the same pitch. Therefore, even when two people create the same musical pitch by an identical combination of mass, frequency, tension and shape, they do not sound the same; their voices have different timbres, each of which we recognise as belonging to and expressive of a particular person.

The tonal quality or timbre produced by an instrument such as the piano is fixed. No matter what pitch you play, it will have the timbre that is unique to a piano. This means that you can play over seven octaves, from the deepest note on the keyboard up to the highest, all within one quality of sound; and if you were to close your eyes and listen, you would not notice any difference in this quality. Furthermore, the pianist could change pianos half-way through playing the scales and you would probably still not notice.

The timbre produced by a single human voice, however, is not fixed. Unlike the shell of a piano, which is held fast and sturdy by wood and iron, the 'vessel' and 'sounding boards' which house the vocal cords are engaged in a dance of continuous motion, much of which arises from the activity necessary to make changes in pitch. For example, to move from a deep pitch to a higher one, tensile adjustments in the laryngeal musculature have to be instigated in order to slacken the tension in the vocal cords, and the necessary muscular movements naturally alter the shape of the resonators and thereby change the vocal timbre.

Unlike the pianist who can play seven octaves from the keyboard's lowest pitch to its highest without any change in timbre, the human voice cannot do this. If a person begins to sing the lowest note possible and rises one note at a time up to the highest he or she can sing, it will be possible to discern changes in the timbre at certain points, as though the person has 'changed voices'.

# Register

The most familiar and easily recognisable of these changes occurs in men when they ascend upwards from a deep pitch to higher ones. At a certain point a break occurs and their voice shifts into what we call 'falsetto'. This is only one example of what is known as a 'change in register' or a 'register break'. The more usual register used by a man, in speaking and in singing, is called the 'modal register'. The change which often occurs when ascending in pitch is referred to as a register break from modal to falsetto.

A register is any series of notes or pitches which have the same continuous timbre. The term 'register' therefore refers not only to the notes that you sing, but to the quality with which you sing them and it is important to recognise that the same pitch can be sung in different registers. For example, in a man there are usually three or four notes which mark the transition from his modal register to falsetto and these pitches can usually be sung in either of the two registers. That is, he can sing the same musical pitch with two distinct timbres.

Just as there is a change in register as a man ascends the scale, so too there is a register break when he reaches very low pitches. At a certain point low in the scales the voice takes on a growling quality, a timbre that has been termed 'pulse register' or 'vocal fry'. But as with the transition from modal to falsetto, there are a set of overlap notes which can be sung in either register.

Women too have different identifiable registers which have historically been described as 'head register', which sounds like a man's falsetto, 'middle register' and 'chest register', each of which have their own consistent timbre and a number of overlap notes which can be produced in either of the registers which lie each side. In addition, some women have a further register very high in the scale which has been referred to as a 'whistle register' because of its fine and piercing timbre.

So the notion of register break is intimately connected to the concept of pitch range. However, what the ear notices is more than just a change of pitch, which after all occurs within one register. It also notices a fundamental change of timbre, for register is a combination of pitch and timbre.

## Country and Western, the Swiss Yodel and the Operatic Voice

The ability to shift dramatically and obviously from one register to another is an integral part of certain styles of singing. For example, the yodelling practised by the women of the Swiss Alps and by the indigenous folksingers of Argentina involves speedy shifts from chest to head register. In men the same yodelling technique may be described as containing shifts from the modal register to falsetto. The same register shifts are used by both male and female Country and Western singers. Kenny Rogers, for instance, makes clear shifts from modal to falsetto and Dolly Parton from middle to head register.

However, the aim of singing training in Western Europe has always been to reduce or even eliminate the changes in timbre between one register and another. This has led to the production of voices which can sing the widest possible pitch range without any audible change in timbre. Opera singers are trained to be able to sing a set pitch range without any audible change in register and without any major change of timbre. The operatic voice has six of these specialisations, three for men and three for women.

SOPRANO
This is the highest female voice and usually ranges upwards for two octaves from middle C on the piano.

MEZZO-SOPRANO
The word *mezzo* is Italian for 'middle' and the mezzo-soprano is the middle female voice, ranging two octaves upwards from the A just below middle C.

CONTRALTO
This is the lowest female voice, ranging from the F below middle C to F an octave and a half above.

TENOR
Tenor is the highest male voice in opera and ranges from the C below middle C to the C above it.

BARITONE
This is the middle male voice and ranges from G an octave and a half below middle C to the F above it.

BASS
This is the lowest male voice. It ranges from middle C down to E almost two octaves below.

# Specialisation as Synthesis of Pitch Range and Timbre

It will be apparent that there is some overlap between these classifications on the piano. While one person may sing middle C as a tenor, another may sing it as a baritone. Therefore operatic specialisations cannot be described only as pitch ranges; they also constitute particular timbres. The same note can also be sung in timbres which do not correspond to any of the operatic registers; both Elton John and Phil Collins have the same range as a tenor, but their voices would not be described as tenors in the operatic sense. The operatic voice is one which operates within given pitch ranges and at the same time has a particular timbre.

Scientific instrumentational investigation has not yet been able to explain exactly what causes the audible shifts in timbre which give rise to particular registers or what creates the difference in timbre between the various operatic specialisations. What remains certain is that there is considerable chaos among singing teachers about the nature of registers and the terminology used to describe them. In one of the most thorough and precise books on the science of the singing voice, Johan Sundberg proposes that the chaos in register terminology merely reflects a regrettable lack of objective knowledge and that voice research has not yet reached a stage where it can show the anatomical and physiological changes in the larynx which give rise to audible changes in vocal timbre.[1]

But there is research which suggests that this lack of objective knowledge is due to the fact that no scientific instrumentation or process can ever fully account for the unique characteristics of a voice which we readily recognise as belonging to a particular person.[2] This is supported by Margaret Greene and Lesley Mathieson in *The Voice and its Disorders*, which has for many years been the seminal text on the functioning and malfunctioning of the human voice.[3]

What we do know is that the mass, frequency, tension and shape of the vocal cords, along with the shape, mass and constitution of the resonators, play some part in determining vocal timbre.

## *The Psychological Chemistry of Vocal Timbre*

As we have established, while listening to two instruments, say the clarinet and the saxophone, we notice that even when both instruments are playing the same note, there is a difference in timbre which enables us to tell them apart. This difference is caused by the material of which the instrument is made and the shape to which it has been moulded, which in turn causes it to accentuate particular harmonics. If two simple whistles are made to the same dimensions, but one in metal and one in wood, they will sound unalike as a result of their different materials. If the whistles are both made of wood but the dimensions of the tube are different, the sounds again will be different on account of their dissimilar dimensions. The same principles apply to the human voice.

During phonation the sound resonates in different cavities of the body, particularly in the face, head and mouth, in the same way that the vibrating string of a guitar resonates in the hollow wooden shell, or the puffs of air which pass down the clarinet resonate in the length of its tubular body. However, one of the differences between the human voice and a musical instrument is that a person can change the shape of these cavities at will by articulating the mouth and face and by reorganising the muscular architecture of the larynx and vocal resonators; this makes it possible to sing the same note with different timbres. We know, for example, that if we open our mouth wide as though to yawn and then phonate, we get a very different sound to that produced if our lips are pursed. Because the face is used to communicate emotions, physiognomical expression plays an important role in forming the affective element of vocal timbres, and muscular changes which we make with our face influence the quality of the voice to some measure. (See Figures 20 and 21.)

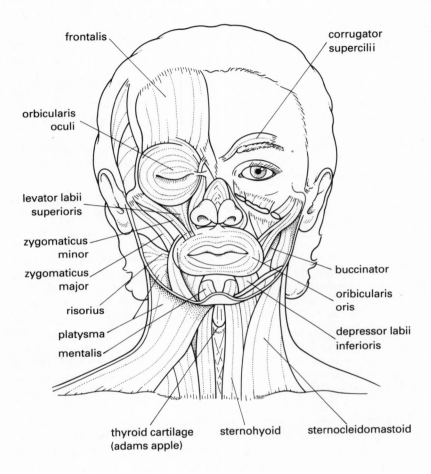

*Figure 20*  Muscles of facial expression (a)

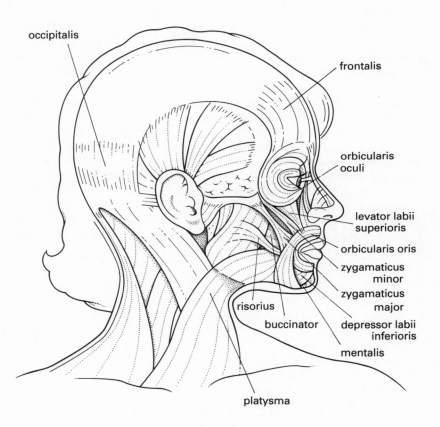

*Figure 21*   Muscles of facial expression (b)

A good state of health and malleability in the muscles of the face and those which constitute the walls of the resonators is vital for liberated vocal function. However, these muscles are also called upon to initiate other tasks besides serving as sounding boards and animating facial expression. For example, they move the head, the lower jaw and the tongue, and faulty use of the muscles to initiate such actions has a negative effect on the operation and acoustic quality of the voice. (See Figures 22, 23 and 24.)

In addition to the shape of the resonating cavities, vocal quality is also affected by the constitution of the resonating cavities and is also in constant change as a result of chemical secretions. We know, for instance, that during influenza, when the nasal passages are full of catarrh, the voice quality changes considerably; and more subtle chemical and hormonal changes are occurring all the time. For example, we know that the endocrine glands secrete hormones in response to emotional stimuli, such as adrenalin when we are anxious. Many of these secretions impregnate the nasal passages, which, being resonating cavities, in turn affect the voice.

Because the quality of the voice depends on both the shape and chemical constitution of the resonating cavities, it is apparent that any chemical or physical change which affects these cavities will cause a change in vocal timbre.

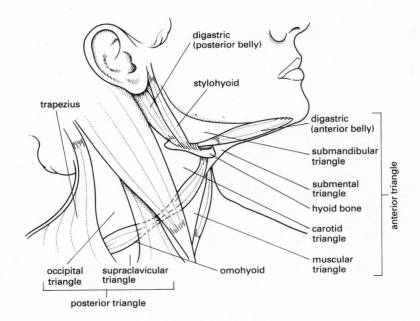

*Figure 22*   Muscles which move the head

130

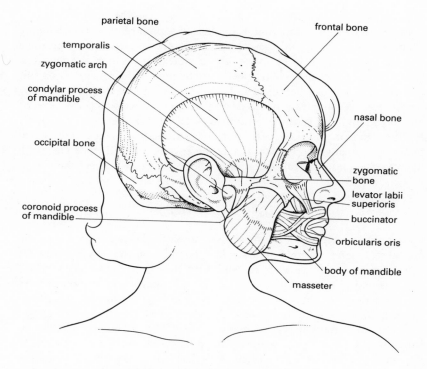

*Figure 23* Muscles which move the lower jaw

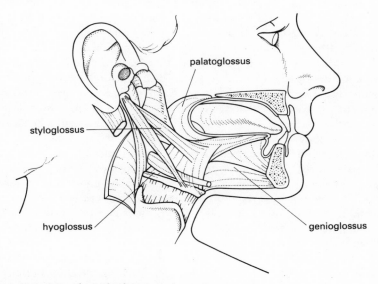

*Figure 24* Muscles which move the tongue

It is therefore the combination of skeletal structure and ever-changing chemical constitution and muscular architecture that gives each person's voice a unique quality. However, the chemical and physical alterations which cause change in vocal timbre do not happen of their own accord, but as a result of our psychological and emotional reactions to events and circumstances. We become anxious or excited in response to an event or set of memories, and the resulting responsive changes in chemical secretions, facial expression and other actions in turn stimulate a change in the vocal quality. Thus anything which affects the psyche will influence chemical, neurological and physical operations, which in turn will affect the voice.

# *Endocrinology*

An extreme example of a chemical effect upon the voice occurs during the period from ten to fourteen years, when the pubertal changes in hormonal development occurs. In girls the length of the vocal cords may increase from around 15 mm. before puberty to 17 mm. afterwards, and this lowers the pitch range of the voice. In addition, the larynx enlarges, which enriches and deepens the timbre of the pitch produced.

The vocal changes in a boy are more overt. The vocal cords increase in length to a greater degree, lowering the pitch more considerably than in a girl; in a boy who has the potential to develop a bass singing voice the cords may be as long as 23 mm. The position of the thyroid cartilage also shifts more dramatically in a boy, and as a result the larynx not only grows but drops in position. Furthermore, the resonating cavities of chest and pharynx enlarge, which gives the male voice a quality distinct from the female even when both are phonating on the same pitch.

The healthy development of the boy's larynx at puberty, as with all masculine characteristics, is dependent on the release of certain hormones by the endocrine glands. The main glands which control the development and maintenance of the voice in a male are the thyroid and testicles; and if these are damaged prior to puberty, the mutation of the larynx which deepens and enriches the voice does not occur, leaving the adult with a boy's voice in a man's body.

In seventeenth- and eighteenth-century Europe such a voice was greatly admired and the castration of pre-pubescent boys was common practice, producing the so-called 'castrati' singers. Due to the prevention of hormonal release by removing the testicles, these singers conserved the quality of a child's voice in an adult body, which, according to musicians of the period, gave the castrato's voice a unique quality, neither male nor female but angel-like and androgynous.

As well as singing in concerts and at the courts, the castrati were also employed by the Vatican, who needed high voices in the choir but did not admit women choristers. However, Pope Leo XIII (1878–1903) banned the castrati from the Church. The most renowned castrato is Farinelli, who was employed by the Queen of Spain to cure her husband, Philip V, of madness. There are obviously no recordings of what this type of voice sounded like, though Gluck's opera *Orfeo* has a role written for a castrato and thus gives an idea of its range. Adoration of the voice of the castrati is also eloquently expressed in Balzac's story *Sarasine*, and though the castrati no longer exist, we come close to its sound in the male falsetto.

The hormonal secretions of the thyroid also affect a woman's voice, not only at puberty but throughout life, particularly during menstruation, pregnancy and menopause, all of which can be accompanied by changes in the audible qualities of the voice.[4] There is also some evidence to suggest that the hormonal activity stimulated by sexual excitement causes changes in vocal timbre and pitch, and there may therefore be some scientific basis for the popular conception of the rich and fruity timbre of the stereotypical 'sexy' voice accompanying a highly developed sexual appetite.[5]

In a man, however, puberty marks the climax of his hormonal upheaval, and when the pubertal period is fully over, the vocal instrument assumes its mature state. For both men and women, once puberty is over, if the voice is looked after and treated properly, it can not only maintain the expressive function which it possesses innately, but can be trained to enhance its pliability.

# The Physical Voice

Respiration, phonation and resonation involve an intricate structure of cells, tissues, nerves and blood vessels in a continual process of mechanical and electrochemical activity. Consequently the human voice is just as susceptible to all manner of diseases, injuries and impairments as any other part of the body. There are many things which can go wrong with the voice as a result of injury or sickness which change or mutate, hinder or damage the anatomical structure and acoustic operations of the vocal instrument.

Like all disease or injury, the first sign is usually pain or discomfort. A patient with a vocal problem may experience soreness, an ache, a difficulty in swallowing or a lump in the throat. A further sign of difficulty is a change in the sound of the voice; it may become wispy, breathy, harsh or gruff, descriptions which all come under the heading of 'dysphonia', audible disruption in vocal quality which impairs the smooth tonal clarity of phonation.

The first action a person usually takes in this situation is to visit the doctor, who takes a look at the larynx and the vocal cords – the first stage in the process of diagnosis, treatment and cure. The fact that the doctor can actually have a look at what the voice is doing owes much to a man called Manuel Garcia, who was born in 1805, the son of a Sevillian tenor and composer, and who lived to be a hundred and one.

Garcia won a brilliant reputation as a singing teacher in both Paris and London, and the key points to his approach are contained in his book *Hints on Singing*.[6] Garcia's most important achievement, however, was the invention in 1854 of the laryngoscope, that familiar metal tongue with a built-in light that allows the doctor to observe your throat while you say 'ah'.

If the laryngoscope reveals symptoms such as inflammation or discolouring, the patient will often be referred to an ENT specialist, a phoniatrist or a laryngologist, who is likely to use an advanced version of the laryngoscope to have a closer look. One of the most remarkable technological developments upon Garcia's original idea is the fibre-optic camera. This consists of a flexible tube with a beam of light passing through it. The tube is passed up the nasal passage and down into the larynx and enables the laryngologist to observe on a screen an enlarged colour image of the working vocal cords. If this image shows evidence of organic disturbance, it is possible that the treatment may involve surgery, the administration of drugs or both. The practice of surgical procedures and the prescription and administration of drugs are solely the domain of the *medical* voice specialist i.e. the E.N.T. specialist or laryngologist.

Whether or not surgical or medicinal procedures are necessary, the latter stage of vocal treatment regularly consists of a process of retraining the patient to make healthy use of the voice which does not place demands upon it which are likely to generate problems again in the future. This latter stage, which is crucial to a patient's recovery, is usually administered by professionals who in Great Britain are called speech and language therapists, though the work they do is often described as speech therapy and their title is therefore often shortened in everyday communication to speech therapists; in the U.S.A. such professionals are more often referred to as speech-language pathologists. Though the work of such therapists is not *medical*, it is however *clinical*, sharing the medical specialist's diagnostic criteria and therapeutic aims. The speech and language therapist is therefore often a significant contributor to the patient's recovery from organic voice disorders. One example of such an organic disturbance is paralysis of the vocal cords.

The vocal cords, laryngeal musculature and adjoining cartilages are served by a complex and highly delicate matrix of nerves which transmit the electrochemical impulses necessary to initiate the physical movement that in turn promotes phonation. The coordinated vibration of the two vocal cords which brings them to adduct and abduct is therefore dependent on the healthy functioning of these nerves. But if they become badly damaged, for example by cancer or during thyroid surgery or following a severe neck injury, and they are no longer able to transmit impulses, then as a result one or both of the vocal cords may become paralysed.

The left vocal cord is the most commonly affected because of the greater vulnerability of the left laryngeal nerve, and paralysis of this gives rise to a situation in which only the right cord opens and closes. One way of treating this is for the medical specialist to inject Teflon paste into the paralysed cord, which increases its bulk and therefore moves its edge nearer to the mid-line, so that the working cord can be trained to meet the treated cord during phonation.

If the damage is to both left and right nerves but is less severe, then both the vocal cords might be rendered partially paralysed, being capable of some movement but unable to adduct fully. One way of treating this is for the medical specialist to fix one of the cords surgically with a stainless-steel suture and then retrain the other vocal cord to cross the mid-line to meet it during phonation.[7] In both of these cases of paralysis, the retraining is a major contributor to the patient's regained vocal function, and although the laryngologist may initiate this process post-surgery, it constitutes one of the speech and language therapist's many skills.

Another pathological condition which affects vocal function is laryngeal carcinoma, which occurs most frequently in those who smoke. It can affect any part of the larynx, including the vocal cords themselves. If the tumour is growing on the edge of the vocal cords, it is referred to as glottic carcinoma. If it continues untreated, it can block the windpipe and result in a distressing death.

The most popular and successful cure is radiotherapy, which in the UK successfully and permanently cures between 80 and 90 per cent of those it treats. In cases where the tumour is considered too advanced for radiotherapy, chemotherapy is often administered, in the form of cytotoxic drugs given intravenously.

If treatment is unsuccessful and the windpipe is dangerously blocked, then it is sometimes necessary to perform a surgical operation known as a laryngectomy, in which the larynx is partially or totally removed and the patient breathes through an opening made in the neck through which it is also possible to speak with the aid of mechanical devices.[8] Whilst the administration of the drugs and the surgical removal of the larynx is the domain of the medical specialist, it is often the speech and language therapist who teaches the patient how to use the mechanical devices and who accompanies the patient through a time of delicate and often traumatic transition.

## Vocal Abuse

Organic disturbances of the voice, such as in the two examples given above, make up a small percentage of the vocal difficulties which patients regularly bring to the doctor. The most common origin of vocal problems is not illness or accident, but abuse and misuse of the voice which results in pathological condition.

A common example of such 'self-induced' conditions are vocal-cord polyps, which arise when vocal misuse is so great that a haemorrhage arises, causing tissue to congeal into a round globule on the vocal cord. Polyps can be removed by surgery, after which the speech and language therapist must retrain the patient to use the voice efficiently.

A haemorrhage does not by any means always produce a polyp. A particularly demanding singing concert, or a psychological trauma which causes someone to shout or scream, may provoke a haemorrhage that disappears after a few day's rest. It is persistent misuse which produces the polyp and a host of other physical malfunctions which can make us sound hoarse, croaky, squeaky or husky, which can cause us to feel a burning, a soreness or a strain in the throat or which can cause us to lose our voice altogether.

Another form of swelling on the vocal cords is vocal nodules, minute bumps which protrude from the edge of vocal cords, preventing them from closing properly. These arise when the cords are brought together under great force, and often rest and retraining are sufficient to clear up the nodules.

It follows that if a vocal condition such as nodules or polyps is caused by misuse then short-term alleviation, either by rest, surgery or other means, will not prevent the condition arising again. The patient must be re-educated to use his or her voice in a healthy fashion. However, this situation is complicated by the fact that the way people use their voice is affected by their psychological condition and social situation. A probationary teacher who has to keep her unruly class of remand adolescents under control may be using her voice badly in response to a continual need to be heard above those in her charge. Laryngologists, phoniatrists and speech and language therapists must therefore take into consideration the demands she places upon her voice, or else the teacher should change her job. A man who misuses his voice by giving vent to his aggression and anxiety may be cured of polyps by surgery in the short term, but any lasting effective therapy will have to address his psychological predicament and either help to change it, or help the voice withstand the demands placed upon its expressive function.

# Soma and Psyche in the Voice Clinic: The Holistic Revolution

The connection between the psychological condition of a speaker and the resulting vocal misuse and damage first began to be recognised in the 1950s, when an increasing number of medical practitioners became interested in a holistic approach to vocal treatment. One of the earliest references to this was made in 1958 by Lynwood Heaver, a medical doctor who called for 'a holistic consideration of all laryngeal disease'. He stated:

Vocal abuse which results in nodes and polyps appears in patients who use their voice for the expression of their excessive hostility and aggressive impulses.

What then are the goals and limits of vocal analysis? The larynx should always be judged by the voice it produces, and the voice should always be interpreted as a relentless [expression?] of the speaker's personality. The axiom of a holistic consideration of all laryngeal disease cannot be limited to the specialised activities of the phoniatrist. It should guide the philosophical orientation of the entire laryngologic profession and ought to be well understood by all specialists, just as medicine in general has come to understand the need for the consideration of the sick patient as a living person and not as an assembly of dissociated organs.[9]

Since these remarks were made, a number of laryngologists have noted similarities in the personality types who display nodes and polyps; qualities ascribed to patients include 'ambitious', 'aggressive', 'highly motivated', 'hard-working' and 'perfectionist'.[10]

But polyps and nodules constitute only two examples of the way in which vocal ill-health can result from the misuse of the voice, which in turn arises from the expression of psychological state. There are many other less specific manifestations of the same process which give rise to discomfort, inflammation or strain, all of which impair vocal function.

In recognition of this and in further support of a holistic view of the vocal dysfunction, a medical phoniatrist called Pedro Bloch made a continual plea in the early 1960s for doctors to incorporate more of a psychological interpretation and analysis of vocal disorders, stating that:

in our era of psychosomatic medicine it should be obvious that the conscientious voice specialist can never be satisfied with merely examining the larynx. Rather we are actually studying a person, a human being, an organism, a biotype, a constitution, a temperament, a character, a living individual who has a problem with his throat or with his voice. Very often this problem does not even pertain to the larynx because it is a general problem of emotional maladjustment. But the psycho-dynamics of the underlying imbalance, and perhaps environmental circumstances, have channelled the psychic disorder into vocal expression . . . We have occupied ourselves too much with the movement of the vocal cords which are so much less important than the emotional cords.[11]

In 1962 Friedrich Brodnitz, one of the most famous medical voice specialists, referred to the importance of understanding the voice as a 'holistic' phenomenon analysable from a number of different perspectives, including the psychological; he said that 'voice is more than a mechanical or acoustic phenomenon. It is a mirror of the personality, a carrier of moods and emotions, a key to neurotic and psychotic tendencies.'[12] Brodnitz further stated that:

> the difficulty with the psychological approach to vocal analysis lies in the ambivalence of vocal symptoms. It requires great experience in listening, and a considerable amount of intuition, to obtain a correct over-all picture of the personality of a voice patient out of a multitude of observations . . .
>
> For the voice therapist this means that he must learn to understand voice as a unified function produced by many forces and shaped by many influences. Too often, voice is described and judged by easily defined characteristics, such as hoarseness . . . nasality, or pitch. Too often, correction of impaired voices is attempted by the manipulation of these single factors. . . . abnormal pitch, faulty nasality, or hoarseness are nothing but symptoms, and the therapist must try to deal with the underlying factors that produce these symptoms. He must learn to evaluate symptoms as part of a larger over-all picture, and must keep in mind the relationship between the voice he hears and the total personality of the individual who produces it.[13]

In cases where the voice problem is not organic, such as carcinoma, polyps or paralysis, but functional, such as the case of a teacher who becomes frequently hoarse as a result of shouting at a class of unruly pupils, the patient will work with a speech and language therapist whose task it is to assess, treat and retrain the use of the voice; and this training can be aimed not only at the physical process of phonation, but at the psychological process of expression. Up to the 1950s, laryngologists were solely concerned with making a visual diagnosis of the problem and providing medical or surgical treatment. However, the vocal organ is essentially an expressive faculty employed as a tool to communicate what we are, what we feel. If a voice is being used badly, it goes without saying that the psychology of the person has to be taken into consideration. A man does not yell for nothing. It is not a heart that has a cardiac arrest but the man in whom the heart lives; the heart gives up under the pressure of the man's life. In the same way the voice does not become ill of its own accord, but in response to a life-pattern.

The significance of psychology for the voice is further highlighted by the fact that many patients who go to the medical doctor with a vocal complaint actually show no physical signs of disturbance – just as patients of Freud's had pains and paralyses for which there was no somatic explanation. In these cases the problem is psychogenic or psychosomatic, the voice becoming the locus for the expression of unresolved psychological difficulties. Furthermore, because the voice, more than any other part of the body, is essentially used to communicate the state of the mind, we might say that all voice disorders caused through misuse reflect to some degree a psychological dynamic, and today the psychological factors which have a bearing on the health and quality of the voice are more readily contemplated by medical specialists and clinicians of different orientations.

## Voice Therapy as Psychotherapy

The central aim, and the most time-consuming, of any professional attending to the voice is to retrain the patient to make healthy use of the voice in order to prevent damage. Now that the psychological influences upon the voice are more readily acknowledged, it should also be a part of any vocal programme of therapy to help treat a patient's psychological condition where this has a direct bearing on the vocal function.

Furthermore, any vocal training, whether it is singing lessons, a vocal coaching lesson, a voice workshop, a rehearsal of *Hamlet*, incorporates or should incorporate the same fundamental processes – physiological, mechanical, acoustic and psychological – which underpin the therapeutic rehabilitation or preservational education of a voice in clinical treatment. When all these processes are included, in vocal coaching and in therapy, there are positive effects not only upon the vocal instrument, but upon the psychological state of the individual. Therefore to treat, retrain, rehabilitate and re-educate a person's voice is one means of helping to efface the deeply ingrained psychological patterns which produced the unhealthy vocal patterns in the first place. An effective investigation of psychological dynamics will be vocally therapeutic; and an effective therapy for the voice should be psychologically beneficial.

In 1955 D. A. Weiss, speech-language pathologist, set out to analyse the 'rather neglected relationship of the speaker or singer to his own voice'.[14] Weiss regarded the speaking and singing voice as a 'psychologically determined and controlled function',[15] and drawing on his clinical observations of patients, he observed that 'a radical change of the speaking voice . . . has a great impact upon the personality itself. Sometimes it approaches a thoroughgoing change of personality, mainly from a shy and timid one to a more self-assured and assertive one'.[16] Observing the psychological benefits of voice therapy reported by patients, Weiss further proposed that 'a successful therapy of the voice might be equivalent to the effects of a thoroughgoing psychotherapy'.[17] Weiss's paper was an important landmark in the development of the notion of a relationship between the aims and effects of psychotherapy, those of voice training and those of clinical voice therapy, in that it introduced into the field of medical science a notion which had been a part of theatre and psychotherapy for some years, as has been shown by the work of Wolfsohn, Lowen, Grotowski and others described in Chapter Three. Weiss's most eloquent and precise rendition of this principle is contained in the following words:

The voice and the psychological make-up of an individual mutually influence each other. If a person is psychologically disturbed, the voice suffers, and in turn the deterioration of the voice exerts a negative influence upon the psyche. We can approach this vicious circle from either the psychological or the vocal angle. Psychotherapy is often a hazardous and always lengthy procedure and . . . the voice would have to be treated in any case. On the other hand, in the treatment of the voice we feel on pretty firm ground. Attacking the formerly vicious circle from this point of view, we arrive, by improving the phonation, at influencing the psyche in a favourable manner. This, in turn, creates more favourable conditions for the voice itself. Thus the vicious circle has been converted into a 'virtuous' one.[18]

At the same time, the voice clinician Augusta Jellinek observed that 'the psychotherapeutic effect inherent in the success of vocal rehabilitation and in the treatment situation itself is often sufficient to restore the well-being of the patient',[19] and the idea that vocal work can be psychologically as well as vocally liberating has now gained currency in Europe and America.

The increasing interest in the liberating aspects of working with the voice has highlighted the fact that there are many people for whom the existing structure of treatment and therapy does not respond. Although a speech and language therapist is equipped to deal with voice problems which are functional and organic, and which can be alleviated through retraining and rehabilitation, work on the voice is a relatively small part of an extensive schedule which also includes attendance to disorders of speech and language, where the problem is not with the quality of phonation and resonation but with the articulation of these sounds into words.

There are many people who have perfectly adequate speech and language skills, are without organic or severe functional voice disorders but who are dissatisfied with the restricted and unmalleable qualities of their voice. The nature of the restriction is however often such that the person does not want or need to be clinically treated for a specific vocal problem, but wishes to have the extension and expansion of vocal range enhanced and facilitated in the context of his or her whole self – body and mind. Even if there was room in the fully committed schedule of a speech and language therapist for attendance to such persons, it is in my experience usually the case that a creative approach to vocal development is required by such people.

It should, however, be clear that vocal expression consists of complex interdependent factors that must all be borne in mind during treatment. On the one hand, the voice is a physiological and mechanical operation, and any process which involves working with it should remain responsive and responsible to the preservation and development of the organic functioning of this system. It is also a psychological phenomenon, arising from the voluntary or involuntary tendency to emit acoustic signals which communicate the essence of our mental condition to others; and any process by which these signals are developed should accommodate a genuine and delicate appreciation of the importance of nurturing mental health. In addition, the human voice has a political dimension; it is the means by which a person asserts his or her rights within the social order. To develop a voice represents the provision of a power that is everyone's right and which ensures the maintenance of democracy.

Practical applications of the principles derived from such an integrative understanding of the human voice are described in the following chapters. They do not constitute a programme of clinical voice therapy, neither are they intended to respond to specific diagnosed pathologies which demand medical or surgical attention. They are instead designed to facilitate the development of a completely liberated and malleable voice in those people whose vocal condition is restricted but for whom clinical ministration is inappropriate or undesirable. They form part of a therapeutic strategy which I have called 'voice movement therapy', and the tenets upon which it is based have arisen from a process of development that has remained responsive to the fundamental principles of vocal health and function which scientific, artistic and psychological investigation has established over many years.

The aim of voice movement therapy is to train a voice to be capable of giving expression to the gamut of human emotions and images which constitute psychological and creative processes. It seeks to benefit a person's psychological and physical state of being. The descriptions given in the following pages are not intended to be a substitute for the rigorous practical work and supervision which constitute the training in voice movement therapy. Neither are they intended to provide a self-help programme for prospective clients. They provide merely the opportunity to gain an initial insight into the practical application of the work; those interested in finding out more about it should write to the International Association for Voice Movement Therapy, the address for which is given at the end of this book.

# CHAPTER FIVE

# The Practical Elements of Vocal Liberation

## The Five Elements

There are five main therapeutic and educational strategies by which liberated vocal function may be achieved: ideokinesis, breathing enhancement, placement, movement and massage. In the voice movement therapy session, whether in a group or working individually, these five aspects are unified into one process; but in order to provide an initial insight into this process, let us begin by outlining each separately.

## Ideokinesis

Ideokinesis is an educational method by which kinesthetic imagery – that is, images of the body in motion – is used to stimulate specific muscular responses. The purpose of ideokinesis is to encourage a client to use the body in a way that is in tune with the healthy functioning of anatomical mechanics. Given that many clients find these processes complex and difficult to visualise, ideokinesis translates them into pictures based on everyday experience. Ideokinesis therefore denotes the 'psycho-physical process in which imagery and kinesthetic sense stimulate bodily change'.[1]

Ideokinesis has been most widely used in the teaching of dance and originates in the work of Mabel Todd.[2] The principles of her work, developed during the 1930s, are simple; their execution, however, places rigorous demands upon the dance teacher.

Todd proposed that first the teacher should come to understand the precise mechanical operations of the muscular and skeletal system. Secondly, the teacher must be able to translate these complex operations into images which the student recognises and can enjoy, but which none the less support and encourage the free play of mechanical operations according to scientific principles. Her premise was that 'concentration upon a picture involving movement results in responses in the neuromusculature as necessary to carry out specific movements with the least effort'.[3] The picture may be of a parasol, a dinosaur's tail, an opening gate hung on well-oiled hinges, a concertina – anything which provides a kinetic image that accords with the physical mechanics of anatomical motion. Todd described this process as 'psycho-physical and psycho-physiological'.

The legacy of Todd's work gave rise to a new generation of dancers and movement teachers, including Barbara Clark[4] and Lulu Sweigard[5], among whom ideokinesis became an accepted term. However, the process was not confined to dance and began to be used by music teachers also.[6]

Ideokinesis was central to the movement and body-release work taught by Mary Fulkerson at Dartington College of Arts from the early 1970s until the mid-1980s, and I was fortunate to have the opportunity to be her pupil for four years.[7]

Experience has taught me how essential it is to use images when helping clients to liberate their voice from constriction, and indeed the process of ideokinesis permeates every aspect of voice movement therapy. Asking clients to imagine that their voice resembles tiny fragments of broken glass which rub together producing red hot sparks when they sing is bound to produce a dysphonic quality which ends in inflammation. Evoking the image of a ping-pong ball coated with honey which is supported by a jet of water (a most popular image with singing teachers) is, on the other hand, more likely to produce an unhampered quality.

The surgeon William Faulkner discovered in 1942 that suggesting imaginary situations of a pleasant or unpleasant quality affected the activity of the oesophagus, the diaphragm, the nature of the breathing and the audible characteristics of the voice. Faulkner found that unpleasant suggestions caused an oesophageal tightening, while pleasant suggestions caused relaxation and relief of spasm. Following this, Faulkner declared that, without either telling patients which organ was being examined or giving instruction in breathing technique, he had demonstrated conclusively that the 'range of diaphragmatic movement in patients can be altered by suggesting situations which arouse strong emotions. If these emotions are pleasant, they cause increased amplitude of diaphragmatic movement; while the unpleasant type restrict it.'[8]

Augusta Jellinek also found some success in alleviating vocal disorders, improving voice quality and production and relieving stuttering through the use of 'guided imagery'[9] in which 'the subject closes his eyes and reports aloud to a listener what he sees as it appears before him'.[10] The therapist then influences what the patient sees by suggesting a collection of ideas and pictures which together form a positive image of vocal function. Working with singers, Jellinek enabled them to improve their performance by holding in mind 'vivid pictures' of their 'ideal of perfect singing'[11] so that 'when these pictures are recalled before a later performance, the subject's function is at its best, his level is higher than usual'.[12]

Faulkner and Jellinek took the principles of ideokinesis beyond the realms of anatomy and drew upon images of all kinds – emotional, figurative and sensory – to influence vocal function. This process of visualisation was developed in some detail and employed for its psychotherapeutic use by Roberto Assagioli,[13] founder of psychosynthesis, and it is still used as an aid to psychological excavation in therapeutic strategies which draw on Assagioli's work, such as in transpersonal psychology. The patient closes his eyes and imagines himself in an environment populated by objects, characters and animals which he describes aloud; the therapist meanwhile not only interprets but may suggest certain events or obstacles, arrivals or departures which the patient must visualise and report simultaneously how he deals with these suggestions.

The difference between ideokinesis and the application of a wide range of imagistic suggestions such as those used by Faulkner, Jellinek, Assagioli and others is that ideokinesis, as Todd and her students conceived of it, utilises images of a strictly mechanical nature. It is a non-emotive process. Furthermore, ideokinesis was developed not as a therapeutic strategy but as an educational procedure designed to enhance and facilitate healthy movement.

Though not intended for therapeutic use, ideokinesis incorporates a principle which psychotherapy established during the early twentieth century: that each individual has a mental picture of his or her own body which conforms to a greater or lesser extent to the physical appearance of that body when viewed 'objectively' by a third party. Freud had observed how being overly susceptible to this body image could lead the patient to experience bodily symptoms with no organic genesis in no lesser degree than if they were genuinely somatic. Meanwhile, Jung had paid particular attention to the way in which no bodily action or mental thought can be brought to consciousness unless it takes the form of an image by which it can be represented in the psyche.[14]

But the process of making use of the psychologically generated body image to enhance physiological functioning is not so simple as it may sound, neither is it a process which should be employed without considerable care and attention. The images used must be based on an understanding of what, according to scientific analysis, is actually going on. This means that the voice therapist, vocal coach or singing teacher must have an understanding of anatomy. Of course, images plucked out of nowhere have been seen to work; for many years singing teachers have intuitively responded with all manner of idiosyncratic pictures, thereby encouraging many of their students to produce good voices. However, other teachers with less intuitive genius have also caused many students to produce bad or even malfunctioning voices. Ideokinesis is an attempt to establish the physiological facts from which the individual teacher or therapist may draw appropriate and 'safe' imagery when helping to free the client's voice from psycho-physical constraint.

## Breathing Enhancement

As I have explained, there are two bodily regions which expand during inspiration to accommodate the inflated lungs. One is the thoracic cavity, expanded by the raising of the ribs; the other is the abdominal cavity, expanded by movement of the diaphragm and muscles of the abdominal wall.

When breathing, most people combine both of these movements, which can be seen in the simultaneous rising of the chest and the stomach during the course of normal respiration. The visible enlargement of the chest and the abdomen is called 'thoracic expansion' and 'abdominal expansion' respectively, and each person uses one more than the other, sometimes to such an extent that the lesser-used cavity barely expands at all. These two types of expansion are often also referred to as 'thoracic (or chest) breathing' (sometimes referred to as 'clavicular breathing') and 'abdominal (or stomach) breathing'.

It is in fact possible to extend considerably the expanded dimensions of both cavities and thereby increase the amount of air you inhale. For, although it feels as though you are 'full up' with air when you have inhaled, there is always the potential for further capacity by shifting the area of expansion from the predominant to the secondary one.

Singers and actors do this because they need to take in more air than usual in order to sustain the long phrases contained in classical plays and in songs. In order to achieve this, they combine both thoracic and abdominal expansion during the same inspiration. They begin expanding the chest and then, when they feel full, instead of exhaling, as we would normally, they carry on inhaling by expanding the abdomen. This provides an increased volume of air with which to sustain phonation and is referred to as increasing the 'vital capacity'. Though this technique takes training in order to perfect it, some people can get a basic grasp of it quite quickly.

Locating the two areas of expansion is not only of benefit to performers; it is crucial to the maintenance of a balanced relationship of mind and body, because the two different breathing methods have different psychological and emotional connotations. As a rule, people will employ thoracic breathing when in a state of fear, anxiety or worry, while abdominal breathing is used when we are relaxed, calm and secure and is the form of breathing which we employ unconsciously when we are asleep.

Thoracic breathing is often more shallow than abdominal breathing, and as a result you have to breathe more rapidly in order to inspire the same volume of air as when breathing abdominally at a slower rate. Thus, when we become anxious, afraid or worried, we also breathe more quickly.

The relationship between breathing and state of mind works both ways. As certain emotions stimulate a corresponding change in the emphasis of breathing from abdomen to thorax, or vice versa, so conversely a change in breathing method can help to induce emotional change. If we continually breathe at a deliberately heightened pace with the primary area of expansion in the chest, we will eventually begin to experience symptoms which often accompany anxiety; while to breathe with the area of expansion focused in the abdomen at a slow, even rate helps to bring about and maintain equanimity.

Whether a person is overtly calm, collected and peaceful or keyed up, distracted and volatile is reflected in the degree to which he or she breathes abdominally or thoracically. By teaching someone to rearrange the emphasis of expansion between thorax and abdomen, it is possible to assist in and facilitate the process of decreasing or increasing an overriding sense of stillness or activity, tranquillity or anxiety.

The aim of breathing enhancement is therefore to redirect the ratio of chest and abdominal expansion towards a balance which responds to the degree of anxiety expressed, described or complained of by the client. But it is important to recognise that this does not always mean decreasing thoracic and enhancing abdominal breathing; for a certain amount of what we may describe as anxiety is in fact absolutely necessary to physical and mental health.

Like all psychological elements, anxiety stands at one end of a spectrum at the other end of which is its complementary opposite – depression. Between the two extremes is a calibrated range of emotive impulses, which, while tending towards either the depressive or the anxious end, occupy a place on the scale that is healthy and necessary. The emotions on the 'anxious' side provide us with our verve and impulsiveness; they keep us enlivened, spirited and engaged. Falling in love, the experience of peaks of excitement and joy, the exhilarated euphoria of great achievement, the feeling of elated anticipation as we wait for the arrival of important news, the thrilling identification with the tightrope walker at the circus, all these emanate from the 'anxious' side of the scale. But even the extreme end of the spectrum has its positive contribution to make to human experience: if anxiety becomes the mainstay of our feelings, drowning out all else, then although we might not say that it was overtly positive, it none the less serves the valuable function of bringing us to recognise that something in our lives requires attention.

The other side of the spectrum contains the moods which have depression at their extreme end: stillness, a sense of calm and quietude, sorrow, contemplative reflection. Someone whose tendency is predominantly inclined towards this end may find it difficult to experience and express emotions of an impulsive, effervescent and reactive nature, while someone tending towards anxiety may experience equal alienation from a sense of calm and ease.

While anxiety is associated with and usually accompanied by thoracic breathing, depression manifests itself in a predominant expansion of the abdomen. The misinterpretations, mass pillaging and commercial dissemination of a number of Eastern forms of meditation by the boom in psychotherapy have unfortunately led to a dangerous popularisation of the depressive end of the emotional spectrum, enforced by physical practices which encourage abdominal breathing. The result is that, while many people find a certain leisure and comfort in such practices, they are misled into believing that a nullification of anxious tendencies is desirable or healthy. This of course is not true, and neither has it been propounded to be so by the philosophic traditions from which many of these popular activities have been uprooted. Meditation and Eastern forms of movement which are based on the notion of 'balancing energies', especially those which achieve this partially through attendance to the development of abdominal breathing, should therefore be perceived in the context of the philosophic and spiritual context of which they are a part, so that their aims can be properly understood. Otherwise they should be left alone and respected as an expression of a cultural history and medical ethos other than our own Western one.

It is true that nurturing an increased abdominal emphasis in breathing can contribute to the alleviation of an anxious disposition by helping to induce a feeling of calm. But it may be equally important in a predominantly depressed person to increase the emphasis on thoracic breathing and so help to mobilise a fresh verve and vitality. There is nothing mystical in this process; it is borne out purely by the fact that medical research in the West has shown that those prone to anxiety or depression have a tendency to emphasise thoracic and abdominal breathing respectively, and that encouraging a shift in emphasis helps to alleviate the emotional experience. It is a technique that can be taught to clients in a relatively short space of time in order that they may practise it in an effort to achieve a balanced emotional state. But, like all the techniques described here, breathing enhancement is something that must be introduced with detailed care and under proper instruction. Breathing primarily through thoracic expansion without following careful instruction may lead to hyperventilation and may have the effect of enhancing those very muscular patterns which have caused a one-sided emphasis in the first place. Indeed, just as abdominal breathing has been overemphasised by some practices in order to promote a state of inaction, so too there are hideous misuses of more vigorous respiratory activities, such as those employed in a number of contemporary therapeutic strategies, where the clients breathe themselves into a state of euphoric excitement and are encouraged to believe that they have surmounted traumas suffered in the dim and unremembered past.

Consumption by emotions which lie at the extreme ends of a spectrum can often occur as a result of an experience, a set of occurrences or an undesirable social or domestic situation. But anxiety or depression which is admitted verbally by a client and supported by signs of a severely unbalanced ratio between thoracic and abdominal expansion cannot be dealt with by breathing enhancement alone. It must be combined with an understanding of the client's personality and environment.

In addition to the predominance of one of the two areas of expansion, another important variable in breathing is the depth of inhalation. There is always a portion of air which is left remaining in the lungs when we breathe out, but in some people this portion is far in excess of what it should be, due to overly shallow inhalation. Breathing too shallowly is often part of the process by which we retain our feelings 'inside us' and 'locked away', so to speak. It is the reverse of the extended breathing which takes the form of a sigh, and which serves to give us the feeling of emotional release. Breathing enhancement is aimed not only at nurturing increased thoracic and abdominal expansion, but at extending the volume of inspired and expired air. Its effect resembles that of a prolonged sigh; it is essentially a cathartic process. However, its benefits are not only psychological, but physiological also. An increased tidal capacity encourages an increased expressive vitality, providing the voice with a support for sustaining sound and therefore for the communication and conveyance of feeling, mood and image.

The breathing pattern of a number of clients with whom I have worked has been dictated by an extreme physical condition. One of the more common conditions is partial paralysis of the intercostal muscles, which forces the client to depend heavily on abdominal expansion. The decreased or disabled capacity for thoracic expansion puts pressure on the muscles responsible for abdominal expansion to work more quickly than they would if sharing responsibility for the respiratory cycle with the intercostal muscles responsible for thoracic expansion. In order to maintain conversations at a speed equivalent to that used by an able-bodied person, the client will often gasp air in sudden convulsive movements visible in the abdominal region, leaving him or her exhausted. In cases where physical predicaments have an overriding influence on the process of breathing, as in the case of paralysis of the intercostal muscles, an overtly psychological interpretation of respiratory activity is much less relevant. Instead the emphasis should be on nurturing an even respiratory cycle which is not caused to convulse in response to the psychological and physical need to compensate for lack of function.

Regardless of the physical and psychological influences upon breathing, it is unusual to be able to observe either the dominant area of expansion or the depth of the respiratory cycle when the client is inactive. Therefore the initial stage of instruction in voice movement therapy is to get the client to reveal his or her habitual pattern of breathing as related to the use of the voice. Clients who have no history of vocal dysfunction, admit no complaints of discomfort or pain in the laryngeal area and who display no acoustic signals which belie underlying problems, should be first asked to call out. Unless the client is chair-bound or bed-bound, he or she should stand with arms held loosely at the sides and should be instructed to breathe in and to let out a call, as if trying to alert someone's attention across a distance of 50 yards. The client should repeat this process while the breathing pattern is observed.

The importance of this activity of calling cannot be overestimated and is not only an essential starting point because it shows up a person's breathing pattern particularly clearly, but because it is the most efficient way of overcoming one of the most common early hurdles in the process of working on the voice.

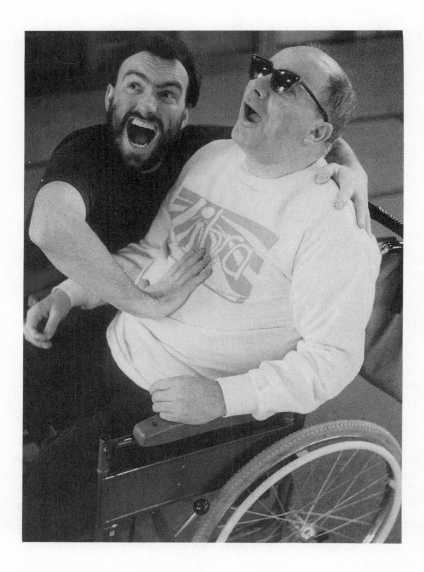

## EDDIE AND PAUL

This client has multiple sclerosis which has left him unable to walk and unable to see very much. He also has a very short memory span. However, his voice issues forth with a thunderous and highly enabled tone. An image which he has found particularly facilitating is an African tribal chief calling his people to feast. This relieves him of the pressure to make linguistic sense and gives him the physical sensation of being enthroned rather than chair bound.

EDDIE, PAUL AND MOLLIE
When he is joined by this second client, who is also unable to walk, an improvised duet ensues which enjoins and unites them in the wedding song of chief and chiefess, which bears no reference to their so-called disability. Close your eyes and you would hear only the dance of liberated voices.

---

The first thing which prevents the liberation of the voice is in most cases a reticence, a lack of confidence or shyness in letting the voice out. Though the client will be genuinely committed to developing the voice, he or she is often deeply restrained by a semi-conscious fear of letting sound out. In vocal terms we might call this state 'phonophobia' – a fear of voicing – and the first aim of any vocal work should be to overcome it.

Phonophobia, or extreme shyness, is both a psychological and a vocal problem, the one aspect feeding the other in a cyclical syndrome from which the person feels he or she cannot escape. It is an excruciating condition which affects thousands of people and yet it has never been taken seriously by therapists of voice, speech or mind.

Phonophobia is the means by which individuals deny themselves the right to speak out, and those who experience it are usually found to be suffering from the repercussions of having been continually silenced, either by a dominating parent, by a school teacher, by the overpowering success of an elder sibling or by a series of suffocating circumstances which denied their right to self-expression and thus silenced their voice.

PAUL (*above and opposite*)
It is absolutely essential that any voice worker maintains a regular
programme of vocal self investigation and training. A Voice Movement
Therapist in particular must be able to follow every client around the
contours of the vocal canvas. The therapist's voice must be malleable
and robust, capable of withstanding the heavy schedule imposed by the
diversity of voices with which he must work.

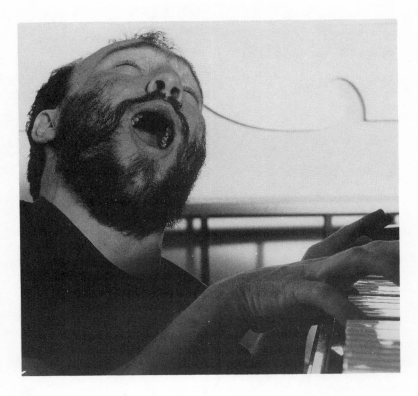

Shyness is the result of a quashing of confidence, and it is usually the parent who is responsible for this. This silencing is achieved almost exclusively by deliberately inhibiting the voice of the child, this being the main medium of her self-expression. 'Don't whine', 'Don't whimper', 'Don't pester', 'Don't be cheeky', 'Don't be rude', 'Don't give me any lip' – all these are the phrases by which the child's right to speak out is undermined and all of them represent the vestiges of the abominable Victorian dictum that 'children should be seen and not heard'.

Later in life, when the mother and father are absent or dead, the oppressive parent or parents live on inside the adult's psyche. The parent becomes absorbed as a little critical voice which inhibits and censors the voice of the adult. The shy person thus sits in silence while those around her speak. However, people who are shy almost exclusively complain not of an inner silence, as one might expect, but of an internal mindscape of unbearable noise: the noise of their own reactions which they dare not and do not vocalise but instead bottle up.

Shy people know exactly what they think and feel and what they have to say, but between the conception and the word falls their shadow, the sum of all those parts of themselves which they hide, which they do not want to associate themselves with. The shy person's shadow is the critical judge, the bombastic extrovert who dominates the stage of the unconscious and comes down like a ton of bricks, preventing the words from coming out. The phonophobic is dominated and tyrannised by a mental judge absorbed from the overbearing critical nature of the parent but which has now become a part of herself. The internal world of noise is populated with silent verdicts, and this inner critical nature combined with the shy person's outward silence may give her an arrogant appearance; many of those who suffer from phonophobia are wrongly perceived as being so secure as not to give a damn for communication.

In the early stages of infantile development, expression is aimed at demonstrating needs to the mother through sound, and confidence is established through having these cacophonous expressions accepted and answered by her. But, as we grow up and our mother becomes more distant, we have to tend to our own needs. The word 'confidence' comes from 'to confide', and to have self-confidence is to confide in oneself. Many people who lack confidence and audacity also find it difficult to confide in people, to share themselves with friends, either because they undervalue the substance of their personality or else they fear betrayal.

The first stage in overcoming phonophobia involves learning to confide in oneself by displaying the inner aspects of the psyche via the sounds of the voice, regardless of the way they appear to the inner critical judge, who may regard them as ugly, untuneful, harsh or weak and condemn them to strangulation.

The most immediate way of achieving this is through the call. The call is not related to singing in the Western sense of the term; it is a phonational expression of emotion, heard in its most stirring manifestation among the folk traditions of Argentina, Brazil, Hungary and Egypt, where it has a raw vitality which surpasses and defies any interpretation which employs the rules of continuous pitch. Frankie Armstrong has for many years been reviving this relaxed and emotive use of the voice through workshops in Britain and worldwide with a range of people whose attitude towards 'what singing is' radically changes while their singing voice extends.

In order for the client to overcome phonophobia, the teacher or therapist must be able to use his or her own voice in a completely free and unhindered way in order that a process of 'calling' conversation can be set up between client and practitioner. Integral to the working process of Jill Purce and Frankie Armstrong is the way that they both demonstrate what they ask their clients to do. If only all vocal practitioners could practise what they preach!

In this early stage practitioner and client call to one another in a series of utterances and replies, and it is during this simple process that all the client's respiratory secrets will out. The range of different breathing patterns is astounding. There are clients who carefully and methodically breathe in with acute concentration, taking four or five seconds before phonating. Then there are clients who gasp so suddenly and have uttered and completed their call in such a little time that it seems as though they were being given a speed test. Regardless of the response, just enough instruction should be given by the practitioner to allow, on the one hand, the patient's natural breathing tendency to be exaggerated by the act of calling and, on the other hand, to arrive at a result which is sufficiently visible to permit diagnosis. Having made an assessment, the next stage is to encourage a depth of inhalation and nurture increased expansion in the thoracic and/or abdominal regions.

There is a third aspect of respiratory activity which has a direct bearing on the quality of the human voice, and which can also be identified during this initial process of diagnosing and retraining the pattern of breathing. As described earlier, the human voice is created by the abduction and adduction of the vocal cords which causes the expired breath to be released in a series of puffs which in turn cause the sound of the voice. But it is possible to push more breath through the glottis than is actually necessary to form the puff which makes the sound. This does not alter the pitch of the note, but it gives it an airy, breathy quality. When there is so much 'superfluous' air that it is possible to detect a breathiness in the timbre of the voice, I refer to the presence of 'free air' in the voice. This audible breathiness was termed 'wild air' during the 1940s by a well-known voice clinician called Froeschels, and was one of the qualities which Moses looked for in his psychological analysis of the voice.[15] With the advent of modern technology it has become possible to make precise quantitative measurements of the amount of air released through the vocal cords during its cycle of adduction and abduction, and the terms used to describe the various acoustic qualities which correlate with different patterns of air flow have become various and more technically sophisticated.[16] However, Froeschels's original phrase has the advantage of making perfect intuitive sense to the voice-user, without recourse to scientific complexity, and I have found it possible to instruct clients in varying the amount of audible 'wind' or 'free air' to therapeutic and artistic effect. To diagnose the degree of free air in the client's natural voice it is necessary to abandon the calling, which will have served to have overcome any phonophobia, and to phonate more in the style of singing in the western sense.

If you phonate with a high proportion of free air, the voice acquires a breathy, soft, velvety and husky quality. However, when you make a sound with only the release of the necessary amount of air needed for phonation, the voice is solid, dense, metallic and hard. Between these two extremes is a wide spectrum that forms an important part of determining the character of a voice.

The amount of free air present in the voice is directly related to the process of breathing. A person who releases a large quantity of free air will not be able to sustain phonation for very long. This will make long phrases in singing or speaking very difficult, and one of the first stages in training the voice of a performer is to adjust the quantity of 'escaping breath'. On the other hand, someone who can sing a note which lasts a long and seemingly impressive amount of time by restricting the amount of air used for phonation to the bare minimum is not necessarily to be rewarded by lack of instruction. It could well imply a reluctance to release a degree of air that would reveal any degree of emotion. We do not sigh for nothing; the emission of sounds which contain a high portion of free air serve to convey a certain potency of affect. As with all forms of expert control, those people who yearn to impress with their long phonation times may well be keeping their emotional skeletons hidden in the cupboard. Though, again, the psychological interpretation of the degree of free air in the voice should proceed with caution and in the context provided by all the other physical and psychological signals revealed consciously and unconsciously by the client.

Based on an observation and analysis of these signals, a further aim of breathing enhancement is to enable the client to phonate with a widely varying amount of free air. Just as there is a scale of pitches from A to G, so too within each individual pitch there is a scale of degree of free air with which it is sung; and this should be taught as much for its artistic as for its emotional applications.

Through careful instruction the client is then able to sing a range of pitches with varying degrees of free air, and the malleability of the voice begins to emerge, along with an accompanying confidence. The next stage is to discover the further malleability possible through the 'placement' of the voice.

# Placement

The notion of the placement of a voice has been used for centuries by singing teachers to denote where the singer imagines the voice is coming from. Imagining that the sound emanates from the top of the head produces a very different timbre to that which arises when the same pitch is sung while imagining that the voice is placed in the stomach, or in the centre of the breast or from between the eyes or from the sacrum.

While singing teachers have for a long time made use of placement happily and with fine results, the idea has not been taken on board so readily by the laryngologic and other clinical professions, primarily because in their hands it tends to become confused with the notion of resonators.

The question of bodily resonators has always been a contentious issue among voice researchers in all fields. Throughout the twentieth century different experiments have been carried out to determine which parts of the body act as a resonator for the voice. Jerzy Grotowski, on the one hand, claimed that his actors could make their voices resonate in the stomach, in different parts of the back, in the groin and at the top of the head; and after Michael Kustow had watched Grotowski's group rehearsing Marlowe's *The Tragical History of Dr Faustus* in 1963, he wrote that the 'voice work aims at discovering extra resonators, rarely used by the European theatre'.[17] On the other hand, notions of the type propounded by Grotowski have been dismissed as nonsense by those who argue that vibration can only be measured in the upper half of the body in close proximity to the vocal cords.

One of the earliest advocates of this latter opinion was Charles Lindsley,[18] who in 1934 published results of experiments which aimed to measure vocal resonance in different parts of the body in order to ascertain what role these vibrations played in determining the quality of a speaker's voice. By recording electrically the vibrations generated in different parts of the body, Lindsley was able to show that the vocal cords generate tones which produce resonating vibrations throughout a wide area of the chest, throat, face and head but nowhere else. Through a comparative measurement of different speakers Lindsley found that the term 'head tones' is not justified, because the amount of vibration produced in this area by the vowels of ordinary speech is negligible. Furthermore, though extra vibration is heard in the head region from singers in soprano and contralto pitch ranges, this alone does not account for the production of head tones.

Despite the endless acoustic experiments which have followed Lindsley's, singing teachers have continued to speak of the voice as being placed in other parts of the body besides those in which vibration has been physically measured. Moreover, they have taught pupils to move the placement of the voice at will up and down the so-called 'resonating ladder'.[19] However, clinically orientated voice therapists rarely employ this language and are unlikely to do so until the disputes of terminology between teachers and themselves are nearer a resolution.

These altercations, which will probably never be completely settled, are fortunately becoming the subject of analysis and dialogue in the UK between the practitioners of all voice-related professions, from actors to audiologists, from singing teachers to speech therapists, as a result of the ground-breaking work of the British Voice Association (BVA).

One of the most enlightening issues to be raised repeatedly at the BVA annual symposia is the incredible variety of terminology used by vocal practitioners of all orientations which bears no relation to objective analysis and often originates in a subjective interpretation of voice quality. At the 1991 symposium Dianne Bless pointed out that 'the terms used to describe voice quality vary not only between professions but also *within* the medical profession, and indeed amongst clinicians of the same discipline'.[20] Much of this terminology involves reference to parts of the human anatomy, yet faith in the medical profession to produce a definitive description of the anatomical and physiological processes involved in voice production is somewhat unfounded; and while doctors, therapists, clients, patients, singers and voice teachers wait for a resolution of the inter-clinical and inter-professional divergences in anatomical terminology, they have to get on with the job.

Fortunately, from a therapeutic and practical point of view, what is important is not so much the terminology involved but whether the idea or the image of sound resonating in, emanating from or being placed in a part of the body helps the client overcome restriction of vocal malleability.

Common aspirin, along with many other useful reliefs and remedies, would have to be thrown out if we would insist upon knowing exactly how they work on the nervous system before we used them to good effect. If something works to improve our well-being, we should be — and medicine for centuries has been — content to use it and hope that we will understand later *how* it works. We make practical use of mysteries every day, and indeed become very adept at handling processes we understand dimly if at all. We would remain in the darkness for a long time if we refused go flip the light switch before we knew exactly what electricity is, or how it does what it does.[21]

We are again in the realm of imagination, or ideokinesis, that elusive and all-powerful ability of the human psyche to generate images to which the body responds. Often these images take poetic liberties with physiological evidence; they translate the discursive language of science into the non-discursive symbols of colour, shape, form, mood, action and above all sensation. As the medical doctor Anne Hollings said in the BVA newsletter of 1989:

The semantics of singing have used descriptions of the sensations a sound gives the vocalist. The teacher manipulates the vocal coordination by asking the pupil to imagine the voice or breath is performing some activity. Perhaps the voice has to be like a ping-pong ball on a jet of water; perhaps rippling over waves, etc. All this is subjective. It may mean one action to one pupil but something different to another. However, under supervision, the effect is real in producing physiological adjustments. Scientific appraisal has often taken singing terms literally and discredited them as not meaning what they say. The best-known example is the idea of 'singing from the diaphragm' — a complete misnomer but often a good term to convey an action to a pupil.

Vocal placement is another singing concept of probable importance to vocal health, but descriptions of where to 'place' a voice are difficult for a scientist to identify with . . .

The brain takes instructions in terms of collections of actions it recognises from experience and not individually, muscle by muscle, like an anatomy book. Teaching phrases cannot use direct physiological jargon. What pupil could respond to requests such as: 'Alter the opening quotient of your larynx please'? . . .

That the languages of vocal training and science are not the same does not invalidate methods of teaching singing but the differences may lead to a mutual suspicion between disciplines.[22]

This suspicion between disciplines can only be dissolved through collaboration and inter-professional cooperation such as that facilitated by the BVA. It is also only by way of such cooperation that the artistically orientated practitioner can be sure that the sensory images he or she is utilising in the teaching process encourage the healthy functioning of the vocal apparatus. Whether the voice can be said to be placed in different bodily areas according to the vibrations which instruments can measure is unknown. Indeed, the video stroboscopy recording which Garfield-Davies made of my voice in 1990 would suggest that the cause for the changes in vocal timbre which appear to result from the ideokinesis of shifting placement actually arise as a result of complex and minute changes in the structural positioning and fibre tensions of the laryngeal musculature. But, as Anne Hollings has implied, what student would be able to respond to instructions based on these complex notions? What is important is that healthy vocal functioning is achieved through images which a client can understand.

In my own early research into developing voice movement therapy I derived the most useful approach to vocal placement from the work of Alfred Wolfsohn, who divided the body into three main areas which he employed as images to help students to expand the expressive potential of the voice. This way of developing and analysing the voice has been used effectively by those working within Wolfsohn's framework for many years, and I am indebted to Enrique Pardo for first introducing them to me.

According to this view, there are three main cavities in which the voice can be imagined to be placed: the head, the chest and the abdominal region. The sound produced by the first placement can be compared to that of a violin and is focused primarily in the head and face. The second is more like that of a viola and is focused in the cavities of the chest and upper back. The third is like that of a cello and is placed in the stomach, womb, intestines and lower back. Wolfsohn showed how it is possible to sing the same pitch in all three of these placements with an audible acoustic difference that is surprisingly great, and in 1956 Folkways Records released a record which demonstrated his students' extended vocal range achieved through the use of these metaphors of stringed instruments and parts of the body.[23]

Although originally inspired by this notion, I found that using the image of a stringed instrument does not encapsulate the actual physio-mechanical process of emitting air from the lungs through the trachea and into the vocal tract via the vocal cords. Furthermore, through an analysis of many clients I discovered that Wolfsohn's image of the viola voice is actually composed of two grades or magnitudes which are experienced as being placed in the upper and the lower chest. Consequently I have adapted Wolfsohn's imagery towards imagining the voice to be a wind instrument which, with practice, can change its dimensions and material constitution. One thinks of a flute quality placed in the upper chest, a clarinet quality placed in the lower chest and a saxophone quality placed in the abdominal region. I have retained Wolfsohn's violin metaphor to describe the twangy instrumental quality which I have discovered to be produced when the sound is imagined to be placed in the head.

The student imagines that the mouth, larynx and trachea form a malleable muscular funnel which can alter in diameter to correspond to the tubular dimensions of a flute, clarinet and saxophone, whose notes resonate in the upper chest, lower chest and abdomen respectively. When this has been achieved, the student then has enough flexibility of the laryngeal musculature to be able to produce the higher, more 'stringy' sounds which Wolfsohn termed violin or head placement.

With training, the voice can be placed in one or more of these cavities by mental will and physical agility; and by taking a single note and imagining that the sound originates in one of the three placements, while simultaneously adjusting the laryngeal musculature in response to the idea of an expandable tube, it is possible to alter its quality radically. Those interested in developing a malleable singing voice need to accomplish this skill in order to be able to move between different styles.

I have given many demonstrations of this technique to clinical and non-clinical practitioners, and the amazement which follows is always further enhanced when they realise that the technique can be used to produce the same results in anybody. It takes mental concentration and a commitment to improving vocal agility, but it does not require any special innate skill. It has also proved to be an important tool in releasing vocal function from physical restriction in many clients.

## THE VIOLIN VOICE OR HEAD PLACEMENT

One of the most famous 'head' or 'violin' voices in singing is that of Billie Holiday. It has a hardness to it, a brittle quality that sounds as though it echoes inside an oak box. Billie Holiday's voice is placed almost exclusively in the region of the head and possesses hardly any free breath, which distinguishes it from, for example, the later work of Marianne Faithful, which is also sung in the head voice, but with more free air, which gives it its gruffness. Bob Dylan's early work was also sung from a head placement with varying degrees of free air. Other examples of the head placement can be heard in the singing voice of Neil Young, Al Jolson and that of Joel Grey in the film *Cabaret*.

The violin voice also has a feline character to it and is brought into play naturally when we impersonate the 'meow' of a cat. This feline quality can be heard in its purest form among the women folksingers of Bulgaria, where it is both passionate and immensely powerful. Finally, the violin voice accompanies old age and most people in their latter years speak with the same focus in their head as do children in their early years. This gives the head voice its particular paradoxical quality: it is at once innocent and yet full of bitter experience, a quality heard nowhere more clearly than in the voice of Billie Holiday.

In speaking, the pure head placement is most commonly heard in children, especially in heightened moods such as petulance and ill temper; very young infants also display a lot of free breath, the best example being in their early cooing. The violin voice is used in the portrayal of classically evil characters, and children exaggerate their head voice when playing the parts of witches and wicked old men in pantomime. In the theatre one of the most famous examples of such head voices is to be heard in Laurence Olivier's portrayal of Richard III. His voice is embittered, vicious and has a brittle quality like burnt wood. The same placement is also used by John Hurt in his role as Quentin Crisp in *The Naked Civil Servant*. Indeed, many homosexual men develop a vocal affectation that we refer to as 'camp' and which can be described as an overdevelopment and emphasis of the violin voice or head placement.

The violin voice is thus characterised by qualities that evoke certain images which are brought into being by mentally focusing the placement, resonation or origination of vocal sound in the head.

## THE FLUTE AND CLARINET VOICE OR CHEST PLACEMENT

The flute and clarinet voices arise from the image of resonation being placed in the chest, with the flute being produced through the ideokinesis of a tube of smaller diameter than that which produces the clarinet. In addition, the flute is imagined to occupy the upper chest while the clarinet sits further down the sternum, as if one had swallowed first a clarinet and then a flute, which now join together in the centre of the torso. The chest voice is less solid and dense than the head voice and has more fluidity about it.

Like the head placement, the chest voice can be sung with a greater or lesser degree of free air. Phil Collins, Elvis Costello, Debbie Harry, Chris de Burgh, Diana Ross, Kate Bush and Paul Simon all have a chest voice with varying amounts of free air detectable in an audible emission of breath which sounds as though it runs parallel to their phonated sound. Elton John, George Michael, Liza Minnelli, Jim Kerr from Simple Minds, Marvin Gaye and Paul McCartney all have a chest-placed voice with no free air, while Suzanne Vega has a chest placement with just enough free air to give it its lightness.

In a woman free air combined with the chest voice can give rise to a certain childlike innocence, particularly at the flute end as in the voice of

Melanie, Cindy Wilson, the lead singer from the B 52's, and Stevie Nicks from Fleetwood Mac. Perhaps the clearest example of the innocence inherent in the airy quality of the chest voice is that of Karen Carpenter, whose voice has just enough free air to give it its soft and melancholy purity but enough density to give it projection. One of the finest examples of a singer with control over the amount of free air in the chest placement is Joni Mitchell, who moves with speed and grace from the reflective and introspective breathy sounds to the higher, assertive and more condensed notes in which the amount of free air is minimalised. She also shifts between flute and clarinet on a single note.

The relationship between head and chest placement, and between flute and clarinet within the chest, is not one of a leap or a jump, but one of gradation, and some voices are placed between the two. Barbra Streisand, for instance, has a voice mid-way between head and chest with no free air, as did Robert Plant when he was lead singer with Led Zeppelin. Sinead O'Connor is a good example of a singer who moves freely between chest and head in the course of singing a single song; the chest placement gives it a certain vulnerability while the head gives it the density it needs to maintain its strength of conviction.

## THE SAXOPHONE VOICE OR ABDOMINAL PLACEMENT

The 'saxophone' voice is focused in the abdonimal region and is best suited to expressing emotions of a mellow and a 'blues' nature. Both Elvis Presley and Joan Armatrading use predominantly the abdominal placement, though Armatrading mixes it with the chest and varies the amount of free breath. Tracy Chapman, who has often been compared to Armatrading, also uses an abdominal placement, but it is combined with a head placement, which lends it a more bony and nutty quality. Another example of this mixing can be heard in the voice of David Bowie, whose leaps from the deeply rounded saxophone to the twanging head or violin sounds are clearly audible; the same transformations can be heard to a lesser extent in the voice of Robert Smith, lead singer of The Cure. Meanwhile, Van Morrison sings mainly in the saxophone voice or abdominal placement with an audible amount of free air, while Brian Ferry sings in the abdomen with hardly any.

In the theatre the saxophone voice is mainly used to portray stupidity; it is the gentle giant, the harmless ignoramus. The saxophone voice also has a certain primitive quality about it. In speaking, we sometimes adopt the saxophone voice spontaneously when we become depressed or deeply sombre. Singing saxophone makes us feel as though our abdomen has enlarged, almost as though we have a cave in our bellies, and much of the physical work involved in releasing it consists of imagining expansion of the space in the abdominal region.

This contact with the saxophone register in the abdomen should not be confused with the grating sounds made in the bass register, such as those used by Barry White. This rough edge or gruffness which White possesses is imitated by a number of singers many of whom have caused themselves vocal problems. Rod Stewart, Bruce Springsteen, Tina Turner, Shane Mac-Gowan from The Pogues and a host of singers from the heavy-metal genre of bands such as Def Leppard deliberately utilise a frictional quality by compressing the laryneal musculature against the glottis and adducting the vocal cords under great pressure while forcing free air through the glottis at the same time. Despite the problems encountered by many of these singers, they have been loath to seek treatment as their fortunes depend upon their pathology. This is a great shame, because there are ways of producing such sounds which do not demand an excess of muscle-fibre tension or an inordinate amount of vocal-cord pressure. Neither does a singer have to have a particularly low voice to achieve this; Louis Armstrong's style of singing is perhaps the best example of an instinctive but healthy way of producing such a voice.

Although one can sing high sounds in the abdominal placement just as well as deep sounds, it is easier to sing low sounds in the saxophone range, while the head placement is meanwhile more encouraging of upper pitches. Part of the training process for any modern singer therefore involves being able to move up and down the placements without changing the pitch.

In order to find out the placement into which the client's voice naturally falls, it is necessary to ask him or her to change the sound from a call to a sung note, because calling tends to give rise to a particularly vigorous phonational quality which, while perfect for diagnosis of the breathing pattern, obscures the natural qualitative tendency of the singing voice. It should then be possible to ascertain whether the natural tendency of the voice is to be placed in the head, chest or abdomen.

Instruction now should take the form of developing that which is absent. For a voice with a head placement this means opening up the lower, warmer qualities of the chest and lower regions. For someone with a voice placed in the abdomen this means working upwards towards the clear icy qualities of the head. Remember, these anatomical references to head, chest and stomach are merely images, pictures to hold in mind when striving towards vocal liberation.

The client should now be taught to phonate on the same pitch with varying degrees of free air in each of the three placements, enabling him or her to express a wide vocal spectrum without even changing note.

These manoeuvres up and down the resonating ladder are not produced by will-power alone, but require a profound physical agility and malleability of the laryngeal musculature, and it is very common for a client, when asked to make a sound using the violin or head placement, or when asked to sing the sound deep from the stomach, to squeeze the face and neck into a contortion which completely inhibits free vocal function of any kind. Hence it is at this stage that the client displays faulty muscular patterns which require attention and remodelling; and this is where movement is of crucial importance.

# Movement

Using the voice, as we have seen in the previous chapter, requires the activation of the laryngeal musculature; therefore vocal patterns give rise to muscular habits and vice versa.

Unfortunately, many of those who wish to partake of the non-clinical physical therapies, either as practitioners or as clients, have been completely misled by the conveniently simplified teachings of biology teachers or handbooks for the lay person, which, though offering easily digestible explanations of the muscular system, none the less fail to deal with the points most salient to the preservation of health.

Central to this teaching is the idea that the human body is composed of a collection of independent muscles which cooporate in antagonistic pairs in such a way that when one contracts the other expands, causing movement of the skeleton at its joints. Though this dualistic idea of compensatory movement localised in an identifiable part of the body facilitates the understanding of highly complex phenomena, it also unfortunately obscures from view those aspects of neuromuscular functioning which relate directly to the significance of movement retraining in relation to vocal function.[24]

If you were to take a scalpel to your leg, cut out a cube of muscle and place it under a powerful microscope, you would see that it is composed of thousands of individual fibres, stretched longitudinally like the individual fibres which make up a piece of elastic. If you were to further magnify this cube of muscle, you would see that each of these fibres is, like all matter, made up of individual cells. The contraction or extension of a muscle results from the degree of tension in these fibres which is set and maintained by the nervous system.

Running from the brain down the spinal cord and out into the various parts of the body are nerves, some of which are designated purely to serve the muscles and are called motor nerves. At the peripheral end, where they meet the muscle, these nerves split like a frayed piece of wool into a number of very fine filaments called axons; and these axons are then attached to the cells of the muscle fibres by what is called an endplate. Each muscle cell receives only one endplate; however, one endplate has to serve more than one muscle cell. A single motor nerve with its group of muscle cells attached at the axon is called a motor unit.

When the brain is stimulated, the semi-permeable membrane forming the cell walls of the nerves alters in constitution and allows positively charged sodium to pass from the intercellular fluid into the cell, creating a ripple of polarity alterations which constitutes the so-called neurological message. When a message is transmitted down a particular nerve, all the muscle fibres whose cells are attached to the axons of that nerve will be forced to respond. It follows, then, that in parts of the body where very precise movements are required, such as in the eye, a single motor nerve controls only a small number of cells; while in a part of the body which does not utilise precisely controlled movement, such as the buttocks, many hundreds of cells will be served by the same nerve.

There are millions upon millions of these muscle fibres attached to motor nerves all over the body which tend to gather into units. The compartmentalising needs of anatomical description have classified these as individual muscles, such as the trapezius, the biceps and the pectorals. However, this terminology is misleading because these muscle units cannot and do not function on their own. The moment the muscle fibres in one part of the body are contracted, the muscle fibres in another part are immediately expanded, which in turn causes adjacent fibres in another part to contract, and so on throughout the body, creating a ripple of compensatory movement.

When you raise an arm, fibres of the upper trapezius, the deltoid and the supraspinatus contract, causing fibres of the pectorals and latissimus to expand. However, the raising of the right arm creates an imbalance in the distribution of weight about the body's axis and pulls the torso to one side. In order to keep the body centrally vertical, therefore, fibres of the erector spinae muscles contract. At the same time, fibres of the various individually named muscles of the neck will contract to maintain the head in a vertical position and this in turn requires other fibres of the trapezius to expand. This all tends to pull the pelvis to one side and therefore other fibres must contract to keep the hips in place. This contraction in turn affects the legs which remain in pose as a result of further responsive expansion, and so on throughout the entire body, creating a push-me-pull-you of contraction and expansion maintaining bodily balance in response to a singular muscular intention towards activity. The simple action of raising one arm therefore instigates a highly complex cat's cradle of expanding and contracting muscle fibres; and it would be a simplification bordering on a lie to pin any single bodily movement down to the action of a single pair of muscle units.

No so-called individual muscle contracts or expands all of its fibres at one time. It is true only that some muscle fibres controlled by one motor nerve contract, while other muscle fibres controlled by another motor nerve expand or remain motionless. But a fibre neither contracts nor expands completely, in the same way that a piece of elastic is neither fully stretched nor fully contracted. There are degrees of contraction and expansion within each muscle fibre; and it is this degree which we refer to as 'tension'.

Contraction of a muscle does not only occur in the movement of the body, such as in raising an arm. A degree of tension is required among some fibres all the time to maintain a position, otherwise we would be a helpless mass of tissue lying on the floor. Even when we are asleep there is a degree of tension distributed throughout various muscle fibres, and in fact the only time all the muscle fibres of the body are completely without tension is under a general anaesthetic. So what does it mean when a therapist comments that a client is overly tense?

In the course of day-to-day activities many muscle fibres are involved in an ever-adjusting process of contraction and expansion, while many of them are maintained in a constant degree of tension in order for the body to hold pose. It is this constant tension of some muscle fibres which give rise to what we call 'muscle tone'. However, it is very common for a person to contract more muscle fibres than is necessary to execute a particular action or to maintain a position. For example, imagine that early one Friday morning a man is preparing to go to work, preoccupied with the impending likelihood of delayed rail service and a subsequently disrupted schedule at the office. He goes into the bathroom and cleans his teeth; he grips the toothbrush hard in his hand and brushes with such a pressure that an observer might notice a bulge in his biceps. Later that night, relaxed and preparing for bed, looking forward to the lie-in on Saturday morning, he cleans his teeth again. Only this time he doesn't grip so hard and he exerts less pressure on his teeth. When he brushed his teeth in the morning, there would have been thousands more muscle fibres held at a greater degree of tension than during the same activity in the evening. We would therefore describe him as having been more tense in the morning.

Muscular activity, such as teeth cleaning, is an acquired habit; it is something we learn to do. There are, however, other degrees of contraction and expansion within certain combinations of muscle fibres which a human being inherits in the form of a natural instinct to execute a particular motor activity. These automatic responses include suckling, breathing, crying and defecating.

Some of the neurological messages which organise and orchestrate muscular activity are conscious and executed by volition. We are usually fully aware that we raise our arm, or move our hands in an up-and-down motion to clean our teeth. Others, however, continue their activities without our being conscious of them. Blinking, breathing, the muscular process of digestion are inherited functions that can occur outside our conscious control or recognition. Most animals live their lives satisfied with the automatic motor activities innate to them and do not progress to execute any more precise or complex muscular movements than those with which they were born. Shortly after birth the young zebra can already stand, run, drink and do all the things that he will ever do. Furthermore, he will already be programmed to execute certain motor activities in response to visual images with which he is completely unfamiliar – such as running away from an approaching lion. However, a human being acquires the coordinated proficiency with which to accomplish actions of incredible virtuosity and precision. Speaking, walking, writing, cleaning teeth, playing the piano, riding a bicycle, all these activities involve a series of contractions

and expansions within muscle fibres which have to be voluntarily instigated by consciously engaging the impulse-sending capacity of the motor
nerves.

If the same motor activity is repeated sufficiently over a long period of
time, the degree of conscious volition involved in its execution depletes and
the muscular movement becomes what we refer to as 'second nature',
barely distinguishable from those automatic motor activities which we
were born to do. This is why it is possible to drive a car or play the piano
without really 'thinking about it'.

If generation upon generation of people acquire and repeat the same
motor activities, eventually an infant may be born with the ability in the
form of an inherited automatic response. This constitutes the evolution of
behaviour and is, for example, the means by which a species adapts to the
ever-shifting face of danger. The process by which an originally volitional
motor action becomes automatic is not understood by neurologists, and
this field of research still leaves thousands of questions unanswered. What
is agreed is that neuromuscular activities which in the first place require
constant conscious application can, after a time, become unconscious.

During the process of acquisition of a motor activity, a person often continually instigates more volitional nervous impulses and therefore stimulates contraction of more muscle fibres than is necessary to execute the
action effectively; and when this motor activity becomes 'second nature',
the unnecessary level of neuromuscular activity is maintained. The un-
necessarily tight grip and powerful pressure becomes as integral to the
motor activity of cleaning the teeth as the action of gently opening the
bathroom cabinet. But why should a human being engage more effort than
necessary in executing a muscular action?

During the process of acquisition, an unfamiliar motor activity is controlled not only by the motor nerves whose task it is to instigate and maintain the precise settings of tension in the various muscle fibres, whether in
order to maintain a pose or to execute a precise action, but also by other
nerves which have a sensory function. The sensory nerves repond to both
physical and emotional phenomena; they are equally receptive to a touch
upon the skin or a change in temperature as to a swiping insult or shocking
news. At the level of sensory-nerve impulses there is no division between
psyche and soma, between mind and matter.

The sensory-nerve messages travel in the opposite direction to those of
the motor nerves, and are sent towards the brain, which as a result is able
to produce an appropriate motor response, such as withdrawing the face
from the descending fist.

The nerves respond not only to our conscious instructions, or to those of
the parent whom we seek to please, but also to our emotional state. Influences which cause us to experience fear, anxiety or sorrow are processed
by the sensory nervous system, which in turn stimulates motor activity.
Fear makes the zebra run away from the lion. Sorrow makes the shoulders

droop at the funeral. Anxiety makes muscle fibres throughout the body increase in tension. Therefore, if the acquisition of a motor activity, such as learning to walk, is continually accompanied by an undesirable emotional state, such as anxiety, then the increased nervous stimulation instigates a higher degree of tension in a higher quantity of muscle fibres than is either necessary or comfortable. If, for example, you continually raise your hand threatening to strike a child every time she eats, those muscle fibres and tensions which the child requires to execute the motor activity of shying away will become engaged in anticipatory tension, ready to move her head clear of your fist should it fall. When the motor activity of dexterously combining use of knife and fork becomes ingrained and second nature, this muscle tension acquired in the face of the danger which accompanied eating will continue, even after the threatening parent is long since dead and buried.

Of course, few children are unfortunate enough to be raised in circumstances subjecting them to such calculated sadism; but none the less we are all prey to impinging emotional conditions at the period of our lives during which we are acquiring new muscular patterns, and these take their toll in the form of muscle-fibre tension in excess of that required for efficient, healthy and comfortable action.

One of the most difficult and demanding of these acquired motor activities is learning to speak, which requires a complexity of neurological signalling more sophisticated than almost any other acquired human activity. Moreover, the acquisition of speech is a learning experience more consistently couched in an emotional environment of punishment and reward, success and failure than any other. Children are rewarded or punished, encouraged or thwarted as much for what they say as for what they do. The act of phonation and speaking, as much as any other acquired habit, is therefore prone to incorporate unnecessary degrees of tension within an excess of muscle fibres. Furthermore, because the use of the voice is couched in so many fears and anxieties and is so ultimately connected with our sense of well-being, our sense of worth and our communicative efficiency, it is probably more prone to the accumulation of muscular ramifications of stress than any other expressive faculty; and these muscular patterns can continue to operate unconsciously long after the specific events which instigated the stress have disappeared. To quote Melba Hurd Duncan:

> Like facial expression, vocal cues are not entirely personal. Constitutional build is a determinant apart from 'the life within', as is convention, and conditioning by habits of speech in the environment. Furthermore, the various aspects of expression have different significance for different individuals. Another fact about voice should be noted, in which it resembles other habits of behaviour: if the vocal pattern seems dominated by undesirable social or emotional adjustment, it is not necessarily the present attitude which is

reflected in the voice. Because muscular habits become well entrenched over a period of years, it is entirely possible that the tension
pattern causing unsatisfactory speech may persist long after the atti-
tudinal cause (assuming such a factor was present) has disappeared.[25]

Fortunately, these patterns of overly increased fibre tension can be un-
learnt, but only by reintroducing to the body sensory and physical experiences which are as potently ingrained upon the nervous system as the
ones by which the habits were originally learnt. If you teach the brain that a
certain degree of fibre tension is necessary to instigate motor activity, this is
what the brain will insist upon when the motor skill becomes second
nature. The brain will not be satisfied that it is eating unless the muscle
fibres involved in moving the head to one side are engaged in a degree of
tension, so used has the brain become to the close association of eating and
the threat of a blow to the face.

Telling a grown woman that she has nothing more to fear from an impending blow and that she can enjoy her meals in peace is of very limited
value to her on account of the psychological effects which have become ingrained in muscular habits, a point that both Reich and Lowen made so
abundantly clear. To release the muscular patterning from such effects involves retraining the neuromuscular system, in particular re-educating the
brain to accept that the same motor activity can be more comfortably and
more efficiently achieved with less tension.

This means that the process of 'de-patterning' can only be accomplished
through the same process by which the patterns were originally instilled;
that is, through movement. Everything that we have learnt to do with our
muscles we have learnt through movement. We observe an activity in
someone else and our intention to imitate it stimulates a motor nerve message which in turn instigates muscular movement; and knowledge of the
execution of this movement is established in the brain by the return message of the sensory nerves. The aim of movement in any therapeutic context is to satisfy the brain with a different neurological message which reports a different motor action.

Those who could be especially helped by a 'de-patterning' therapy are
the blind and visually impaired. On the one hand, they rely to a great extent upon touch as a source of information and sensory stimulation, having
a need for tactile affirmation of their environment. But, on the other hand,
contact with an object spells for them the potential for injury and consequently instils an eventually unconscious muscular withdrawal. The sensory nerves are trained to generate impulses to the brain which transform
into motor messages to move away. The effect this has upon the general
neuromuscular state of the body causes permanent predisposition to extreme contraction of the muscle fibres concerned with retreat.

In the UK one of the most innovative research programmes in the field of 'de-patterning' therapy for the visually challenged is the Touchdown Dance Project, led by Anne Kilcoyne and Steve Paxton. Its work seeks to dismantle the defensive pattern of motor actions with which many blind and visually impaired people respond to touch.

In the mid-1960s Steve Paxton founded a dance form called 'contact improvisation', which explored the intuitive free-play of weight-sharing between two people. The training of these dancers involved exactly the opposite to that established by the neuromuscular conditioning of retreat in people without sight. Two dancers move together in constant physical contact, taking it in turns to lift, carry, release and support each other in a process of intuitive decision-making conducted without recourse to optical information. Since contact improvisation often demands that the students keep their eyes closed, so it was realised that the technique could be applied to the retraining of people with little or no sight.[26]

Paxton's innovative dance form has been integrated into the physcial vocabulary of many contemporary dance companies, but Touchdown Dance uses contact improvisation not for its aesthetic potential as the material for entertainment, but as the process by which the physical and psychological tension associated with touch may be depleted in the blind or visually impaired.[27] I myself was highly privileged to be Steve Paxton's pupil during the early 1980s, and his work on human movement has had a profound influence on my understanding of the role of bodily movement in singing.

The use of movement in voice movement therapy is to reverse unnecessary muscular habits relating to vocalisation by giving the body a new sensory experience. By retraining the muscles involved directly and indirectly in vocalisation, it is possible to re-educate the brain to accept that the task has been achieved by the activation of fewer motor units and consequently the contraction of fewer muscle fibres. The purpose is to enable the client to experience that it is possible to communicate effective vocal signals without the habitual accompaniment of a high degree of muscle-fibre tension throughout the whole body, particularly the neck and upper back.

The importance of retraining muscular patterns associated with vocal function was researched in depth by Frederick Matthias Alexander who, while working as an actor, found that on many occasions he would begin to lose his voice half-way through a recital; it would become weak and strained and on one occasion he lost it completely. Despite consultations with numerous doctors, Alexander could not find the cause of his intermittent voice loss and so, like Alfred Wolfsohn, he began to search for his own answers.

He began by setting up mirrors in which he watched himself recite, noticing the physical movements which accompanied the use of his voice, and he observed particularly that he pulled his head backwards and downwards whenever he spoke. Eventually Alexander realised that this pulling of the head had a direct influence and effect on all the other muscles, which became cramped as a result. He therefore developed a technique of resisting these and other habitual movements and of relearning a more natural use of the musculature.

It is often forgotten that it was a vocal problem that initiated the techniques founded by Alexander, and his work serves as a constant reminder of how important the postural state of the body is to voice production.

As with all voice movement therapy techniques, the use of imagery plays an important role in retraining muscular activity. Manipulation and instruction in the mechanics of motion emanate from a translation of healthy physiological functioning into potent and accessible images and is a process to which the client or recipient must remain committed outside therapy sessions.

# *Massage*

The contraction or tension of muscle fibres requires nutrients and oxygen, both of which are supplied by the blood, which absorbs these essential ingredients from the lungs and digestive system respectively, transporting them around the body. As a result of the muscle fibres' consumption of oxygen and nutrients, there is a continual accumulation of carbon dioxide and other toxic waste matter, some of which is absorbed by the lymph vessels. The lymph vessels clean and break down toxic waste before reintroducing it to the blood stream for eventual expulsion in expired air, sweat and urine.

Muscular activity thus involves a continual exchange of great volumes of fluid. But, contrary to the picture acquired by most people as a result of faulty teaching, these fluids do not pass straight to and from the muscle fibres. They pass through what is called connective tissue; and an appreciation of the role which connective tissue plays in bodily processes is very important to an understanding of the therapeutic benefits of massage.

Connective tissue is the packing which keeps the body's internal parts supported. It surrounds every nerve, every bone and every organ. It cushions the heart, the liver and the kidneys; it protects the cartilages and the bones.

For blood to get to muscle fibre it must pass through connective tissue. For waste to get back to the blood it must pass through connective tissue. For waste to get into the lymph vessels it must pass through connective tissue. Connective tissue is thus being constantly impregnated, drenched, infused with liquids and gases which are on their way out or on their way in.

This connective tissue may be compared to gelatin. If you take a piece of gelatin and leave it in the fridge to go cold, it will become set and hardened. However, if you place it in a bowl and beat it, whip it up, or else warm it gently on a stove, it will soon soften and become more liquid. Connective tissue too is capable of hardening and softening, depending on its temperature and the degree to which it is kept moving.

Physical activity which generates muscle movement and in turn creates heat causes the connective tissue to become more molten and fluid. Stasis and lack of exercise meanwhile allows the gelatin-like connective tissue to become solidified.

Chemical and gaseous substances move more easily and more rapidly through a substance the more fluid it is. Therefore the more pliable and supple the connective tissue, the more easily and efficiently substances pass through it and so the more the muscles can be assisted in their work. If the connective tissue becomes too set, then many of the toxic waste products do not pass through but are retained by the connective tissue where they become woven into its constituting fabric, like the pieces of dust that get clogged in the filter of a vacuum cleaner.

How does this relate to massage? Massage has the same effect on the connective tissue as whipping or heating has upon gelatin; it softens and warms, reviving its suppleness and thereby assisting the free-flow of substances through it. This is why some people who receive massage feel nauseous afterwards, or come up in spots or get a headache. Toxic waste, hitherto kept bound by the connective tissue, is suddenly released into the blood stream via the lymphatic system. However, the result of the treatment, if followed through, is genuinely cleansing; and one of the most significant areas of research into the transformative and liberating effects of connective tissue massage is that conducted by Ida Rolf, whose work initiated a therapeutic strategy known as 'Rolfing'.[28]

The role of massage in voice movement therapy is therefore to instigate a process of detoxification and to help maintain the fluidity of the connective tissue. It seeks to nurture in the body of the client an ease of movement and a pliability of tissue, so that the kinetic potential of the body may be as great as the acoustic potential of the voice in order that both may express the multiplicity of imaginative and psychological processes.

The techniques of ideokinesis, breathing enhancement, voice placement, movement and massage are not applied in succession according to a formula, but are rather the artificial subdivisions of an integrated process which seeks to facilitate a client's ability to overcome the shadows and resistances, the fears and inhibitions, the constrictions and the restraints which prevent liberated vocal function.

CHAPTER SIX

# The Liberated Voice

## Therapy or Personal Growth?

The processes which I have described in the previous chapter are designed to mobilise an effortless tonal and timbral vitality in the voice by dismantling those physical and psychological constructs which impair liberated vocal function.

For some people this may take a considerable amount of time, demanding of the therapist a committed and unwavering attention to the developmental changes which occur in the client's voice, body and sense of self during the process. For others the restrictive psycho-physical patterning may be less entrenched and liberation of the voice may therefore be achieved relatively quickly; and there are a few whose vocal flexibility emerges almost immediately. Regardless of how long it takes, arriving at the point of a liberated voice does not mark the end of the process. Having retrained muscular and respiratory habits, facilitated the ideokinetic use of placement, taught the control of free air, established a postural ease and kinetic fluidity, and provided for accompanying cathartic abreaction, it is possible to approach the second stage of voice movement therapy.

Whereas the first stage may be referred to as primarily therapeutic, in that it helps to put right those faulty muscle patterns which impair the innate health of the voice, the second stage is more appropriately described as educative because the emphasis is on developing expressive potential.

The relationship between a curative programme of therapy and an educative programme of self-development is an ambiguous one, and the way in which individual clients view themselves often contributes more to the definition of a process than the nature of the programme itself. This is particularly noticeable within the widespread culture of the 'workshop', which may be traced to the so-called 'human potential movement' which grew up in the USA in the 1960s and shows no signs of receding. It began as the distinctly Californian concept of the 'group encounter', in which those seeking to overcome inhibiting psychological factors would explore and interpret aspects of their personality within an ensemble of other participants, under the influence of a leader, director or *agent provocateur*. The therapeutic strategies of the 'group encounter' are as various as the names associated with them: Jacob Moreno and the 'psychodrama', Fritz Perls and the 'Gestalt', Eric Berne and transactional analysis are just some of those who helped to mint the common currency of group therapy, the styles of which ranged from the use of dramatic scenes to replicate recent events, to a cacophonous and *ad hoc* confusion of cathartic dance and breathing which was believed to expend the affects associated with a tortured childhood.

The shift in emphasis from the intense one-to-one verbal encounter founded by Freud to the participatory groups which began to take hold in the mid-1960s had the effect of socialising the therapeutic procedure to such an extent that the notion of therapy became as much associated with leisure as with medicine. The participants went not so much to remove something negative, but to increase that which was positive, hoping to acquire what Joel Kovel describes as 'the means through which the focus of therapy widens beyond neurosis itself to include all the unfilled promises, the loneliness, the loss of meaning, the whole well of unhappiness'[1] which humans are born to experience. The ramifications of this group promise of freedom from common unhappiness are various and, says Kovel, 'it would be hard to think of an approach to human life that has not found its way into the group setting and has been called "therapeutic", from multiple psychoanalysis to women's consciousness-raising, satanism rituals, mass bioenergetic sessions, primals, nude marathons and heaven knows what else'.[2] There are also a number of self-help books based on the synthesis of therapy and personal development, offering an easily digestible therapeutic strategy which promises, either explicitly or implicitly, that joy, happiness, freedom from depression, misery and strife are not only possible, but are achievable via a course of workshops and an accompanying text.

What began as an all-American concept of 'group therapy' has grown to become a Western concept of 'the workshop', and the synthesis of leisure and medicine has found its ultimate expression in the holiday-resort centre, which offers an integrated programme of meditative, analytic, artistic, physical, social and psychological pursuits only minutes from the beach. The books, the centres, the consultations, the workshops, the tapes, the T-shirts all combine to form one of the few commercial enterprises not only to withstand national and global recession but to increase its clientele as a result of it.

Most of those who participate regularly in workshops do not consider themselves ill or even as requiring therapy, but rather seek to extend their sense of potential, or their sense of calm, their sense of energy or of creativity, their perception or self-knowledge.

Although workshops in various 'self-orientated' processes have made 'therapy' economically and socially accessible to a wider range of people, they have also diluted the analytic content and confused respite with confrontation. The workshop acts as an 'out-road' from the burdensome routine of daily life, offering a momentary amnesty, as opposed to the in-road of consistent self-scrutiny which one-to-one psychotherapy provided and which was originally intended to be an integral part of the very life-circumstances from which the patient sought relief. This is not to imply that the one-off workshop does not contribute to the process of recovery, self-development, or even cure, but it is usually of another order because of the different intentions of the participants.

Integral to many of the group approaches to developing human potential was a shift away from an overtly verbal strategy and a move towards procedures which invited other forms of expression, dispensation and investigation. Non-Western forms of meditation and movement such as yoga and *t'ai chi* became employed for their seemingly therapeutic effect; and, in addition, the arts found a new function in the workshop. Drama, dance, painting, sculpture and music were all incorporated, not as entertainment or decorative icons, but as processes which yielded psychological results.

Because use of the human voice, especially in singing, is an artistic operation, the second stage of voice movement therapy may be considered in the context of this tradition of self-development through artistically orientated psycho-investigatory processes. However, the process of further developing the voice beyond the initial liberation described in the previous chapter is as much work as it is leisure; it is as analytical as it is spontaneously creative and it requires a commitment in excess of that associated with the short, sharp workshop shock. In order to understand the aim of this second stage, and to relate it to the overall development of therapeutic strategies since the genesis of the artistically orientated group workshops in the mid-1960s, it is necessary first to return to the conceptual framework of Jung's analytical psychology and survey the way this has been developed by some of the so-called post-Jungians; and, secondly, to describe the principles underlying the therapeutic use of the arts.

# How Many People are You?

As we have seen, Jung's fundamental vision was that there is a level of the psyche which houses a gallery of moods, ideas, fancies, instincts, characters, geometric patterns, animals and stories which manifest themselves in various forms. They appear visually in dreams and in paintings; they appear linguistically in stories and poems; they appear as motifs and acoustic structures in music and in opera; they appear as characters in drama; they appeared in the religious rituals and mythical narratives of ancient peoples; and they appear through the behavioural tendencies manifested in our everyday actions.

Jung observed two sources of these psychological phenomena. First, they arise from the residue of our own personal memories, the fairy-tales we were read as children, the films we have seen, the events of bygone days and from a host of other environmental stimuli which we have knowingly or unwittingly absorbed. Secondly, they arise from psychological blueprints established in the deepest and most distant past, way beyond our individual life; they are the archetypes.

Jung thus perceived the psyche as essentially multiple, a matrix of individual images, part personal, part archetypal, which do not form a self-orientated unity, but are 'a contradictory multiplicity of complexes'.[3] He observed the most overt example of this disorientated mass of images in the behavioural manifestations of the so-called psychotic, in whom the extreme degree of autonomy inherent in the various image matrices led to the appearance of a number of separate personalities, 'autonomous complexes', 'splinter psyches' or 'little people'.[4] Jung's later work brought him to realise that these different 'personalities', far from being constituted of idiosyncratic components arising solely from the patient's experience, in fact demonstrated elemental similarities. The multiple personalities of psychotic patients world-wide tended to include similar individual 'characters', perhaps the most familiar of which is the Christ figure or Saviour, who still populates the bodies and minds of many acutely affected psychiatric patients.

These mental eruptions and disintegrations were, for Jung, a result of too wide an abyss between the unconscious treasure-house of images and the conscious process of assimilating and understanding the impulses which motivate our behaviour. The more the mental chasm widens, the more likely that the images from the depths will burst forth upon us, arresting all reasonable faculties. This is why Jung was intent upon encouraging any process which helped to bring the unconscious store of images into consciousness, such as painting, writing, fantasising, talking to oneself or, ultimately, psychotherapy. Such processes enabled the sequestered images of the deeps to be unearthed, observed, wrought, formulated and incorporated into conscious life, rendering neutral their tendency to burst forth pathologically.

It would be a misunderstanding, however, to assume Jung believed that therapy should nurture the multiplicity and disorientation of psychological elements, producing people who could not maintain any consistent sense of identity but were this one minute and that the next. Far from this, Jung believed that, despite the innate tendency for personal and archetypal characteristics to cluster into complex structures which appear as distinct personalities, there is an equally strong, or perhaps stronger, tendency for the psyche as a whole to hold all these elements in orbit around a single centre, the unifying presence of which should override the identities of any of the smaller parts.

Jung called the sense of being a single entity, in the face of continual disruptions and interruptions from the unconscious, 'the self', and this term is widely used by psychologists, psychiatrists and psychotherapists from the most diverse fields to denote this 'sense of I' which remains constant, regardless of the transient quality of internal or external circumstances.

But Jung's notion of 'the self' was more than a 'sense of I'. First, he proposed that as the ego is for the conscious, so the self is for the unconscious. While the ego acts as the central point around which the feelings and actions of which we are conscious orbit, the self provides the focal point for all those influences of which we are unaware. He described the self as the 'most important and most central of archetypes'[5] with 'the significance of a ruler of the inner world, i.e., of the collective unconscious'.[6] While the ego maintains the integrity of our conscious world of abstract thought and sensible impressions, the self, we hope, will organise the inhabitants of our deepest mental canyons; it will stop us falling apart at the seams.

But, to complicate matters, Jung proposed that while the self acts as a centre, it also represents the psyche as a whole: it contains the conscious, and therefore along with it the ego; and as we cannot perceive anything except through the ego's faculties, it is in fact impossible to have a complete sense of self, because the parts cannot comprehend the whole.

However, this sense of whole which accommodates but does not yield to the dominance of the parts was for Jung something that we must none the less forever strive for in a process that is comparable to the Buddhist's search for nirvana or the Christian's search for God.

The search for the self was, for Jung, as much a spiritual journey as it was a therapeutic procedure; it represents our striving for wholeness and unity, the universal quest for the true sense of who we are and the promise of the reward of having found ourselves. The self embodies a longed-for perspective, a place from which we will be able to see with an inner eye and perceive the order of things. In Jung's words:

> I have called this centre the *self*. Intellectually the self is no more than a psychological concept, a construct that serves to express an unknowable essence which we cannot grasp as such, since by definition it transcends our powers of comprehension. It might equally well be called the 'God within us.' The beginnings of our whole psychic life seem to be inextricably rooted in this point, and all our highest and ultimate purposes seem to be striving towards it.[7]

Jung's notion of the self can perhaps be understood as the inevitable complementary antidote to a body of psychological research which points so continually, so relentlessly and so profoundly at the uncentred and multiple nature of the human psyche, as Jung's research surely does. The degree to which Jung believed either in its existence, its attainability or its comprehensibility can perhaps be ascertained only by those who knew him, for his published works leave the reader only with a sense of ambiguity, a not inappropriate sentiment when one considers how the psyche resists logical interpretation. In 1959, when Jung was nearing the end of his life, he said:

> So far, I have found no stable or definite centre in the unconscious and I don't believe such a centre exists. I believe that the thing which I call the Self is an ideal centre, equidistant between the Ego and the Unconscious, and it is probably equivalent to the maximum natural expression of individuality, in a state of fulfilment or totality. As nature aspires to express itself, so does man, and the Self is that dream of totality.[8]

In recent years this dream of totality, which remained central to Jung's psychotherapeutic practice, has been publicly questioned, challenged and

dismantled by a number of renowned therapists working within the framework of analytical psychology, namely Michael Fordham, Joseph Redfearn
and James Hillman. It would be wrong to imply that these therapists share
an identical vision or even a common terminology, but all of them are striving to achieve a fundamental reappraisal of the notion of mental health, in
which the concept of totality is substituted by that of multiplicity. In other
words, the tendency for the constituting material of the psyche to fragment
into partially autonomous units appearing as discrete personalities which
impregnate the 'sense of I' is not viewed as pathological, but as the natural
and intended state of mental functioning. In this view, the psyche is composed of many 'I's' or many selves, which Fordham calls 'de-integrates',
Redfearn refers to as 'sub-personalities' and which Hillman refrains from
naming in any consistent fashion. Common to all is the steering of the therapeutic process towards tolerance of multiplicity, which Fordham
describes thus:

> Any concept of mental health must include the consideration of
> variables and emergent possibilities in a periodically unstable system.
> What is healthy, and what is not, will depend upon the dynamic
> deintegration of the self into the component structures of the ego and
> archetypes and the integration of them into the whole organism. The
> two processes lead to the development of an ego whose growth must
> involve periodic experiences of disorder felt as dangerous or even
> chaotic. These states, however, need to be negotiated and can be ren-
> dered creative if they function healthily. Only the periods of in-
> tegration can be relatively stable and, it might be added, adapted, in
> the sense that the organism fits into the environment and influences it
> effectively. The states arising from deintegration are often unadapted
> in the first place, since they arise when a new development is required
> under the stress of internal or external dynamisms. Therefore mental
> health must be considered in relation to externally unadapted as well
> as states adapted to social requirements and in relation to the inner
> growth processes known as individuation.[9]

Joseph Redfearn, who was Fordham's analysand, has also investigated a
polycentric model of the psyche in which it is accepted as a factor of mental
health that 'the basic feeling of unity and continuity and of being a person
is subject to marked fluctuations and disruptions'[10] by which a person experiences himself or herself not as one person, but as a different person at
different times.

Further to this, James Hillman's work not only redirects the psychotherapeutic procedure to tolerate multiplicity, but he transforms such a
goal into the code for a way of life, implying the futility of a search for any
kind of exclusive centre. For Hillman no individual can 'provide a norm
even for himself'[11] because the psyche is deliberately structured by the grace
of the gods 'to save the diversity and autonomy of the psyche from domina-

tion by any single power'.[12] Hillman, like Fordham and Redfearn, stresses that the manifestation of multiplicity is not a sign of pathology: 'Because we have come to realize that each of us is normally a flux of figures, we no longer need to be menaced by the notion of multiple personality. I may see visions and hear voices; I may talk with them and they with each other without at all being insane.'[13]

# I Don't Know What Came Over Me – Honest, Officer

Beyond the field of psychotherapy, in the wards of psychiatric hospitals, and in the consulting rooms of psychiatrists and clinical psychologists, the notion of being composed of many selves still retains its pathological colouring, so that any philosophy advocating such a model of health appears dangerous and morally irresponsible. Recently, R. Aldridge-Morris has published a study of people who have had a tendency to behave as different personalities to such a marked degree that one 'personality' does not remember what the other has done; and many of these cases have involved criminal activity. In the USA multiple-personality syndrome has been the source of extensive investigation by lawyers and psychologists, and Aldridge-Morris suggests that, because of the lenience with which the United States legal profession treats those diagnosed as mentally ill, intelligent criminals are potentially able to use the guise of multiplicity to shield themselves from execution or imprisonment.[14]

Hillman refrains from approaching the subject of criminology, or extreme manifestations of multiplicity which cause pain and suffering to the person afflicted. Redfearn, on the other hand, has recognised that 'many destructive actions' seem to be performed as though 'the person is possessed by a violent sub-personality . . . or in a state of which he says afterwards "I don't know what came over me"'.[15]

However, while Fordham and Redfearn have included clinical material from their own studies to support the case of tolerance towards multiplicity, the various branches of post-Jungian psychology are disunited over the issue and its implications in the field of psychiatry and the treatment of psychoses.

It should be pointed out, though, that those patients who select or who are referred for psychotherapy as their main treatment tend not to be those whose 'little people' manifest themselves in behavioural tendencies with criminal or heavily anti-social consequences, or who do not remember what one of their selves has done. In fact, one of the most common conditions which emerges in the course of psychotherapy is precisely the reverse: it is what we might call a 'monophrenia', a state in which a person becomes stifled by the dominating influence of a single aspect of him or her self. In Redfearn's words:

If all one's sub-personalities were spread out like a map or landscape, or a vast world of happenings and relationships, there would be places or scenes which were often visited by the conscious 'I', and others which would never have been visited, or have even been avoided. The feeling of 'I', as I have so often pointed out, may inhabit one role for a moment, then another. Other roles might be avoided especially in certain circumstances. Some people are stuck in one role much of the time, especially if that role has paid dividends in the past.[16]

One of the primary aims of a polycentric analytical psychology, such as that propounded by Fordham, Redfearn and Hillman, has therefore been to entice the patient's 'sense of I' to embark upon a journey during which it may temporarily identify with the various free-floating images of the unconscious. This brings the patient in close relation to the actor by playing different roles, all of which manifest different aspects of the person he or she is; aspects, however, which are so diverse that many of them appear to be incompatible or even mutually exclusive.

While a polycentric psychology may differ from Jung's original vision by way of its shift of emphasis from wholeness to decentralisation, it remains faithful to Jung's notion of encouraging the unconscious images to be admitted into consciousness.

The negative aspect of a large part of the post-Jungian polycentric psychology lies not in its dislocation from the field of psychiatric research into multiple personality, but in its strict adherence to the classical relationship between analyst and patient, the primary medium of communication between whom remains verbal discourse. It is innovative in its willingness to admit to a dramatic model of psychological functioning, one in which the individual is seen as being the player of many parts. But it does not go far enough, as shown by its unwillingness to realise that a dramatic model of functioning necessitates a dramatic model of expression.

However, to each discipline its own mode of execution, and while the mainstay of so-called 'respectable' Jungian psychology in Britain and the USA remains committed to this essentially 'talking cure', there has been a complementary development of more practical applications of polycentricity in other therapeutic practices, of which dramatherapy, dance movement therapy, art therapy and music therapy remain the most significant.

## The Arts Therapies

While for Jung the pursuit of fine art provided a welcome adjunct and complementary contribution to the process of verbal therapy, the therapeutic and analytic use of painting has since become a strategy in itself; and over half of the registered art therapists in Britain work in the National Health Service.[17] Music therapy is also now a formally recognised procedure by which to facilitate the personal well-being and psycho-social development of people with widely differing needs.

Both art and music therapy have a lengthy history of use in mental hospitals throughout Britain and Europe, but the transition from providing background music, nostalgic sing-songs or a box of paints to distract confined patients from boredom, to the analytically creative use of musical and artistic processes is one which has been widely disseminated only in the last forty years.[18]

Dramatherapy, now a recognised therapeutic strategy, cannot claim such a long-established presence in the field of mental health as can painting and music, though we know plays to have been performed by the inmates of certain French asylums during the eighteenth century. It owes its origin, in conception at least, to the work of Jacob Moreno, who developed what he called 'psychodrama' in the 1920s and 1930s. Psychodrama was a process by which a person acted out various roles in improvised situations taken from his or her life and which provided an opportunity to complete an action or ventilate the accompanying emotion that had been inhibited during its actual occurrence. Its philosophy was primarily a cathartic one – the talking cure became the acting cure.[19] It also offered an opportunity for patients to become the actor not only in notion but in action, by which they assumed the role of other people in their own life who were not present, or other patients in the psychodrama group. This encouraged the patients' 'sense of I' not only to recognise the different roles it played in the face of certain situations, but also to empathise with the feelings of others, to see things from the other person's view. It was through this process of entering the character of another person that the patients of Moreno's therapeutic theatre were encouraged to recognise their problems as arising from an essentially social cause.

For Moreno psychological degeneration originates in our inability to comprehend and appropriately respond to the complex social dynamics in which human behaviour is contextualised, and in order for progress to be made in this direction, the dynamics contained in family and other relationships have to be recreated. Although your mother, with whom you have a problem, cannot be present in the psychodrama workshop, a fellow actor can play her part and enable you to 'work through' and interpret the role that you tend to play in her presence. Furthermore, you too can play the part of your mother and experience how you think she feels. It was from this game of role-playing that the Gestalt therapy of Fritz Perls grew.[20]

Perls encouraged patients not only to use other actors as makeshift mothers, but to use objects – chairs, pillows and curtains. A patient could whip the chair with a stick to express the repressed revenge he felt at his mother for dying when he was a child, or crawl across the floor to demonstrate the way he felt hindered in his ambitions, staggering towards his future without reward. Perls's therapeutic procedure was predominantly dramatic, employing props, scenes and role-playing. By setting up dialogues between the significant characters of the participant's life or between different parts of the self, represented by inanimate objects, Perls was furthering the dramatic brand of therapy initiated by Moreno, in which the now widely established practice of dramatherapy has its roots.[21]

But while Moreno focused on the social causes of psychological disorders, Perls was concerned with causes arising from within the individual. Perls was keen to prove that there were certain 'roles' adopted by all people, such as those of the 'top dog' and the 'under dog'. The top dog is the role we play when we are in charge, dominant and leading the way. The underdog is our frightened, subservient response to danger or authority. In addition, Perls encouraged patients to view parts of their body as personalities; they could speak to the chair as if it was their penis, for example, or their legs or their acne.

In fact, this process of relating to body parts as psychic facets of the self was not an invention of Perls, but had occupied the attention of a number of therapists, including a number of Post-Freudian analysts, among whom the most renowned is Melanie Klein.[22]

## Psychoanalysis as Playtime

Klein's particular contribution to psychoanalysis was that she pioneered a method of analysing children. Because she could not hold in-depth conversations with her patients, she introduced another form of communication: play. Klein invited children to play with toys, to paint or to draw and to talk to her simultaneously, so she might understand what the child believed he or she was displaying with pen and paper or with a particular arrangement of dolls. Klein observed how inanimate objects came to represent parts of the child's own body as well as other people and the child's relationship to them; and it was the interpretation of the nature, structure and intentions inherent in play that yielded the analysis.

This introduction of a new element to the therapeutic procedure also generated two new channels of communication. Now there was not only the verbal disclosure between patient and therapist, but also the patient's manner of relating to the play-object, and the therapist's interpretive analysis of that relationship.

Klein's pioneering work with children's play is highly relevant to the operational dynamics of art therapy, where there are also three lines of communication: 'between therapist and client, client and painting, therapist and painting'.[23] In art therapy the canvas acts as the blank screen upon which the contents of psychological functioning may be given visual representation, and the therapist's analytical conclusions regarding the patient's predicament come as much from an interpretation of the visual image as they do from the decoding of the patient's text about the painting.

The demands upon the art therapist's faculties of interpretation therefore differ from those which are placed upon the psychotherapist. The former must be conversant with the non-discursive characteristics of visual imagery, while the latter must be familiar with the discursive nature of linguistic dialogue.

One of the first art therapists to be influenced by psychoanalytic principles, Margaret Naumberg, said that the 'process of art therapy is based on the recognition that man's most fundamental thoughts and feelings, derived from the unconscious, reach expression in images rather than words',[24] and the skill of the analytically orientated art therapist rests in the ability to interpret the psychological significance of these images without projecting on to the canvas aspects of his or her own pathology – that is, without a negative counter-transference.

## Transference and Artistic Interpretation

There are three elements to the traditional psychotherapeutic consultation: the patient, the analyst and the text which is engendered between them. The text may rightfully be seen as a third entity, first, because it cannot exist without the presence of both participants and, secondly, because it can be viewed after the event by another person independent of the presence of either party. It can be set down, recorded, retained and made definitive as the words of a novel or a poem upon the page.

These words form the mainstay of the infamous case study, in which the patient's script is quoted verbatim in the journals of the various schools of thought and interpreted by the author according to the conceptual foundations of that school.

The discourse between patient and therapist during the consultation is not one of equality, but is founded upon a mutual agreement to allow the therapist interpretive rights. The therapist is empowered by the patient's belief in him that he can 'read' the words uttered, see between the lines, understand the undertones and implications which are obscured from the patient's view. If the therapist is continually over-eager to dissect, decipher, analyse and unfold what he believes to be the underlying preoccupations, the patient's words become predominantly influenced by a sense of awe towards the therapist's scalpel-like tongue, and as a result the flow of verbal thought processes emblematic of the patient's predicament is impeded; art therapists Caroline Case and Tessa Dalley describe the 'over-interpretive analyst' as a 'tyrannical mother' whose 'language is integral to her power'.[25]

However, the ideal therapist does not construct a scaffolding of interpretations around each segment of the patient's unfolding text, but helps the patient to analyse the discourse him or herself and to understand the underlying patterns of psychological dynamics. Psychotherapy could not work, however, without some degree of interpretive explanation on the part of the therapist, and this will be inevitably influenced by the perceptive framework within which the therapist's own school of thought operates. Where a Freudian sees unresolved Oedipal conflicts, a Jungian may see attachment to the *puer* – that is, the influence of the child archetype which resides in us all – a Gestaltist inappropriate responses to social demands and a priest a dearth of spiritual faith.

But more fundamental to the analysis than these tools of perception which the therapist acquires is the nature of his own personal view of the world, his fancies and tendencies, his loves, hates, beliefs and convictions. In order that patients be enabled to discover their own world-view, the therapist must refrain from seducing them into sharing his idiosyncratic attitudes and preferences. In psychotherapy this is the aim of the therapist's own therapy. The therapist must become the patient and discover those incentives and persuasions which he holds most dear in order that he may refrain from interpreting his patient's text according to his want. In the therapeutic setting he must retain his feelings as opposed to discharging them as the patient does.[26]

Freud proposed that patients in psychoanalysis use the analyst and their relationship to him as the means to re-captivate and play out strong feelings and patterns of response which originate in childhood experiences of early relationships. By observing the emotive patterns by which the patient responded to the analyst, Freud believed he could see mirrored the patterns which the patient had learnt to use in order to cope with earlier relationships, particularly those with the parents. Freud called this off-loading of feelings and responses on to the relationship with the analyst the 'transference'.

> What are transferences? They are new editions or facsimiles of the tendencies and phantasies which are aroused and made conscious during the progress of the analysis, but they have this peculiarity which is characteristic for their species, that they replace some earlier person by the person of the physician. To put it another way: a whole series of psychological experiences are revived, not as belonging to the past, but applying to the physician at the present moment.[27]

Just as the patient revives past experiences in the form of behavioural responses to the analyst, so too the analyst, by nature of being human, is predisposed to transfer his feelings and habitual patterns of retort on to the relationship with the patient through the 'counter-transference'. Hence it is important that the therapist is trained to be aware of this and to be sufficiently in touch with his own feelings that he may refrain from projecting them on to the patient and seeing them where they do not really exist, other than as a reflection of himself.

Recognition of the phenomenon of counter-transference applies equally to the art therapist's analysis of the visual image, as well as to the drama-therapist's scrutiny of the psychological dynamics expressed through dramatic action.

Dramatherapy took shape in Britain during the 1960s and 1970s, pioneered by Sue Jennings, among others. It began as an attempt to consolidate the principles which had for some time informed the practice of remedial drama – theatre games, trust exercises, improvisation classes and a host of activities derived from the various methodological elements of an actor's training and rehearsal. Dramatherapy sought to apply such practices to the educational and social development of those with divergent physical and emotional needs.

There are now enough dramatherapists to be able to discern a spectrum of approaches almost as extensive as those which constitute the psychotherapies, not least because those practising dramatherapy have been influenced by widely differing analytic frameworks.[28] None the less, at the heart of its practice is the fundamental belief that aspects of the unconscious can be admitted to consciousness through the act of performing. The same may be said about dance movement therapy.

While dramatherapy explores through theatre the psycho-social dynamics of human interaction, dance movement therapy uses physical movement to promote psychological release and also embodies a number of analytic frameworks.[29] Among those using a Jungian approach are Mary Stark Whitehouse,[30] Joan Chodorow[31] and Amelie Noack,[32] all of whom seek to give physical form to images of the unconscious through rhythm, gesture, pose and kinetic geometric configurations.

Some practitioners of both dramatherapy and dance movement therapy have been keen to encourage and respond to the role of the voice in dramatic and physical expression. Dramatherapist Steve Mitchell, influenced primarily by his work with members of Grotowski's theatre laboratory, includes vocal exercises in his group sessions;[33] and a number of dance movement therapists have introduced collective singing alongside dance.[34] But the use of the voice has remained peripheral to both therapeutic procedures.

The fact that vocal work has remained a minimal aspect of the arts therapies is, however, a credit to the specialisation of these psycho-artistic activities. For the use of the voice is not something which can be tacked on to drama or to dance or even to music; it is a complex artistic and expressive function which necessitates its own equally specialised field of therapy.

The four major artistic therapies – drama, dance movement, music and art therapy – all have one fundamental principle and practical procedure in common: they seek to invite and admit unconscious contents into consciousness through an artistic medium. The contents may consist of dream images, personal memories, generalised compounds of feeling and mood, characters, caricatures, animals and symbols of different kinds. Regardless of their shape and form, these contents which gain expression through the dramatic scene, through kinetic gesture, through melody and pitch or through colour and shape are all emblems, icons, representative expressions of different aspects of the psyche. Even when the expression taken is not of human form, the images produced by the client may still be considered as a sub-personality or 'de-integrate'.

Redfearn, Fordham and Hillman have shown that a sub-personality or de-integrate need not necessarily appear as a person; it can be any image which encapsulates one particular aspect of the self. For example, a man may paint or dream of a lion, which may express that part of himself that prowls, dominates and devours or lords it over his family, ready to pounce on them should they make any wrong move. Or a patient may dream of or paint a delicate cut-glass bowl balancing on the edge of the table, ready to tumble to the ground and shatter into a thousand pieces. Just as the lion is partly a reflection of one of the client's sub-personalities, so too is the cut-glass bowl. It represents that little person within who feels fragile, timid, delicate and insecure, percariously balanced and highly vulnerable in life, sensing that the slightest trouble or threat from the outside world would leave him shattered.

In Gestalt therapy Fritz Perls would have asked the client to 'enact' the glass bowl, encouraging him to crouch defensively on the edge of a table or chair in order that he might experience the essence of such an image. The therapeutic procedure would then progress to throw light on other complementary sub-personalities, such as the wind which threatens the bowl with destruction. The patient would be enabled to change roles, to become the all-powerful gale threatening to blow the glass from the table. Through this process a patient would be helped to recognise that he need not always play the glass bowl as though it were the only sub-personality he had, but that he could also play other roles and thereby extend the range of his responses to situations, thus avoiding unnecessary pain and suffering.

But whatever the artistic means of admitting deeply buried psychological contents into consciousness, the process is not a Post-Jungian phenomenon; in fact it was pioneered by Jung, and he called it 'active imagination'.

# Active Imagination and Amplification

Andrew Samuels succinctly describes active imagination as 'a channel for "messages" from the unconscious by any means; for example, by media such as painting, modelling or writing. These products are not viewed aesthetically but valued for the information they contain'[35] about the deeper strata of the psyche. This absence of aesthetic judgement in active imagination constitutes the fundamental difference between the arts and the arts therapies. The client's acting or dancing or painting or musical rendition is not passively witnessed or judged according to the degree to which it entertains, inspires or demonstrates a formal virtuosity, but is actively nurtured to convey honestly the deeper influences, fears, concerns and pre-occupations which usually remain hidden behind the stylised expressions of day-to-day communication. The emphasis, then, is not on the product – painting, dance, musical score or play – but on the process.

In Jung's practice, active imagination was intimately connected with an-other vitally important process, which he called 'amplification'. As we have seen, for Jung the images which emerge from the patient's psyche, in what-ever form, are determined partly by personal factors and partly by ones of a trans-personal, collective or archetypal nature. However, in the therapeutic session the images which emerged tended to be perceived by the patient as largely personal, the embodiment of his or her particular psychological problem. Therefore Jung needed a process by which to make the transition from the saturation of personal associations which an image held, to the point where the patient realised that the image, and problem or dynamic therein represented, was in fact a typical one. This process was what Jung called amplification.

For example, a patient may begin speaking about feeling insecure, fra-gile, lost and frightened, while the therapist asks for an image which cap-tures such a feeling. The patient describes a dream she had about being only eight years old and running through a dense dark wood in which the trees towered above her and appeared to speak to her with their rustling leaves. The therapist asks what she was frightened of, and the patient says that she felt as though she were being pursued by a threatening animal.

So now the patient describes herself in terms of the image of a young girl running scared in a forest while pursued by an animal. When the therapist asks why the girl cannot escape, the patient replies that the animal is too clever and that in the dream it felt as if the animal was everywhere, but that she couldn't identify it.

The therapist now amplifies this personal network of images by com-paring it to the widely known fairy-tale of Little Red Riding Hood, who is threatened by the wolf but does not recognise him because he is in disguise. The image of the wolf vibrates with significance in the patient and she elaborates on her feelings to the point of recognising that she relates to men as though they were wolves 'hot on her tail', disguising themselves in sheep's clothing and waiting to pounce. The therapist now begins to in-troduce motifs from other fairy-tales or myths in which a woman is pur-sued by an animal, until what began as a personal admission becomes a journey of discovery among the world-wide myths and stories which pro-vide examples of the way men pursue women.

But the point of amplification is not simply to make the patient feel better in the knowledge that he or she is not the only one; rather it is to dis-cover a means of overcoming the fear of threat by learning from the images contained in stories of a universal significance.

In many stories and myths where someone is threatened by an awesome creature, the victim triumphs not by violence or retreat but by cunning, as in the case of Oedipus who defeats the Sphinx by answering her riddle, or Brer Rabbit who continually defeats the fox through wily plots. The story of a fearful victim overcoming threat through ingenuity, wit and skilful manipulation of the circumstances has been and still remains a universally popular archetypal idea in all cultures.

Now the patient recognises that the wolf in Little Red Riding Hood is also very cunning and therefore will take some beating, and she further refers to men as being cunning and difficult to ward off. But the therapist points out that the animal in her dream and the wolf in the fairy-tale are also parts of her, because everything we dream is not only a representation of our perception of something outside ourselves, but also a manifestation of a part of our inner life. So now the patient recognises that she too is the pursuing animal, the wolf, and is able to locate potentialities in herself that compare with the qualities of the victor as opposed to the victim.

In the course of this seminar the therapist introduces the Greek goddess Artemis, 'Lady of the Wild Things', who lived in the forest forever chaste and with the power to hunt and tame the most ferocious of beasts. But Artemis was also protectress of young nymphs and had a maternal sovereignty that required no paternal intervention. The patient now begins to relate herself to the qualities of Artemis and, over a period of time, she is able to visit parts of herself that have been hitherto ignored and incorporate them into her life and perception of herself.

The primary strategy by which Jung facilitated active imagination and amplification was verbal discourse, though he did incorporate other forms of expression and encouraged patients to employ artistic media to assist in the process. One of the aims of the arts therapies described above is to make participation in creative activity the cardinal means by which active imagination and amplification can be achieved.

# Active Imagination in Voice Movement Therapy

While vocal expression is peripheral to or absent from the four arts therapies, voice movement therapy seeks to employ the acoustic emissions of phonation as the primary channel through which to lure ostracised and expropriated images and de-integrates of the psyche into consciousness. It is active imagination and amplification through vocal sound and singing, and may perhaps best be described as 'psychophonic'.[36]

'Psychophonics' may be defined as the process of conveying psychological information in the form of non-verbal vocal sound. Such sounds may be called psychophonic when they reveal to the intuitive listener qualities which are the audible manifestations of affect and image. Such sounds do not translate logically into a discursive scheme, but yield to metaphorical amplification; that is, they may be described as creating effects which comprise mood, character, colour, essence and instinct.

Just as therapeutic dance and drama make use of the voice to some extent, so too any therapeutic voice work should incorporate elements of dance and drama that provide a natural accompaniment to vocalisation. But at the same time therapeutic voice work should remain committed to phonation as a primary medium of expression.

The role of the therapist in voice movement therapy is similar to that of the psychotherapist in the example of the little lost girl who discovers the wolf and the huntress within; except that in voice movement therapy the psychological contents emerge through the vocal sounds of the patient. The therapist enables the client to discover parts of herself which she has not visited for a long time, but the mode of transport is the voice. The little lost girl and the devouring wolf emerge from the larynx in sounds which are numinous and charismatic, tear-provoking, terrifying, affecting and arresting and always genuinely expressive of the de-integrates, sub-personalities, complexes, networks of images, moods, emotions that constitute the fabric of the singer's psyche. As with the other artistically orientated therapies, these sounds are not judged for their entertainment value, their musical eloquence or their formal virtuosity, but for their depth of genuineness and authenticity, the degree to which the client can be incontrovertibly heard to express something which rears up from the deep as opposed to mimicking something from the surface.

For example, the therapist asks the client to sing, without effort or tension and without putting on a performance. She sings as herself. The patient utters first this note, then that, ascending and descending a scale in which the therapist can hear distinct emotional qualities. The sound is genial and tender with a wispy emission of free air; the higher the pitch the more gentle, soft and unassertive it becomes. It has a girlish frivolity and fragile delicacy to it. The therapist can see that the client is swaying slightly from side to side and has an ingenuous expression on her face that seems to enhance the innocence of the sound. The therapist asks the patient to exaggerate the swaying as though she were on a swing and to increase the childlike quality of the voice, imagining herself to be only seven years old. The client begins to enter into the embodiment of this image while the therapist leads the pitch of her voice up the scale into a higher octave to assist her in recreating sonically the image of an ever younger child. As the notes begin to get higher and more difficult to sing, the client contorts her face and clenches her fists, which endows the sound with a degree of ruckus and commotion, as though the baby were having a tantrum. The therapist asks the client to sing as though the baby were incensed and protesting, and as a result the spectacle of indignation becomes more animated and multiphonic. The client opens and closes her fists, stamps on the ground, and the therapist now massages and manoeuvres the neck and back in order to ease out any unnecessary tension of the muscle fibres. The client continues to vocalise during this massage; her voice increases considerably in volume and pitch, whistling through the studio like a siren.

In order to recreate more fully the experience and personification of the instinctive, primal quality which is emerging, the client crouches on all fours, dancing the back and shoulders in an undulating motion to ensure freedom of movement. The therapist rhythmically strikes her back with the edge of the palms and asks the client to imagine that she howls from the lower back and that the sound resonates inside her belly, which is lined with white gold.

The sound now assumes a canine quality like that of a howling wolf. The therapist asks the client to imagine that her hackles are up and that she is howling out a protective shield of sound around her cubs, which lie curled beneath her belly. The pitch descends and the sound becomes guttural and marauding and echoes as though in a cave.

In the deeper pitches the sound is wolf-like; in the higher pitches it is feline; in the middle there is an ambiguous, animalistic quality, half wolf, half cat, like a creature from a beguiling bestiary concocted from an amalgam of animal instincts.

The therapist, having observed the client's tendency to open and close her fists during this voice-dance, now asks the client to develop this movement as though she were a creature extending and retracting her claws in preparation for a fight. At the same time she is asked to decrease the volume of the sound and to sing with an alluring, tantalising and ravenous timbre, part lion, part Siamese kitten, part wolf. As the client sings, the therapist continues to suggest tonal images: feline, lustful, devouring, seductive, spiteful, provocative, coquettish. The creature has offspring and is prowling around her young. She spits with venom, with threat and with intimidation. Her voice is made of acid; it is caustic, ungracious and scathing.

The therapist now introduces the piano and directs the melody of the sounds by playing different notes. As the voice-dance assumes a more formal structure, the sounds become more humanised yet without losing their arresting and compelling intensity. The client stands up and the therapist suggests the image of a gigantic and buxom Parisian chain-smoking animal-lover who has six children, who wears furs and who bellows and bawls. The client's voice becomes darkly enfolding, a quality which the therapist amplifies by suggesting a collage of images: mouth full of caviar, red lipstick, a voice like molasses or like tar. The voice is that of a prolific and world-famous Parisian lion-tamer. A new character emerges and the studio thunders with the voice of 'Madame Félineou'. The client now struts around the room singing improvised arias on the words 'I am Madame Félineou', like a prima donna. She mimes smoking with a cigarette-holder. Her facial expression has altered radically since the beginning of the session and any visible or vocal signs of innocence and vulnerability have long since receded. The voice and posture of the client is dominant, proud and unnerving.

The therapist watches the client's arm enact the backward and forward motion of putting cigarette to mouth and asks the client to magnify and inflate the movement. It now becomes the whip that urges the horses on as the client drives a chariot away from the circus into the forest. The voice drops into the abdominal placement and takes on a hot-blooded, retaliatory and barbarous tone. The therapist encourages this tranformation by suggesting tonal images: Boadicea; the wild woman of the forest; a vengeful war cry; leading the warriors into battle; rounding up a tribal mass of agitated protesters. The client's voice and body are now involved in an opera of blood-curdling melody as though the studio were filled with an army of female revolters.

The client is becoming tired, and the therapist slows down the pace with the piano. The dead lie scattered and the wild woman now feels sorrow for the victims. The voice returns to a higher pitch and whimpers. The therapist suggests tonal images: pangs of regret; mourning and melancholy; a prayer for the dying; and a contemplative chant on the futility of war. The client now stands swaying, as she was at the beginning of the session, and the therapist asks her to blend together the different aspects of the acoustic journey. The irritable child, the vulnerable kitten, the howling wolf, the wild woman of the forest, Madame Félineou and the unbridled warrior become less separate and distinct, uniting to form a single tone. The voice now sounds and feels to both therapist and client that it belongs to her, unified yet multifaceted, embracing a spectrum of images any one or combination of which could emerge as dominant at any time.

In the above example of a session the therapist facilitates the process of active imagination in the patient by the following five processes:

1 Verbally suggesting images which the client allows to infiltrate the tones of the voice.

2 Uttering sounds which the client emulates.

3 Massaging and manipulating the client's body.

4 Setting pitch and pace with the piano.

5 Conducting the client's voice and movements through gesture.

As a result of these processes, the client gives form to images which, with the therapist's help, assume an archetypal significance. But the relationship between voice movement therapist and client is more complex than that between Jungian psychotherapist and patient. For the client the experience of voice movement therapy has an added artistic dimension and is comparable to being in a performance under the direction of a conductor and yet not bound by a set score or text. However, the patient is not a passive receptacle for the conductor's whims, slavishly obeying his wishes. She is running ahead, fleshing out each sound with details of taste, colour, character and essence which defy discursive interpretation but demand intuitive engagement instead.

Thus communication between client and therapist in voice movement therapy has more in common with art therapy than with psychoanalysis or analytical psychology, in that it is conducted not through abstract words but through imagery. However, it is unique to itself in that the form which these images assume are non-optical, non-plastic but phonic, acoustic and vocal. Yet despite the non-optical nature of the expressions, the fundamental material of psychophonic activity in voice movement therapy is image.

# Image

Jung made no distinction between a psychic content and an image, neither did he differentiate between psychological processes and the faculty of imagination; because for Jung the psyche is image and the world of images constitutes the imagination.

Although the mental topography of humankind may be perceived as being composed of contents which are more or less personal, more or less archetypal, more or less instinctive, more or less cognitive, none of these contents can be apprehended *in toto* as formal structures. We can only catch glimpses of the free-floating fragments of these psychic contents in the form of images. In Jung's words: 'Every psychic process is an image and an "imagining," otherwise no consciousness could exist . . . imagination is itself a psychic process';[37] 'the psyche consists essentially of images . . . it is a picturing of vital activity'.[38]

The prime embodiment of these images is the dream, where they take the form of optical impressions seemingly etched upon the inner surface of our eyes and recaptured the following day through our verbal recollections. This process of dreaming is not only a psychological function, but a creative process of the imagination. Because images are the language of the psyche, any process of imaginative creativity is by nature also a process of psychological investigation. This is the nub of Jung's analytical psychology and it is what makes his ideas so accessible to the artistic application of psychological principles and the psychological interpretation of artistic activity:

> Not the artist alone, but every creative individual whatsoever owes all that is greatest in his life to fantasy. The dynamic principle of fantasy is *play*, a characteristic also of the child, and as such it appears inconsistent with the principle of serious work. But without this playing with fantasy no creative work has ever yet come to birth. It is therefore short-sighted to treat fantasy, on account of its risky or unacceptable nature, as a thing of little worth. It must not be forgotten that it is just in the imagination that a man's highest value may lie.[39]

The function of the strategic relationship between therapist and patient in Jung's view of psychotherapy is to stimulate this 'creative work' by which the imagination may be encouraged to fantasise, actively imagining and amplifying the contents of the psyche in words as an artist is wont to do with paint upon the canvas. There is an aspect of this relationship which is fundamentally akin to playing; as Donald Winnicott has said, 'psychotherapy has to do with two people playing together',[40] and the materials of this play are images. It is this aspect of the therapeutic relationship that has been deliberately intensified in art therapy, where the interaction between client and therapist is essentially playful and in which imagery is given optical and plastic representation.[41]

In the late 1970s James Hillman wrote a number of articles, equally relevant today as at their original appearance, which questioned the overall tendency to equate the notion of image with an optical construct:

> Why do we talk about images as if they were pictures? Is this mix-up just one of easy talk? Is it inherent, like the German word *Bild*, which means both an image and a picture, even a painting? . . . Or is the confusion of images with pictures a residue of sensationist psychology that understands images and even imagination to be left-overs of actual things seen?
>
> In therapy the muddling of image and picture gives trouble: patients think they have to see pictures in their minds in order to have an image. If I ask them for an image of what is going on in a problem (of family, of sexual relations, of anger), they try to *see* something, and when they don't find anything to see, they say they have no image, no fantasy. The confusion gives trouble to theory too. People accuse imagistic therapy of being mainly visual, hence optical, and intellectually distant, hence gutless . . . the complaint that imagistic therapy is gutless is the complaint of a consciousness that *pictures* its images and regards them optically. It is a consciousness that hasn't got into the image as body.[42]

Hillman answers his own plea for a trans-optical understanding of image by concentrating on the imagistic quality of words in the therapeutic consultation, and his strategy remains a verbal one. The originality in this attitude is, says Hillman, that he is concerned not with words as concepts but with words as images.[43] This approach pays no heed to the grammatical, syntactical or narrative context in which the patient couches the words, but instead expands them to take into consideration 'the full extension of any word, all its meanings and possibilities . . . any context in which the word occurs'.[44]

This means that the image of a girl being chased by a wolf may be seen as containing multiple notions. The morpheme 'wolf' appears also in the term 'wolfing it down', describing ravenous and frantic eating. The word 'chased' also occurs in association with the notion of ingestion – we talk of a 'chaser', an alcoholic spirit which we 'chase' down; and perhaps underlying the girl's fear of the wolf is the idea that it will ingest, devour and chase her down his own gullet. But the sound of the word 'chased' is also equivalent to that of 'chaste', signifying an abstinence from sex, and the image of running from the wolf may be expanded to incorporate the notion of virginity and innocence.

This process of reading the patient's words involves an imagistic perception which liberates the parts of speech 'from their narrational obligations which link them into time sequences for story-telling. The imagistic view of words frees them from having to submit to logical reason and operational definition.'[45] So the image of the wolf also contains the residual experiences of all those 'wolfy' people the patient has known, all those experiences of being chased and chaste which are not translatable into definitive concepts or memories but simply remain as images. It is a transformation of the discursive nature of words into a non-discursive mode of reading them.

The non-discursive, non-conceptual and imagistic approach to words has been further investigated by Paul Kugler, a practitioner concerned with linguistics who has published two papers which propose that the sounds of words carry meaning and stimulate images in the mind of the reader or hearer independent of their linguistic signification and semantic context.[46]

The purpose of Hillman's and Kugler's non-narrative and ontological perception is not to tie the image down to a single meaning, but to tolerate and entertain the 'unfathomable analogical richness of the image'.[47]

> A poetic understanding does not consider the dream as a report or message giving information about something other than, or prior to, the dream. Rather, the dream is like a poem or a painting which is not about anything, not even about the poet or the painter. The painted lemons on the plate must not refer to the lemons on a plate which the painter used as a model; the painted lemons can be experienced altogether without reference to those lemons, or any lemons, anywhere. (Nor do they refer to an invisible archetypal essence of lemons – lemonhood, lemonness; they refer neither to physical lemons nor to metaphysical ones.) They may analogize with and evoke all sorts of lemony experiences; but the image transcends such referent evocations – that is, we might buy the painting, not because it so well represents lemons on a plate, but because it speaks so well to and of our soul.
>
> So, too, with the lemon in the dream. The poetic view does not need to posit an objective psyche to which the lemon refers and from which it is a message. The psyche is there in the lemon, located nowhere else than in the actual presented image.[48]

Hillman's paradigm departs from Jung's not only by way of its polycentricity and insistence on non-conceptual and non-referential relationships between word and concept, but in its intention to 'make specific' as opposed to 'make typical'. In Jung's work the process of amplification sought, in a sense, to generalise the patient's images in order to arrive at the archetypal roots. The particular individual wolf became the archetype of the wolf, 'wolfness'. Hillman, on the other hand, uses the therapeutic dialogue to make the wolf more distinctly idiosyncratic, more specific and more precisely emblematic of the client's unique conception of it. What sort of eyes? What sort of fur? How fast is it running. How does it prowl, sit, turn and look? How does it feel, smell and sound? 'Images that are generalized and conventionalized . . . have had their characteristic peculiarity erased[49] . . . the more precision, the more actual insight'.[50]

According to Hillman, in order to detect the multitudinous resonances of the images, the therapist requires a special kind of insight that has more to do with artistic erudition than with clinical proficiency and science: 'We are forced toward the field of those who are specialists in images – the field of aesthetics in its broadest sense.'[51]

Many of the prominent and published members of Hillman's school are indeed aestheticians in one sense or another, and the ideas propounded are more applicable to artistic practice and cultural analysis than to the therapeutic rehabilitation of those suffering from extreme pathological conditions. This does not make their approach more or less viable than a more clinically orientated therapy, but it makes it different in aim and in nature, for it occupies the borderland between the philosophy of cultural analysis and the precepts of psychological investigation.

Since the mid-1980s James Hillman and Paul Kugler have been looking to the theatre as a means of generating image, in collaboration with Enrique Pardo, a pupil of Roy Hart, with whom he researched the vocal work initiated by Alfred Wolfsohn.

Pardo's specific contribution, both to the theatrical application of voice and to the psychological understanding of image, lies in his experiments to show how images can be conveyed to an audience through the non-verbal channel of vocal sound and bodily movement. Applying Hillman's view of a polycentric psyche to an extensive malleability of the human voice, Pardo uses a dance of vocal sound to create images which, to an audience, resound with an uncanny recognisability and yet defy reduction to a linguistic or otherwise codified schema. A reviewer writing about one of Pardo's performances states:

> With his *Hymn to Pan*, Enrique Pardo has shown how one can discover an artistic form with an unbelievably enriched and enlivened character, with this extended vocal range, which not only finds its own corporal, bodily expressions, but which also lives in symbiosis with them. Enrique Pardo has created a mythological and poetic language.[52]

This mythological and poetic language consists of using the singing voice, incorporating both the ugly and the beautiful, to 'embody' the images of the psyche:

> Image at this level means personified archetypes, creatures, charac-

ters, elements. Such personifications carry very strong psychological and cultural meanings. In the following, embodiments (personifications) emphasize *vocal* images: the screeching witch, the fat dirty baritone, a laser-beam tenor, a broken-motor sound, a multiphonic ghost, a high-alto laughing hysteric, a feeble hermaphroditic soprano, an inhuman robot, a cracking rock.[53]

In short, Pardo's work, which spans over twenty years, probably represents the most sophisticated and deeply researched psycho-theatrical investigation since Grotowski's, and central to it is a concern with image.

## Image in Voice Movement Therapy

As I have stated, in voice movement therapy image is paramount. The work of both Hillman and Pardo has shaped my own understanding of the psychophonic aspect of vocal expression.

The patient makes a sound that appears wolf-like; it has a howling quality to it. The aim of voice movement therapy is not to amplify the image towards the archetypal, but to request of the client that it becomes *a* wolf, *her* wolf, with its particular teeth and legs and glistening eyes and gnashing jaws. The client repeats the sound over and over until it assumes a personalised precision; what Pardo calls an 'imagistic eloquence'. The client is on all fours, the head turns with a languid fluidity, the eyes blink slowly and menacingly and a sound emerges from somewhere deep in the client's body that is unmistakably rooted in a sensible and somatic embodiment of the image of wolf and all it means to her.

The evolution from this wolf image to the image of Madame Félineou is a slow one, in which every stage of the transformation from the howling wolf to the meowing cat-woman is fleshed out, filled in and made specific through precise alterations in phonational quality and kinetic gesture. From wolf to wolf-dog and then to wolf-cat; from wolf-cat to cat and from cat to cat-woman; and finally from cat-woman to the cat-like woman, Madame Félineou. This has nothing to do with merely putting on different voices, such as that heard in cabaret or on the television, for when the vocalist succumbs to the superficial option of mimicry, not only the attuned therapist but anyone else who may be present can hear that it is not genuine.

The relationship between client and therapist in a voice movement therapy session is delicately balanced. The therapist must help to amplify, embellish, enrich and refine the timbral qualities which are present in the voice, yet he must not generalise and abstract all detail, but remain attentive to specifics – what Hillman and Pardo call 'sticking to the image'. Furthermore, the therapist must not be influenced by his own modalities or image associations, nor must he impose upon the client his own tastes or prejudices. A therapist with a subdued but unresolved sexual preoccupation with the image of a domineering and sadistic woman would be prone to suggesting this image to the client so that it appeared in her voice-dance. He might therefore tease the wild woman of the forest into a character clothed in leather with high heels and black stockings, brandishing a whip and emitting tones that are tantalising and manipulative. This would be both ethically irresponsible and therapeutically irrelevant. The images supplied by the therapist must originate in the acoustic information supplied by the client and must be amplified to embody images of a genuine significance, culturally and personally, and not to reflect the widespread social stereotypes to which modern men and women have become prey.

The issue of training in this field of working with image is therefore, as Hillman has pointed out, a contentious one. There is no training process which will guarantee the client's freedom from the therapist's projection of his or her preoccupations; neither is there a training that will ensure that the therapist is able to respond extensively and analytically to what he or she hears in the client's voice. Instead the therapist must strive diligently to increase the reservoir of images from which to draw in the process of nurturing a voice. Films, books, plays, music, songs, paintings, dreams, myths – all these are important sources of images for the voice movement therapist.

## Image and Range

Often, despite the success of stage one of the process, which should have achieved a psychological and physical freedom from constriction, the client is unable to give vocal expression to the full range of psychological contents on account of a limited range. Pardo could not have achieved his phonational expression of image without an extensive range of pitch. This ability to extend the range of the voice to mirror the breadth of the imagination is something which few teachers of voice have bothered to pursue, because it takes time, commitment and courage on the part of both teacher and pupil. But it has to be done; the process of working upon the voice can never stop.

There are some images of a personal and archetypal significance which, by their nature, can only be expressed in a pitch range that is higher or lower than used in normal speech or in most kinds of singing. Consequently the second stage of voice movement therapy should aim in part at extending the pitch range, which for men usually means developing a higher voice and for women a lower one, by cultivating an awareness of the images associated with height and depth in the voice.

### THE HIGH VOICE IN MEN
In singing, the high voice of the male has always attracted the greatest fasci-

nation. There is something in the sound which is unreal; hence the term *falsetto*, from the Latin for 'false'. Its aura of falsity comes, however, not from a faked worldliness but from the opposite; it has a celestial quality of spirituality, of transcendence, as though the gods themselves were singing. It is unreal because it is not of this world.

Because a high voice is normally associated with a woman, there is something apparently feminine about the falsetto voice. Castration did indeed deprive its subject of virility, and the falsetto singer also sounds as though he has suspended his masculinity and entered into the role of a woman. However, the overt masculinity shown in his face and body creates not so much the image of a woman, but of an androgyne or hermaphrodite, a perfect blend of male and female.

The androgynous character figures widely in the mythology of many cultures as an expression of the unity of male and female in every human being. For, just as biologically the male possesses female genes and the woman male, so too, psychologically speaking, we each possess elements of the other sex.

As we have seen in Chapter Three, Jung named the male part of a woman the 'animus' and the female part of a man the 'anima'. The anima and animus are dormant and unconscious, rising up out of the sleeping soul in our dreams. The women that appear in a man's dreams carry with them not so much the vestiges of the women from the man's daily life, but more the aspects of his own femininity. So too, with a woman, the men in her dreams represent parts of the man in her.

Accepting qualities normally associated with the other sex is often a difficult process and meets with greater resistance the more we consciously stress our given gender. In men the usual difficulty encountered when attempting to sing in the higher registers has much to do, not with a lack of physical proficiency, but with this psychological resistance against contacting and expressing the feminine.

The androgynous figure is not only a synthesis of male and female, but is also connected to the spirit and to God, which gives the sound its mythical and spiritual dimension. God, in transcending the world, transcends all opposites and is neither male nor female but both. Behind the Christian patriarchy which worships an all-male God there is a wealth of mythology which stresses the androgynous aspect of God, and all these mythologies tell that the world was created by a sexless being who was heaven and embodied earth, fire and water, male and female. Plato proposed that it was from such an androgynous original God that human beings descended, and he believed that in earlier times all people were androgynous and only later became divided into opposite sexes. Thus, for a man to sing falsetto, he has to unite his masculinity with the dormant anima, to rise above the conscious one-sidedness of his male gender and enter a fusion of opposites which creates an audible symbol for the spirit.

Because the high voice has its roots in the pre-pubescent stage of our development, it is naturally associated with the child in us, and the ability to sing in this register requires contacting the inner child and giving it expression.

For a man to achieve the clear falsetto voice, he therefore has to contact the female, the childlike and the spiritual parts of himself. This is a difficult task, but when finally he reaches the sound, it gives him a special sense of achievement on a very deep level. He feels he has awakened something long since repressed, which, once reawakened, endows his voice and his self with a revivified energy and passion.

## THE DEEP VOICE IN WOMEN

Just as with the highest voice, the falsetto, there are certain psychological motifs to be confronted in order to achieve it, so too with the bass voice we are dealing with a complex or network of images which underlie the sound. The notion of a bass voice has its psychological equivalent in the 'base' aspects of the personality.

To sing bass is to confront all that is 'base' in us, a notion that has two aspects. First, the 'base' is the foundation, the bedrock, that which underpins and forms the very foundation of our character. Thus with the bass voice there is a sense of deep-rootedness, of contact with the earth, of underlying strength and of support. Therefore to sing bass a woman must make contact with part of herself that is the most secure and possesses a sense of stillness and authority. It is a regal sound, domineering yet with a paternal warmth to it.

Secondly, 'base' means crude, unrefined, flagrant, obscene and coarse, and as such it represents our animal instinct. The deeply primitive noises of belching and grunting are associated with masculinity, not because women cannot utter such sounds, but because social tradition and conditioning have prohibited it. Just as the upper register represents a feminine quality in its ethereal nature, so the bass voice is its opposite; it is masculine and, in the classical tradition, the bass voice is the lowest in pitch and is assigned exclusively to the male.

For a woman to sing bass, she must contact and express a certain primeval barbarism, which means arousing her most animalistic and savage nature, tapping into those instincts which society has denied her under the name of femininity.

But the 'base' is also the earth and as such has much to do with death. Ashes to ashes, dust to dust, from earth we are born and to earth we will return. The earth is that from which things grow, and it is that into which the rotting compost of dead matter is absorbed. When singing bass there is a sense of this earth, of death, of going down into the deeps, a descent not only in the musical scale but in the emotional scale also. The bass voice feels low in the same way that we feel 'down in the dumps', 'in the pits', 'in the doldrums'. The bass voice therefore touches upon depression.

It is for this reason that those prone to anxiety have particular difficulty in reaching the lower voice. Anxious states are always expressed through a heightening of the voice, and seeking the lower register requires a drop in this vocal and emotional scale.

To express means to 'ex-press', to press outwards, and all forms of expression require a certain pressure: the pressure of air which leads to exhalation, a build-up in the toxic pressure which leads to excretion. Through expression we exude, exhibit; it is an extroverted activity concerned with depositing something of ourselves upon the world.

The reverse of 'ex-pression' is 'de-pression'. To 'de-press' is to 'un-press', to relieve ourselves of the pressure of expression. To be depressed is to abstain from expression. It is impossible to live under the constant pressure to express, and depression is therefore a necessary ingredient of a balanced life. Depression is the saviour, the antidote to the cultural manic-mood disorder from which we all suffer. Singing low sounds is thus a fine alternative to the tranquilliser, for when an anxiously disposed person reaches the base of the scale, there is a new-found sense of calm and of security.

Thus, in order to sing bass, one has to touch upon three aspects of psychology. First, one must locate a certain security, a sense of stability and sureness; any major uncertainty or sense of unease in the personality will manifest itself as an involuntary shake or tremor in the voice and will not provide the necessary bedrock for the bass voice. Secondly, one has to contact the capacity for producing crude and primal sounds; to sing low first requires an uttering of swamp-like, belching noises. Any preoccupation with beauty and etiquette will prevent the voice from singing low. Finally, one must be prepared for depression – to invite it in and befriend it.

All these images converge upon a single centre which is the low voice, and whether or not a woman can touch these sounds depends on how readily she can contact these images.

When we 'ex-press', we get something out, we get rid of something. We exhale gases, literally ridding our system of the poisonous substances in our lungs and, at the same time, metaphorically 'getting something off our chest'. The satisfaction of experiencing such relief is comparable to defecating; crude words of an anal or genital nature are often uttered in a low tone and indeed we are often accused of 'talking shit'. The experience of discharge is particularly felt when dealing in low sounds because they are ideokinetically imagined to issue from the stomach and intestines.

Like the earth, the stomach and intestines are full of 'filth', and to sing bass we have to go to the pits of our stomach and to our intestines where putrefaction, digestion and expulsion of waste matter takes place. To assist the release of the bass voice, a certain amount of massage and manipulation of the muscles surrounding the abdominal and intestinal region is therefore needed.

In this contact with the 'lower region' of the body there is a gender complication. The woman's abdominal region is the focal point for two systems, the digestive and the reproductive. Thus for a woman to focus sound in her abdomen brings into play a whole complex of images, which are beyond the somatic experience of a man. A male, unlike a female, does not associate this region of the body with the shedding of blood or with carrying a child.

The whole psychological significance of blood is therefore entirely different in a male and a female. To a man blood invariably signifies illness, injury and war. For a woman it contains the images of transformation, of necessary and unavoidable shedding, of sisterhood, maturity, power and regeneration. For a woman to sing low sounds, the womb and its functioning has to play a role in the process of ideokinesis; for it is not possible to focus sound in the abdominal part of the body without stimulating anatomical images associated with menstruation and birth.

It is in this respect that the low voice not only embraces death but also rebirth, for to die is to be reborn. Thus, while for a man the bass voice is ultimately connected with death, for a woman it offers the basis for rebirth; for the shedding of blood is in itself the eternal reminder of fertility — it is the wise wound.

For a woman to achieve low sounds, it is often necessary to vocalise the pleasure and the pain of giving birth, and when the sounds are achieved, it gives her a sense of deep contact with her ability to create new life.

For a man to find the uplifting and life-giving side of bass, as well as the depression to which it naturally tends, he has at least to come to some degree of understanding of the regenerative aspects of discharge. However, because he can never know this bodily, the bass voice always sounds more depressing in a man than a woman.

The purpose of extending the vocal range to incorporate the extremes is to enable the client to give expression to images of height and depth. It is probably the most exhilarating aspect of the work for most clients and stimulates an amazement in them at having been able to touch parts of the psychological and phonological scale hitherto unexcavated.

# Verbal Analysis

The central principle which unites the diverse practical approaches and theoretical paradigms used by the practitioners described in this book is that the sounds of the human voice act as a metaphor for the dynamics of the human psyche.

Security, femininity, sweetness, innocence, bitterness, revenge and thunderous aggression in the voice all have their parallels in the psyche, and it is by expressing these states of mind that the voice gains its range of timbral qualities. Working with the voice is therefore a means of working with the mind.

In order for clients of voice movement therapy to gain insight into the way that their vocal images reflect significant aspects of their imagination and psychological operations, a degree of verbal analysis is necessary whereby they can consider and discuss the vocal work. Clients who have a particular difficulty in producing warm, hearty and generous sounds in the lower pitch range, for instance, but who can sing such a range with a quality of aggressive retaliation, need an opportunity to reflect upon their problem. In my experience the client nearly always offers further psychological support for the vocal dynamic. There are other reasons in the client's life why deep sounds have become overtly associated with violence as opposed to warmth, and these reasons, when offered by the client, should be discussed, analysed and related to the state of the voice.

An important difference between psychotherapy and voice movement therapy is that in the latter verbal analysis is relegated to the end of the session, when there has been enough vocal work generated to provide the material for investigation. There are of course a number of clients who will at every opportunity wish to stop the working process in order to talk, but this should be discouraged as it is often a way of avoiding sensory confrontation with the real material.

Voice movement therapy also differs from psychotherapy in that it focuses on analysis of non-verbal vocal sounds, while the clients provide the supporting information of their own accord. A good voice movement therapist will always be able to analyse the voice in such a way as to give it a deep significance for the clients, so that they can understand how their acoustic expressions contain psychological components. If clients do not wish to discuss the connection, then that is their right.

If clients do want to discuss the way that their psychological state is revealed in their vocal patterns, then the voice movement therapist must enter into an objective psychotherapeutic relationship with them, subjecting their descriptions to close scrutiny. The aim of this analysis is to give clients insight into themselves and to offer a way of undoing those confining constructs through vocal work. For instance, by providing an opportunity to locate lower pitches possessing a generous and warm timbre, the negative association between depth and aggression can be depleted. The verbal analysis assists clients in understanding what the therapist is trying to achieve through vocal analysis, and helps to demystify the process.

Such mystification of vocal work is not uncommon among vocal practitioners particularly those with a therapeutic bent. The human voice, because of its complexity, is open to endless intricate and meaningless interpretations which, combined with the voice practioner's air of authority, can lead the client into a worshipping and adoring relationship with him or her. The verbal analysis therefore also serves as a reminder that it is the client who provides the material and its authenticity; the practitioner merely abides by the process of education and interpretation with as much perceptive objectivity as is humanly possible. Through this process the client achieves liberation.

Here the client begins the session by establishing a voice with a warm, sympathetic and enfolding quality. The focus of the sound is directed to the palm of the hand which is held close to the body, encouraging a mild and effortless expression of soothing maternity, without projection or extroverted intensity. The client is working with the image of a cat licking her kittens.

By this point in the session, the alkaline quality of gentility has been developed into an acidic and retaliatory quality which warns and protects. The body extends forwards, the fingers claw and retract and the voice intensifies and projects outwards towards those who threaten the object of her sympathy. Now the client is working with the image of a lioness prowling and protecting her cubs.

To assist the humanisation of the primal animality which has emerged, the client moves to standing whilst maintaining focus on the imagined offspring close to the ground. The lifting of the body engenders an uplifting quality to the voice, celebratory and joyously overwhelmed with pride.

The client now departs from an internal matrix of images which are withholding, nurturing and protecting and locates a lightened spontaneity which infuses the voice with a heartful and volatile sprightliness. She works with the image of an eagle seeing her eaglets in departing flight.

The client seeks to locate an unapologetic presence that asserts without dominating or intimidating. Here his body is held from behind by the therapist so he may literally and emotionally 'come forward' without the need for a strident thrusting of the chest. The sound is loud and declamatory with a boyish, servile and inquisitive timbre. The client is working with the image of a young prince animated by the homecoming of his adored father.

Here the client is encouraged to deepen the pitch, maturing and fermenting the quality of the sound to locate a disapproving pomposity. The boyish prince becomes a knight and the inquiring servitude becomes a pioneering bravery. The sound is imagined to emanate from the chest and the client visualises an indestructible jouster on horseback.

In order to locate a capacity to yield and acquiesce which can complement the emerging immovable status, the client is encouraged to experience physical sensations of falling and being carried: a wounded jouster rescued by a brother. The voice retains a strength but becomes infused with a modest recognition of mortality.

Having found in the voice a compositional combination of assertion and recession, bravery and passivity, inquisitive impulsiveness and mature wisdom, the client now extends the pitch range of the vocalisation to ensure that the qualities can be located across the spectrum of the vocal range. The client works with the image of chivalry and gallantry which is explored as a means to achieving a comfortable and undogmatic assertion.

# CHAPTER SEVEN

# From Song to Speech – the Muscle Beneath the Skin

## The Right to Speak: A Socio-physical Model

Literally hundreds of so-called 'drill books' on the practical nature of speech training have been written throughout the nineteenth and twentieth centuries. In the last fifteen years alone a vast number of books have appeared on the subject of voice production and speech training, and many of these describe exercises which the reader can practise in order to improve his or her speech. They include prescriptions for vocal health by scientifically orientated practitioners,[1] generalised and idiosyncratic approaches to vocal training propounded by voice coaches,[2] and detailed descriptions of the significance of phonetics.[3] Some of these investigators of voice or singing wrote in an inspiring and fluent manner and became minor legends in their own right, such as E. H. Caesari[4] and James Rush.[5] The writings of others disappeared from the shelves within weeks. The books which were published during the Victorian era have one thing in common: they all perceive speech as a sociological phenomenon; that is to say, the precision, diction and elocution of the spoken word is taken to be directly proportional to a person's intelligence, status and social worth.

There have since been a great number of experiments, initiated in the early twentieth century by speech trainers, linguists and psychologists, to test how social judgements are made according to the way a person speaks and the way in which amendment of speech habits yields social and behavioural adjustment, both in the speaker and in the listener's reaction to him or her.[6]

Probably the most well-known example of an equation between speech and social standing is revealed in the story of Eliza Doolittle as told in Shaw's *Pygmalion*. Eliza's transformation from a 'sloppy speaker' to a 'posh speaker' is seen to be equivalent and directly related to her transformation from a member of a lower social class to a higher one.

Such an understanding of the sociological function of speech is innately bound up with a certain puritanical view of the English language and of English culture, in which different acoustic signals are allotted varying degrees of social value. Those signals which are valued highly – what Doolittle calls a 'posh accent' – are generated, inculcated and preserved by the privileged members of English society; they are the moneyed, the physically able, the so-called educated and tend to live in the South.

It is not only in Britain that vocal signals are attributed varying degrees of social status. In other European countries, such as France, the dialects of some regions are held in high esteem as representing the perfect emblem of French diction, while other geographical idiosyncrasies are equated with simplicity and simple-mindedness. In the USA, too, the acoustic undulations preserved in the speech of many farming communities carry with them a stigma of unintelligence as against the supposed sophistication of the crisp phonation of the city dwellers.

However, the twentieth century has seen a widespread migration of people, and there are parts of England, Europe and America which are no more populated by an indigenous gentry than by the people of Bangladesh, Istanbul or Pakistan. In English-speaking countries the perpetuation of an equation between the 'posh accent' and social stature becomes not only a means by which to preserve the exclusive rights of the privileged, but also a way of ensuring the prolonged disenfranchising of ethnic minorities, particularly those to whom the mechanical operation of English phonetics is radically different from their mother tongue, and therefore difficult to articulate. The multicultural fabric of modern Britain and of America demands a reconsideration of speech values and the social mores which they supposedly reflect.

Traditionally, one of the places where linguistic snobbery has been most rife is in the theatre, particularly where the classics, such as Shakespeare, are concerned. For many years the English literati viewed Shakespeare as an icon of aesthetic integrity and a symbol of profound linguistic quality. His plays were used in schools as material with which to practise elocution, and the theatre-goers in their furs and in their dinner-jackets expected and yearned for the sharp and incisive articulation of the great Shakespearean actors.

But this belief in the linguistic purity of Shakespeare's work was incongruent with scholarly findings long before the widespread use of elocutionary histrionics died a death. Today not only academics but theatre professionals realise that Shakespeare's actors spoke in a variety of regional accents, some coarse, some creamy, some metallic, some harsh, others slippery, languid and mellow.

One of the most important and certainly the most effective challenges to verbal puritanism in British theatre has come from the work of Cicely Berry at the Royal Shakespeare Company. An important part of Berry's work has been to shift single-handedly the emphasis of the theatrical profession from the formal affectations of mannerism, which has occupied the elocutionists for so long, to highlighting the overriding significance of meaning and emotion inherent in a text.[7] This shift of emphasis has been extended to encompass other forms of speaking, both professional and non-professional, by one of Berry's students and colleagues, Patsy Rodenburg.

Rodenburg's book *The Right to Speak* is particularly significant and timely because it occupies a sociological framework which pays attention to the multicultural context in which the English language is now placed. In her words: 'The English Language, some would say, has been contaminated by other cultures. It is probably truer and more accurate to say it has been enlivened and enriched by being spoken in different groups and ingested back into the mother tongue.'[8]

Rodenburg appreciates what she calls the 'dynamism' of the English language which has arisen from 'its exposure to multiple linguistic habits', and her practical teaching works in opposition to the notion that there is 'only one right sound'.[9] Her aim is to free verbal facility from inhibition, self-consciousness and constriction in order that the musicality unique to its cultural base can be honoured, celebrated and conserved. This is what she calls the 'right to speak', and it is a prerogative which she feels has been stolen, not only from socio-linguistic minorities, but from the female population also. By encouraging a phonational quality in women which can be dominant, tenacious, resolute and robust and a vocal sound in men which can be susceptible, disarmed, tender and tolerant, Rodenburg makes socio-political use of speech training.[10]

Rodenburg proposes that social inequality constitutes one of the two primary means by which people are prevented from the right to speak; the other is habitual physical patterning which she believes is acquired from an early age. According to her, these physiological constructs should remain the focus of the voice worker's attention, and it is through the process of 'de-patterning' these constraints by way of physical exercises that a liberation of vocal expression can be achieved. However, it is in this sense and in this sense only that she considers her work to be therapeutic: 'I would never claim that voice work is psychologically therapeutic (that's one of the dangers to be avoided), but as a kind of physiotherapy it does release hidden memories encased in the body. To that extent it is exceedingly therapeutic.'[11]

It is in its resistance to and abstinence from engaging with psycho-therapeutic phenomena that Rodenburg's model gets into difficulty; for while actively playing down the responsibility of a voice teacher towards the student's psychological material which surfaces in response to the work, Rodenburg none the less repeatedly reveals that she is frequently dealing with the residue of psychological operations. She admits that 'psychic trauma of any sort' can 'shut down the voice',[12] she accepts that certain vocal habits are acquired through the emulation of our parents' behaviour and that therefore there is 'a certain vocal umbilical cord which sometimes needs cutting as a step towards liberating our own voices'.[13] She also admits that the voice teacher is 'in the front line of action' for the release of 'unexploded mines' of emotional material, such as grief, stored up over years and which takes its toll on the voice:[14]

Linked with the denial of grief – the 'lump in the throat' – is the habit of pushing down the voice. In order to block pain and contain it the voice feels literally clumped in the throat like a mass which we neither swallow nor expel. We want to cry out but stop the sound in the process and deny ourselves the right . . .

I once taught a student who had incredible tension in the jaw, throat and high breath. No exercise could shift the physical habits, everything failed even though he seemed so willing to try. Then one day in a text class concentrating on classical Greek drama came a breakthrough. Something in the text touched him and as he went with the emotional discovery his voice suddenly released with sounds I had never heard him make. Suddenly he howled and howled and howled. He could not stop and needed to be given time and space alone. I and the rest of the class discreetly left him and some hours later he came to find me to apologise (not that he needed to).

He had lost both his parents within six months when he was six-teen. Being the eldest child he had to remain firm and cope with the grief of his brothers and sisters. He had never been given the right to mourn but had settled into a steely state of restraint. Still he felt an apology was in order. From that moment of unexpected release his voice never looked back. It got stronger and stronger, never again ex-hibiting any vocal tension. All of it was released in that one session. This is a good instance where work on a text can be keenly related to releasing a long-held habit. For this particular young man the Greek's notion of 'catharsis' or purgation became a key factor in his voice process.[15]

The description of this particular incident in one of Rodenburg's drama-school classes is clearly incongruent with her resistance to claiming that voice work is psychotherapeutic and with her preference for viewing her strategy of release as a physiological process with sociological results. It is doubtful whether any hitherto unexpressed affect resulting from a severe trauma can be, or even should be, released in a single session. When Rodenburg says that this is a 'good instance where work on a text can be keenly related to releasing a long-held habit' and that for this student 'the Greek's notion of "catharsis" or purgation became a key factor in his voice process', she is walking headlong into the field of psychological processes, particularly the relationship between text and affect researched by Freud.

However, her resistance to dealing with this perhaps emanates not from an irresponsibility towards the psychological implications of voice work, but from an ethical unease with the misuse of psychological paradigms in the hands of some voice teachers. She attacks those teachers who 'provoke students to reveal secrets about themselves unwillingly', and 'dangerously probe psyches, in some cases violating privacy and dignity', who 'work without either anatomical training or licensing as therapists and healers' and who approach voice work psychologically and not just physiologically, which is where she thinks 'emphasis must always be anchored'.[16]

Considered in the light of these comments, Rodenburg's anti-psychological stance could be seen as admirable as much as omissive. Indeed, perhaps if more drama-school voice teachers were as impartial to a psychological approach and as responsive to a socio-physical one, fewer students would graduate in a cloud of psychological confusion and women would have more opportunity to play parts other than the maid and the mistress.

However, there are many people who are fully aware that their vocal reticence or encumberment is directly related to a psychological component, and that the extrication of the voice is not *just* a physiological and social process, but a psychological one also. For these people vocal work does not only dismantle faulty muscular patterns, but also discharges the affective dynamics in response to which they were erected. Rodenburg's omission of psychological issues tends therefore to detract from a fully integrated view of the voice as an expression of physical and psychological constructs. At the same time her admission of the inevitable expression of affective psychological material during vocal training implicitly pleads for the inclusion of a psychotherapeutically orientated aspect in the training of voice workers.

## What You Say and How You Say It

Communication between people consists of the simultaneous operation of a number of parts of the body: eye movements, facial expression, gesture and the sounds emitted by the voice. When we seek to understand what someone is communicating, we attend to all of these sounds and movements in order to form a total impression and thereby appreciate what the person 'means'.

However, although gesture, facial expression and eye contact contribute to the 'meaning' of the message which we seek to convey to each other, it is the sophistication of our vocal utterances that separates us from other animals. Of all the means of communication, the oral channel is the most widely used in day-to-day interaction between people; and this oral channel is itself composed of two levels – the vocal and the verbal, or voice and speech.

As early as 1927 Edward Sapir pointed to the differences between voice and speech, proposing that 'speech' relates to the subject-matter and choice of vocabulary, while 'voice' relates to the way in which this is uttered through the use of pitch, rhythm and volume.[17] Later, in 1959, J. R. Davitz and L. J. Davitz applied Susanne Langer's distinction between discursive and non-discursive symbols to vocalisation and suggested that the non-discursive mode of communicating is manifested in the manner with which the message is spoken – that is, through what Sapir called the 'voice'; while the discursive element is made up of the words that are spoken – what Sapir called 'speech'.[18]

These two channels of acoustic signalling operate simultaneously during the act of verbal expression, and the vocal channel is very often responsible for communicating our affective state of mind.[19] B. F. Skinner has proposed that speech can only be used effectively when the voice indicates to the listener the way the words are to be interpreted,[20] and P. F. Ostwald has said that it is the sounds accompanying speech which transmit to the listener the emotional tone of the message.[21]

But, if the speaker is experiencing some kind of personal conflict, the two channels may carry conflicting information, a phenomenon that has been called 'incongruence'.[22] This often occurs, for example, when the words we choose paint the brave face behind which the emotion brews. We say that we are willing to do something for a friend in a tone of voice which, to the attentive listener, reveals a reluctance to help. We say that we are 'doing fine', while we are actually choked with sadness. In cases of mental illness these incongruities are present to a heightened degree and are a highly significant source of information for the therapist or psychiatrist, whose diagnostic conclusions have long-lasting and often irreversible effects on the patient.

Paul Moses asserted that when such an incongruence between the vocal and verbal message occurs, 'the voice is more likely to reveal the truth about the personality'[23] than the speech, and that therefore, 'before attempting to analyse the voice, one must divorce it from the message it seeks to convey'.[24]

A common kind of incongruence can often be heard in the acoustic messages conveyed to children by their mothers and which demands of the listeners a sophistication of interpretation often in excess of their years. John Harris gives a typical example of the mother who has been worn out and irritated by a long hard day and is standing with her child on the platform of a railway station waiting to travel home. Her child is running up and down the platform, jumping about and causing her to feel exasperated. She picks the child up and sits him firmly on the bench, saying: 'You just move from there once more!' Of course, the mother actually intends her message to be decoded to mean 'Do *not* move from there again', despite the fact that the linguistic content of her message requests her child to do exactly the reverse of what she wants.[25] In a situation like this, the melodic stress or prosodic intonation of her voice is likely to leave the child in no doubt as to what she really means. However, there are other less overt cases of incongruence which can often confront children with an impenetrable ambivalence as to what the message intends. Gregory Bateson has carried out considerable research into the unwitting transmission of ambiguous or contradictory signals by parents to their children through an incongruence between the phonic and linguistic dimensions of speech, hypothesising that a high frequency of such 'double binds' sets up fertile ground for the genesis of schizophrenic disturbance.[26]

For the purpose of analysis, then, the vocally produced acoustic signals of communication in the human species can be divided into the phonic and the linguistic, or voice and speech. As we have seen, phonic expression occurs as a result of the vibration of the vocal cords in a process which we call phonation. Linguistic communication, or speech, is achieved by the coordinated articulation of the tongue, mouth, lips and jaw. The term 'linguistic' in fact comes from *lingua*, the Latin word for 'tongue', and indeed the articulation of the tongue is one of the first prerequisites in the production of speech.

It is by producing vocal sounds that a young child first communicates; and it is this form of communication which accompanied the early development of the human species. Language is acquired subsequently. As we become proficient in expressing ourselves verbally, the instinctive phonic sound-making becomes subservient to linguistics, but it retains a certain importance in giving speech its stress, its emotional colour, its melody. The value of this vocal quality in communication cannot be overestimated. The quality of a voice independent of the words it utters reveals much about the personality of the speaker, and a change in phonic characteristics can completely alter the meaning of an otherwise mild-sounding sentence, imbuing it with sarcasm, ferocity, bitterness or defeat. It is the rhythm, melody, pitch and timbre of each other's voice with which the mother and baby communicate before the baby acquires language; it is these qualities which a pet dog understands in the utterances of his master, and which give our words the undertones and overtones required for their correct interpretation.

The linguist J. Lotz has pointed out that if you were to make a quantitative analysis of the acoustic signals emitted by the human voice, only 1 per cent would prove to be of linguistic use and purpose, the remainder being entirely vocal or phonic.[27] In other words, we make a lot of noise that could not be described as speech, but which tell others a great deal about the way we are feeling or the kind of character we are.

If the speech faculty is impaired through illness, disability or because the trauma of the transformation from pre-verbal to linguistic communication has not been successfully achieved, vocal quality may remain the primary acoustic form of communication. There are many people whose verbal capacity is so impaired that their oral utterances convey no linguistic significance but none the less have a definite function in expressing an inner disposition, a mood, a need which deserves to be understood. People who work with non-verbal patients become highly tuned to the inference, instinct, intention and the need implicit in these vocal sounds, and anyone with the patience and the humility to enter into this world of phonic communication would attest to the fact that meaning can be devised at the level of phonation.

In fact, all of us make use of such meaningful but non-verbal vocal expressions through utterances which are termed 'phatic'. These are the vocal sounds we make in response to another speaker — normally written as 'ah', 'er', 'urgh', 'yuk' – and which often serve to convey emotional reactions of an extreme nature.

However, for most 'verbal' adults the primary significance of the vocal quality is in the unique character that it gives to our speech. In the quality of a voice you can hear the vales of depression and the peaks of excitement; you can hear the lulls of concern and self-reflection and the sharp points of provocation and attack. In it you can hear the calm timbres of age and wisdom and the effervescent innocence and enthusiasm of youth; in the voice you can hear the colour of sound – the deep blue of melancholia and the red heat of revenge; and so too can you taste the voice – its citrus tang of jealousy and its sugary-sweet sycophantism. In the voice you can detect resignation, indignation, hope and despair. In short, in the voice you can hear the psyche.

## Is Your Voice Telling the Truth?

Although for sighted individuals vocal quality is only part of a complex series of signals communicated by the face and body of the speaker, for the visually impaired person tone and timbre of voice is crucially important, as it is primarily from this that the listener with limited sight makes sense of what is said by the speaker. Likewise during darkness the voice becomes the central means of transmitting messages, and many people who are mugged or attacked late at night are left only with the sound of the persecutor's voice as a means of identifying him for the police.

In 1937 Frances McGehee, an American psychologist, decided to look closely at this question of voice identification from a legal standpoint, recognising that the human voice 'is the principal and most reliable evidence of crimes committed in the darkness, or upon persons who are blind'.[28] McGehee took a group of participants and asked them to listen to a stranger's voice from behind a screen; they were then asked to remember the voice for a later date. The next day the participants were asked to listen to five voices and to identify which was the one they had heard the day before. This vocal identification parade was repeated at various intervals over the next five months to see for how long people could correctly remember a voice. The experiments showed that the proportion of people who could distinguish the voice which they had first heard was 83 per cent after one day, but only 13 per cent after five months. McGehee made sure that each speaker spoke the same passage of text from behind the screen to ensure that the participants listened to the voice and not to the speech of the person; that is to say, the experiment aimed to test the ability to remember the way something is said and not the particulars of what is said.

Since the first quarter of this century many psychologists have tried to break down and separate out the various channels of human expression in order to discover how significant each one is in the process of communication. They have sought to ascertain what can be communicated about a person by their handwriting, or by their facial expression, or by their bodily movements, and a substantial number of these experiments has been concerned with discovering how effective the voice is, as distinct from speech, in signifying meaning. One of the earliest and most renowned of these experiments into the psychology of the human voice was initiated by an English professor of psychology, T. H. Pear.

In 1927 Pear placed an advertisement in the *Radio Times*[29] announcing an experiment in which he would select nine people to read an identical passage of text over the radio. In the advertisement he asked radio-listeners to guess the readers' age, sex, profession or occupation, the location of birth, the location affecting speech and whether the speaker was accustomed to leading others. Over 4,000 reports were sent in, and many of them were highly accurate. From this experiment Pear deduced that aspects of a personality are communicated effectively to a listener by the voice alone. He published his findings in one of the first books on the psychology of the human voice called *Voice and Personality*, in which he concluded that 'a person's voice often conforms to a stereotype'[30] in the minds of listeners. In other words, certain vocal qualities which are evident in the voice of a speaker tend to conjure up the same notions of personality in many listeners, even though the speaker may not conform to that disposition in real life.

From a very early age we are all influenced by these vocal types. As previously stated, wickedness and wizardry, witches and evil-doers are always portrayed vocally with a hard, brittle and nasal timbre in the games of children; while a deeper, breathy and hollow quality comes to stand for a lack of intelligence and naïveté. These vocal images, consolidated in childhood, later come to permeate adult life, particularly in the theatre, where certain classical roles have been traditionally apportioned specific vocal timbres: the robust and velvety voice of Othello; the metallic and incisive voice of Richard III; the light and wispy voice of Juliet. Radio and television have always made use of the fact that for some reason we regard certain voices stereotypically: the vicar's voice, the cripple's voice, the homosexual's voice. But although certain voice types communicate strongly defined images, do such images truthfully reflect the personality behind the voice?

The work of Pear generated a lot of interest among other psychologists in the relationship between personality and voice. These psychologists conducted more sophisticated experiments based on precise and professionally accepted definitions of personality traits. They began to take what they considered to be 'objective measurements' of aspects of their subjects' personalities. They then asked people to listen to the voices of these subjects and report on the presence of the same aspects as in Pear's experiment, after which they compared these judgements with the so-called 'objective criteria' obtained by the test, to see if the voice could communicate accurately aspects of the personality. For example, in 1933 a psychologist by the name of H. Herzog asked 2,700 listeners to guess the weight, height, sex and occupation of people based on hearing their speaking voices on the radio, and each of the listeners guessed all of the measured aspects with a higher degree of accuracy than could be expected by statistically calculated chance.[31]

The criteria of weight, height, sex and occupation are all easily established with objective accuracy. But how about more subtle and complex aspects of personality, such as introversion, aggression, ambition, depression, generosity?

In order for the psychologists to ascertain how effectively such subtle nuances of character are communicated by the voice, they had first to find ways of obtaining an 'objective' measurement, in the same way as weight can be measured by scales and height by a ruler. This was, and still is, achieved by what have become known as 'standard psychological tests'. We have all, at some time or another, taken part in a variation of these tests. Popular magazines often adapt them to a particular end: 'Discover if You are an Ideal Lover' or 'Are You Over-stressed?'. In these amusing articles a series of questions is asked, in which the reader must state how he or she reacts in a given situation. Often there are three choices, a, b and c, to which are attached numerical values. At the end of the test the participant adds up the points gained from each selected answer and the total gives a generalised character description in relation to the specific subject of the test. These light-hearted tests are merely simplifications of those used by psychologists to determine what sort of person a subject is.

After the publication of Pear's book a vast number of psychologists conducted such tests on different people and then asked others to listen to the subjects' voices and guess the criteria ascertained by each test. The objective measurements of the test and the judgements of the listeners were then compared. For example, in 1934 the psychologists G. H. Allport and H. Cantril subjected eighteen men to three different tests which gave measurements of the degree to which each man was extroverted or introverted, dominant or submissive. In addition, the tests measured the main values of each subject – that is, the kinds of principles by which they lived their life.[32] Allport and Cantril also recorded the political preference, age, height, complexion and vocation of each subject as well as taking photographs and samples of their handwriting. Each of these men were then asked to read out an identical passage for a team of listeners, without face-to-face contact, while the latter had to correlate the test-measurements, handwriting and photographs with the voices. The experiments showed that all aspects were correlated with greater accuracy than could be expected by statistically calculated chance. However, in their conclusion Allport and Cantril, like Pear before them, stated that 'the uniformity of opinion regarding the personalities of the speakers was somewhat in excess of the accuracy of such an opinion, showing the importance of the phenomenon of stereotyped judgment'.[33] For example, nearly all judges would say that they felt the voice of subject C revealed a highly introverted personality even though the so-called 'objective test' defined subject C as highly extroverted. This revealed that certain voices conjure up the same picture in the minds of most people even though the picture does not correspond to the actual personality type.

By far the most detailed series of experimental investigations into the way the voice reveals personal characteristics was first conducted by two famous psychologists, P. J. Fay and W. C. Middleton, between 1939 and 1943. The first of these attempted to determine the degree to which a listener can determine 'Spranger personality types' from the voice of a speaker.[34] Eduard Spranger proposed that a personality can be slotted into one of six fundamental categories: theoretic, social, aesthetic, economic, political and religious.[35] In this experiment two speakers representing each of the Spranger types were chosen to read set passages for forty-five listeners. It was found that listeners were able to guess all types from the sound of their voices more frequently than could be expected by chance.

Fay and Middleton went on to conduct similar experiments to see if the voice could communicate the occupation, intelligence and sociability of a subject, the degree to which the subject was introverted or extroverted, whether the subject was lying or telling the truth and how accustomed the subject was to leadership. They also found that stereotyped vocal images played a large part in the experiments:

> From a practical standpoint, the results of the experiment indicate that certain voices portray a particular personality type to a rather large percentage of listeners. Practical use might be made of stereotyped voices in the broadcasting of dramatic materials. The casting of characters, frequently done ineffectively, could thus be greatly improved. For example, if, in broadcasting a dramatic sketch, it is important that a certain speaker impress his audience as being a religious person, then such a speaker should be chosen because of his stereotyped 'religious voice'; actually, of course, he, or she, may be the economic or the political type rather than the religious. The *actual* type, however, is not important, since in the field of radio broadcasting, as in the field of dramatics, the chief objective is to create a certain type and to produce a certain effect.[36]

The use of voice to communicate psychological ideas is developed to a high degree in the art of acting. The malleability of the actor's voice enables him to convey through a slight twist of timbre or inflection something from the depths of his character. It was this ability of the radio actor to communicate specific personalities with the voice that inspired Pear's book (*Voice and Personality*), which in turn initiated a vast series of experiments that have continued throughout the twentieth century. In these experiments psychologists sought to ascertain the importance of voice as distinct from speech in evoking personality, and in order to minimise the influence of speech on the listeners, steps were taken to emphasise the voice of the subjects. Sometimes this involved asking every subject to read the same passage of text, as in McGehee's experiment, so that the listeners were not influenced by a particular subject's use of words. In other experiments subjects simply spoke the alphabet or numerals from 1 to 100. But all of them, except one, used some kind of speech as the base from which vocal sound was abstracted. The exception to this was an experiment in which subjects read literature that put them in a sad or happy state and then phonated the sound 'ah'. The pitch of the voices were then plotted, by which it was ascertained that 'ahs' of happiness showed higher pitch than those of sadness.[37]

Later, with the advancement of technology, it became possible to reduce further the linguistic content of speech using electronic filters. Subjects spoke into a tape recorder and their recorded speech was then passed through a machine which distorted the linguistic content without changing the idiosyncratic vocal qualities of each subject. For example, in the mid-1950s P. E. Kauffman[38] and J. A. Starkweather[39] each conducted an experiment in which they used electronic filters to reduce the comprehensibility of the verbal content of recorded voice samples. Both of these experiments revealed that the tones and timbres of the human voice are able to communicate emotions independent of its linguistic content. Furthermore, in 1961 W. F. Soskin and Kauffman recorded a series of emotionally charged word samples taken from real life. They subjected these to electronic filtering to reduce the degree to which the verbal content could be recognised and played them to a group of listeners. The experiments concluded that 'voice sounds alone, independently of semantic components of vocal messages, carry important clues to the emotional state of the speaker'.[40]

The psychological experiments of the early twentieth century, such as those described above, have shown how the conclusion we draw about someone based upon their voice often has little to do with the person's actual personality and much more to do with a cultural stereotype. However, it is none the less by way of such stereotypical assumptions based upon the sound of our voice that people make partial assumptions about our character and upon which they make their decisions about how to treat us. To quote Patsy Rodenburg: 'As soon as we open our mouths and speak we are judged. Instant assumptions are made about us by others; about our intelligence, our background, class, race, our education, abilities and ultimately our power.'[41] Changing the way we speak tends to change the way we are received and much of the value of training in public speaking 'may be due as much to the change in the attitude of listeners' as to the change in the subjects themselves.[42]

There is a further and more crucial point regarding this aspect of the voice. The timbral qualities of the voice not only create images, stereotypical and inaccurate through they may be, in the 'mind's ear' of other people, they do the same thing in our own ears.

# Getting Stuck: The Voice and the Mask

The quality that gives a voice its unique character serves an important function in maintaining a sense of identity, for the sound of our voice reminds us of who we are; it affirms and reinforces our self-image. In the same way that our sense of identity is continually reaffirmed by the visual reflection provided by a mirror, so too the sound of our voice enables us to hear reflected an audible expression of our own image, our own sense of self.

However, as time passes we often become over-identified with a single image of ourselves. The self-image is revealed physically in our habitual body language: the way we walk, sit, turn, the way we eat, drink, indeed all of our kinetic activities; it is also revealed in the quality of our voice. This becomes particularly apparent when the make-up of a personality has been informed and affected by a more or less severe set of experiences. In such cases a person's thinking, feeling and behaviour, indeed their whole psyche, may come to be dominated and saturated with a particular emotional tone such as bitterness, defeat, anxiety, fear or rage, and all of these emotional tones find expression in the acoustic tones of the voice.

In addition, a person's psyche may become dominated by a single image of itself as a particular character. A person may become 'stuck' in a childlike image, in a dominating and bombastic image, in a kindly and self-effacing image – often because of an over-identification with a particularly influential person. These character images also find expression through the vocal tones.

Identification with such images can often be heard in the voices of young children, who while playing with their peers assume vocal tones and turns of phrase which are obviously a direct inheritance from their parents and which sound incongruous issuing from such young lips, making them appear grown up before their time.

Because the echo of the tones and timbres of our own voice in our own ears is so important in reaffirming our self-image, we become caught in a vicious circle whereby the bitterness or anxiety which we hear in our voice serves only to reinforce the image of ourselves as bitter or anxious, or whereby the childlikeness or aggressiveness which our voice conveys to us merely reinforces our idea of ourself as a child or an aggressor.

If our psyche becomes saturated with a single emotional tone, it may become difficult for us to communicate, and the voice can, without warning, simply let us down. We may wish to express a particular emotion or image, such as anger or authority; we may need to instil confidence or calm, but our voice has become so identified with a particular aspect of ourselves that it cannot move.

If we are so afflicted, this can cause us some distress; it is as though our voice has become a rigid mask which we are unable to remove. We feel mature but sound childlike; we feel enraged but sound intimidated; we feel saddened but sound unmoved; we seek help but our voice signals self-certainty; we seek warmth and affection but our voice signals guarded detachment; we seek respect but our voice attracts belittlement.

All these notions which so many people unwittingly and unwillingly communicate are contained not in the speech but in the voice. They have nothing to do with diction, dialect, precision or eloquence. They have everything to do with the phonational quality of the voice, the timbre, the music, the melody, the rhythm, the pitch and the substance of that which we call voice as distinct from speech. These emotions and moods, temperaments and characteristics which seem to come out of our mouths of their own accord, often contrary to that which we intend, are woven into the fabric of that part of the oral signals which would remain if you passed the spoken words through the electronic filter used in the experiments cited above. They exist in the voice.

The purpose of voice movement therapy, as with any effective voice work, is to create a vocal flexibility so that, in the terms of archetypal psychology, the speaker can visit and express those parts of the psyche which have hitherto remained under cover. As Rodenburg says: 'Can a bank manager, for instance, easily step outside his or her vocal personality to converse with a child or ticket collector? Can the housewife easily tackle or challenge the doctor? Can the parent express grief in front of the child? Can the teacher be vocally vulnerable in front of students?'[43]

Any effective voice work should enable a client to say 'yes' to these questions. However, the process, though it may have direct sociological effects, is in the first instance a psychological one. The ability to express grief or expose vulnerability often involves raising to the surface aspects of the psyche which have remained buried and permitting them to infiltrate the timbre of the voice. The consequent change in the client's self-image which is provoked by such a process demands of the vocal coach, singing teacher or voice worker a sensitivity and depth of insight capable of encouraging a development which can be both awesome and enlightening. If the new vocal timbre which enables the bank manager to converse with the ticket collector is built merely upon a rearrangement of personal affectations, then the same lack of genuineness is promoted as that which often leads to the stifling singularity of tone and timbre in the first place.

## *The Sensory Voice*

There is a certain muscularity to the voice which gives it a quality analogous to that of physical activity. Words can punch, poke, pierce and undercut; words can stroke, squeeze and envelop. Words can be made to caress, comfort and persuade or they can be uttered with a tone which belittles, condescends and manipulates. If the voice had no relation to physical intent, then Freud would not have been led to discover that words become a substitute for deeds.

When we listen to someone speak, we not only make a cognitive analysis of the linguistic meaning of the words uttered, we also engage in an intuitive interpretation of the physicality inherent in the timbre with which they are spoken. We feel pinched, slapped, compressed, pierced, hammered, stroked, tickled or shaken. The implied physical activity inherent in kinetic expression was investigated thoroughly by Rudolf von Laban, who divided basic human physical expressions into a series of fundamental kinetic actions.

The way that certain physical actions are implied in the manner in which words are spoken was consequently developed by Yat Malmgrem, founder of the movement psychology which has underpinned the teaching of actors at the Drama Centre, London, for many years, and with whom I studied during the late 1970s. That these actions categorised by Laban can also be applied to the singing voice has been explored by Ewan Macoll, one-time husband of and collaborator with Joan Littlewood and the Theatre Workshop.[44] The total effect of these strands of work when drawn together reminds us how the physicality inherent in the timbral qualities of a voice can reveal the subconscious intentions of the person to whom the voice belongs.

But the physicality of the voice is only one of its ideosensory dimensions. We also notice taste and colour in a voice. We say that someone sounds 'bitter' or 'sweet' or that they have an 'acid' tongue. We speak of someone having a 'blue' voice or sounding 'green' with envy. Temperature too is used to describe the quality of a voice. A voice can be warm, cool, red-hot or ice-cold. This process of borrowing a term which applies to one sense, such as sight or touch, and applying it to another, in this case hearing, is called 'synaesthesia'.

Synaesthesia is a key to the mysterious world of images. It is not an objective framework for analysis and therefore is considered by many clinicians to be a fill-in measure until a more objective terminology for voice quality can be established. However, in voice movement therapy it is a fundamental tool which is appropriate precisely because it avoids objective criteria.

People do not speak in images because, consciously or unconsciously, they lack empirical data. They do so because only the slippery, open-ended, metaphorical, multiple and pictorial, intuitive and artistic world of images can adequately represent the way in which the so-called objective world is perceived. And the qualities of the human voice also need to be perceived in terms of imagery in order to be represented fully. It is the control and command of this potential imagistic richness of vocal expression that so many people feel bereaved of.

Many people stake a great deal upon the images which they implicitly or explicitly transmit through the timbral qualities of their voice, a fact which may be attributable to their profession. Teachers, priests, barristers and politicians all rely on their voice as the primary medium by which their integrity is judged; and often the life of an individual, if not of a nation, depends upon its efficacy.

For others the significance of vocal use is a more personal affair. A person wishes to be taken more seriously, or less seriously; or she wants to be treated like a woman and not like a girl; or he wishes to be appreciated for his softer qualities, or for his more authoritative potential.

Whatever the reason, thousands upon thousands of people wish at times to be perceived altogether differently to the way in which they are normally viewed. And many of these people feel prevented from realising this desire due to the inflexibility of their voice.

But the voice is dynamic, not static. It is an instrument, a fluid and adaptable means of expression which responds to exercise in the same fashion as the body. It grows, develops, increases in malleability, fluidity, tone, resilience, pliability, and it can be nourished, educated, retrained and placed back in the hands of the person. This is the aim of voice movement therapy where speech is concerned.

## All Words and No Voice

We saw earlier that in the field of socio-linguistics – the study of the use of words in different situations – the efficient use of speech in order to achieve one's end in a variety of social contexts is referred to as 'communicative competence' (see p. 28). The arrogance and pomposity inherent in this statement is almost beyond belief. It implies that the ability to communicate is equivalent to the ability to speak, which is nonsense. If it were true, then it would mean that all those people to whom an extensive vocabulary is inaccessible – through lack of education, through physical or emotional restriction – would be classed as unable to communicate. It would mean that the more words you knew and the more adept you were at combining them, the better you would be at communicating.

The most verbally saturated people in society are often the ones who themselves complain of feeling vocally inept, inexpressive and misunderstood. Lawyers, sociologists, surgeons and many others whose professional training has equipped them with a vast, precise and intricate vocabulary are often none the less robotic and unmelodic, passionless and unemotive in their speech. The more scientifically orientated one is, the less one's voice uses the affective undulation of music; the facts speak for themselves. Artists, on the other hand, without the support of empirical data to justify their pursuits, are often those who are accused of filling their speech with an excess of emotion.

There is more vocal expression in the non-verbal rantings of a patient with severe brain damage than in the dry semantic manipulations of the philosophy graduate. If those privileged with verbal proficiency had been forced to learn as much from such patients as those patients are forced to learn from the speech-orientated population, perhaps more people would have a conviction of voice to match their sophistication of speech.

This is not to glorify a helpless predicament. Speech therapists spend hour upon hour patiently teaching non-verbal patients to gain control of the speech apparatus, not because of an arrogant belief in the essential dominance of language, but because the acquisition of speech empowers the patient in a world where, whether we like it or not, what you say is what you are.

But we must not forget that, in the history of humankind, language is a relatively new phenomenon, and it would be foolish to claim that meaning did not exist before language. As Peter Brook, Jerzy Grotowski, Enrique Pardo and others have actively proved, there is meaning at the level of phonation, in a grunt, in a sigh, in a sob, in a call.

When we enter the commonroom of a special-education day centre, or when we echo the spontaneous gibberish of a baby, we respond not to the pronunciation of phonemes, morphemes or words, but to the meaning inherent in the phatic, non-discursive phonational quality. When we go to the opera, or to a jazz concert or to hear a great singer, we are moved as much or more by the affective and creative element which radiates from the extended phonation on open vowels than by the lyrics themselves. In fact, in much modern music, you can hardly hear the lyrics, and when you can it is usually something fairly banal. What reaches the audience is not the linguistic sophistication, but the phonational depth of affect.

## Singing Your Way to Better Speech

Great singers of any genre communicate to an audience because they focus wholeheartedly on the way they utter the words. They are vocalists, not verbalists. The same song can be sung by a number of different singers, without a single word or syllable changed, and can be transformed from a trite and ineffectual ditty to a symphonic stirring of the soul.

It is this same vocal art that distinguishes the speaker who moves, provokes and communicates from the one who rattles on and on without effect. A great vocalist can sell a fridge to an Eskimo with fewer words than a three-year-old. Yet a bad vocalist finds it hard to get into Parliament with all the desirable politics in the world.

If our educational system were to be as encouraging and facilitating towards the art of voice as it is towards the acquisition of verbal proficiency, perhaps those less scientifically minded would stand a better chance. Unfortunately, the equation between verbal competence and communicative proficiency still holds. It is perhaps a political aspect of voice movement therapy that it seeks to oppose this equation.

Voice movement therapy is not concerned with enhancing social prowess through extending spoken vocabulary. It is concerned with reinstating the belief that, regardless of the words one uses or the accent with which one speaks, an intended integrity of image can shine through. It is concerned with enabling all people to connect words to the psyche which uses them. It seeks to ensure that the truth comes out, that language is not only spoken but is expressed, with conviction, with emotion, with music. It is concerned with training vocalists. As Kristin Linklater has said, the voice should reveal, not describe, inner impulses of emotion and thought.[45]

Voice movement therapy is not concerned with polishing and perfecting an eloquence of elocution; there are many teachers who can offer this service. It is concerned, rather, with nurturing an eloquence of image, of conviction, of sincerity, of depth, of emotion, of mood and of intent. It does not aim to give someone a 'posh accent' or enhance so-called 'received pronunciation'. It does not 'get rid of' a rich regional accent and replace it with one which cultural prejudice has associated with more intelligence. Voice movement therapy's approach to speech is unmoral and unprejudiced.

A spoken accent or dialect is more than a conditioned use of mouth and lips with greater or lesser decipherability; it is a manifestation of an intricate network of historical, social, aesthetic and cultural dimensions. Nobody committed to a belief in the psychological significance of cultural identity can ignore the importance of maintaining those particular vocal qualities which we associate with Paris or with Berlin, with New York or with Kansas, with Dundee or with Belfast.

Drawing out and working with the images inherent in a dialect is a means of investigating the psychological connection with the culture of which the dialect is a part. However, the further aim of any authentic voice work where speech is concerned is to ensure that the mechanical operation of these dialects support and do not obstruct the psychological operation of meanings which the speaker seeks to convey.

Winston Churchill and Martin Luther King were not great orators because they had mastered the art of elocution, but because they were able to impregnate their unique acoustic cadences with musicality and with conviction. Such conviction is, in the final analysis, a psychological concept, originating from the reservoir of beliefs and passions, instincts and motivations which are capable of moving people to words and actions of tremendous magnitude. It is not only the abominable but so-called requisite acts of war, such as those Churchill spoke of, or the deplorable disasters of so-called democracy, such as those of which Luther King spoke, that can generate a depth of vocal conviction in the speaker. There are notions which we all hold close to our heart, and the voice cannot be mobilised to express eloquence or conviction without first discovering what these notions are in each person.

It is not the job of voice movement therapy to train someone to speak convincingly about the advantages of a new vacuum cleaner. Instead it is the intent of voice movement therapy to unearth and reveal the deeper strata of a person's beliefs so that they may find expression through the timbre and melody of vocal sound.

This process necessitates a deliberate blurring of the boundaries between speaking and singing. And those who view these acts as unrelated should think again. Many of those singers who have been the object of awe and admiration have been able to use their voice in such a way that it is very difficult to draw the line between the two. Listen to the way Marlene Dietrich vocalises and you will see how difficult it is to say exactly what her singing technique is: it appears to hover mid-way between song and speech. The sound is effortless and unadorned; all her work is internal. The same effortless process can be observed at work in the recordings of Frank Sinatra and Bing Crosby, as well as in those of many music-hall artistes. They all sound as though they are at home with their feet up.

To discover the melodic potential of a voice requires a degree of muscular relaxation and a depth of inner contemplation for which the competitive hubbub of daily conversation rarely makes provision. Voice work relieves the client of the pressures of the social arena and invites the exposure of those tones which belie a person's passions. And when clients discover how to voice these passions, it is as though they have achieved a new status in which they can genuinely believe in what they say and therefore in themselves. No voice work could desire more than this.

# CHAPTER EIGHT

# Case Studies

In the following case histories, names and locations have been changed to preserve confidentiality.

## *Mental Handicap, My Foot!*

Jonathan Staves was mentally handicapped. After thirty years in a residential home, who wouldn't be?

In the commonroom of a residential centre for adults with a mental handicap, thirty-seven men and women, ranging in age from twenty-two to sixty-one, gathered obediently in a circle, all seated upon grey chairs from which they were accustomed to eat their dinner, watch television or paint pictures. This time they sat waiting for a voice workshop.

Jonathan sat among his peers: thirty-eight years old, deep-green piercing eyes, gigantic teeth and hands like plates. Jonathan had been classified 'non-verbal'; he had spent some time with a speech therapist when in his early twenties, but to no avail. Though he was non-verbal he was certainly highly vocal; his voice sporadically emitted a stream of guttural sounds accompanied by an undulating and wave-like dance with his arms, as though he was saying goodbye to a departing loved one, knowing he would never see her again.

Jonathan had been abandoned at the age of six; his parents were still alive but had not visited him for twenty-three years. The staff at the centre kept him fed, kept him warm and kept him from danger; they were unconcerned about the noises he made – these were neither considered to be a nuisance nor were they subjected to interpretation. They were thought to be harmless but meaningless.

I was once travelling in Turkey during the festival of Ramadam. It was a hot and dusty evening and the town was deserted. As I turned a corner to buy some water, I heard a sound which grabbed my attention: a moaning, pleading, yearning sound which had a pump-like pulse to it. I could not understand the words uttered, and I do not know even if they were words. The sound was neither despairing nor euphoric; it was neither melodic nor was it lacking in musical form; it was, in essence, spiritual.

I retraced my steps a little way and, with some audacity, peered in through a hole in the blinds of a small house, where I saw a man kneeling with tears in his eyes and beads in his hands. I looked only for a moment; then I turned and listened once more. At this point my entire interpretative faculties went into overdrive in an attempt to classify and comprehend this sound.

Was he crying? Was he singing? Was he praying? And the movements I saw him make with his arms – were they the spontaneous expression of un-controllable grief? Or were they the orderly gestural accompaniment of worship? I could not answer any of these questions, but could only imagine that the ambiguity and unclassifiability of his voice-dance was somehow an important part of why it moved me so much.

Returning to the centre for mentally handicapped adults, each member of the group was asked to call out a sound which the whole group then called back. When it came to Jonathan's turn, something happened that caused me to experience a deep sense of awe. He called out a sound which I had not heard since the time I had stood on that hot dusty street corner in Turkey; and I thought only one thing. If we had taken Jonathan to Turkey and placed him in a room with blinds on the windows and asked him to call out his sound, passers-by may have asked all kinds of questions. Is he praying? Is he chanting? Is he singing? But they would not for a moment have thought to ask: Is he handicapped?

Jonathan's sound was not that of a handicapped person. It was full of re-ligiosity, yearning, needing, pleading and worship. It was also full of music. However, because the linguistic content of Jonathan's day-to-day acoustic emissions were not understandable, 'the baby had been thrown out with the bath water' and his entire vocal faculty had been disqualified and ren-dered insignificant.

In most parts of Europe singing teachers teach with what they consider to be the indispensable aid of the piano; any vocal sounds made by the stu-dent which do not correspond to the black or the white notes are con-sidered unmusical. Western classical music is black and white. It only takes fifteen minutes in Turkey, Egypt, Argentina, India or Bali to discover how limited this view of music is. In those countries, whose musical traditions have been unaffected by the black-and-white philosophy, they bend notes in continual defiance of a single pitch.

This is one of the qualities which Jonathan's voice had in common with the man I had heard in Turkey. Jonathan's sounds were not black and white; neither were they meaningless.

I asked Jonathan to wheel himself into the centre of the circle and I told him that I wanted to work with him for a little while. I had been studying and experimenting with various non-Western forms of singing for some time and I began to employ some of what I had learnt. I began by singing very quietly in such a way as to create the mood and image of a Mohamme-dan prayer. I asked Jonathan to sing with me and to develop the move-ments of his arms into a dance of praying, while bending down from the waist in his wheelchair as though kneeling. The group looked on, amazed, as he composed a voice-dance of exquisite authenticity.

It was clear that the wheelchair was restricting him and preventing fluid and liberated physical expression of the images which Jonathan spontaneously yielded. So we helped him out of the chair and into a comfortable kneeling position on the floor. I knelt behind him and held him around the waist with my cheek resting in the small of his back. Together we arose and descended as though in prayer and chanted together in an improvisation of wavering and undulating notes which turned the commonroom into a sacred space, a temple, a mosque, a synagogue, a church.

After some time, Jonathan became quite excited and enthused by the process, and he expressed this vocally in spasmodic little peeping noises in a falsetto register. I began to mirror these sounds until our musical improvisation gradually transformed into a rhythmical and semi-operatic melody with a xylophone-type quality. In order to ease out the falsetto sounds, I massaged and patted his back, and eventually I was playing his body like a drum. Each time I struck a part of his back, a clear note would emerge.

These notes became stronger, clearer and longer as time went on, and it finally became apparent that not only did Jonathan have an awe-inspiring capacity to work in lower pitches, but he also had a wonderful upper range, akin to a choirboy's.

After the workshop the staff came to thank me before my departure, and all of them asked how I had managed to 'get that out of Jonathan'. This is the kind of question I am asked time and time again.

In order to communicate with someone, you have to speak their language, you have to understand the rules of the game; certain sounds have to be equated with the same things in the minds of both parties. But there is more to this sharing of sounds than mere words. There is the music of the voice. There are sounds which have the same meaning the world over; otherwise how would we know when a foreigner was in pain and how would a mother communicate with her baby and understand its needs?

In order to communicate with non-verbal people, you have to be able to use a non-verbal language. Unfortunately, like many adults, the staff of centres such as the one Jonathan was in were more vocally handicapped than those in their care. When the staff join in the voice workshops at such centres, it is always a significant moment when it comes to their turn to call out a sound; they are invariably far more tentative, embarrassed and constricted than the clients. The sounds of the type uttered by Jonathan are meaningless to them because they do not share his language. But my ability to 'get something out of him' is not a special talent. I can enable Jonathan to work creatively and meaningfully with his voice because I can sing with Jonathan, emulate his sounds genuinely, without constriction and without inhibition, and I can do this only as a result of continual practical work. Such training takes time and commitment. But for this investment we reap the reward of seeing some of the most disenfranchised people invited into the conversational circle of the privileged. Only then do we realise that words can put us to shame.

# The Case of an Eternal Mother

Mary Cook was fifty-two when she first came to work on her voice; she was fifty-four when she left. In that time she underwent a transformation that is both important and rewarding to recount because her case is similar to so many others and may therefore act as a source of encouragement.

Mary Cook had not had the opportunity for formal education beyond her late teens, despite a deep interest and aptitude for the sciences. When she was eighteen, her mother died and she was forced to look after her younger sister. During this period of surrogate motherhood she met and later married a man eight years her senior, to whom she was still married at the time of our meeting.

At twenty-three Mary had her first child, at twenty-five her second and at thirty her third. She had enjoyed motherhood and maintained a close and confident relationship with her children. However, when all her children had left home, she felt completely at a loss.

It is very common for one particular role in life to become so firmly established that it takes us over and pushes out all the other potential roles we once might have played. This is particularly reinforced when the role or 'sub-personality' emanates from an archetypal base, in which case it may take such a firm hold over us that we become stuck, and as a result our life becomes so narrowly identified with a single element that we feel we have shrunk, that we are not presented with the possibilities that we once had, nor do we possess the verve and enthusiasm for change. The 'mother' is a prime example of such an archetypally based role.

The mother cannot be a mother without her children. Thus, when her offspring have grown up and left home, she is thrown back on herself. Those with whom she identified herself have gone; there is no one to mother, and if there are not other focal points to her life, if she cannot ease into another role which gives her equal satisfaction to that of the mother, she will now try to hang on to her children.

The problem is that the mother is such a strong and instinctive, primal and all-enveloping role to play that a woman often gets consumed by the part, a situation made worse by the fact that the grand drama of mother-hood has such a long tour – eighteen years or more. Those apron strings become stronger with time and there is a need for a repeat performance of that umbilical severing that took place at birth. This is what had happened to Mrs Cook: suddenly she found herself stuck in the role of the mother with no children to perform for.

Mary Cook had always wanted to sing but had been positively discour-aged by her husband and her children due to her sounding 'out of tune'. However, it is only possible to be out of tune in relation to something other people recognise; sound cannot be innately untuneful. Indeed, the only per-son Mary Cook was out of tune with was herself, or perhaps I should say her selves.

Her voice was predominantly chest-based and exhibited an uneven use of free air, alternating between a soft and maternal flavour and a metallic and almost aggressive one. She had no difficulty in shifting this quality into the stomach placement, producing a blues sound that had warmth and a tone with a very broody and introverted quality about it. However, the voice flatly refused to break into the head placement and this meant that a whole range of emotional characteristics and figurative images were absent.

I asked Mary to try to imbue her voice with particular images which I knew from experience usually stimulate the violin voice, such as that of the child. However, this was to no avail. When we discussed her difficulty in finding the child's voice, it became apparent that Mary felt that her child-hood had been taken from her and that she had been untimely and pre-maturely propelled into adulthood by the death of her mother, upon which she was forced to assume adult duties before her time. Buried deep beneath Mary's brave face of 'having come to terms with this' was an anger and a bitterness which she had put out of sight.

In a later session, after considerable analysis of the effect of her lost youth, I gave her the image of spiteful resentment and asked her to sing the highest note of her comfortable range with such a tone. When she did this, the sound broke into the head placement and there emerged a voice more intense and emotive than I had heard her sing before. During this time I gradually began to suggest images which contained a quality of spiteful re-taliation and triumphant revenge.

Over the next twenty minutes Mary Cook composed her voice into an extravagant dance, rushing like a tornado up and down the scale of the piano, singing a whole network of images associated with spite and re-sentment. She became a hot-blooded Amazon wading at top-speed through swamp and mire, brandishing spear and shield, bellowing out the cries of war. She became a great jungle cat, injured by the poacher's bullet, prow-ling with intent to ravage and consume her human prey, shrieking out her feline meow. Her voice became venomous and toxic, as if she sang with arsenic and with strychnine, and there emerged the character of a calm, col-lective torturer with an acidic voice which burns and bleaches with every note. She sang like a viper, like an asp.

Contact with this voice involves recognition of that part of the psyche that coldly contemplates destruction of something or someone, and it is one of the most difficult things to recognise in oneself. It is the witch in the tale of Hansel and Gretel or the child who picks the wings from living in-sects; it is the great tormentor.

The capacity to inflict torment, though it is something we should like to ignore, is none the less a human attribute with which we have been lum-bered, and if the energy associated with it is not given a positive creative outlet, it will surely rear its head in some destructive form or another. To release sounds of the tormentor is to give vent to something that otherwise will go on smouldering in the psyche, plaguing our dreams and our fantasies.

In the course of releasing the amalgam of images derived from her repressed resentment, Mary's voice had become louder, more passionate and fully embodied; but it had also become very aggressive. Because this aggressiveness drowned out the subtlety of the vindictive, sadistic element – which was obviously an important but repressed emotion in her – I asked her to decrease the loudness and make the spite more conniving and ensnaring, like a spider slowly and cautiously spinning a web of death, rather than a scorpion quickly and impulsively injecting the poison. The images of insects increased both the quality of spite and the intensity and strength of the voice. Now, as we worked, a fresh network of images unfolded in the voice, building up a picture of premeditated revenge against an oppressor in which she became a character, half insect, half human, with a fatal sting that could inflict a slow, painful death. Gradually these emotions and images 'played themselves out' and we were left with a voice nearly one and a half octaves higher than that with which we had started. When the spite was expended, the voice sounded calm, strong and generous and Mary was now able to vocalise the child when singing in the head placement. So the next time we worked together, we broke into the violin voice with comparative ease and explored sounds associated with childhood. Her voice gurgled and effervesced with innocence and naïveté; she sang with the freshness and purity of a child untouched by trauma, and as she sang, Mary Cook's face took on an open and inquisitive smile which I had not seen before.

Over the next period of our work together Mary integrated the use of head placement into her sound-making, and as a result her voice took on an added dimension which was capable of going in the direction of both innocence and revenge. During our analysis of the work Mary spoke of her memories of the role of surrogate mother which she had played to her sister and which had come back to her during the voice work. She felt that somewhere deep inside herself she had a deep and unexpressed resentment, not only towards her mother for dying, but also towards her sister for requiring care.

Her sister had always accused her of being spiteful and she had in fact been quite malicious during her own childhood. She told me of a recurring day-dream in which she tried to slowly poison her sister in order to release herself from the burden of care-giving. Similarly, during the mothering of her own children, she often experienced moments of spite towards them, feeling that they kept her from 'living her own life'. However, May had repressed all this because it was negative and destructive and because she knew also that without her children she would not really have a role to play.

Mary Cook's avoidance of the head placement in her speaking voice may well have been an unconscious attempt to keep this spite hidden. Only when asked to vocalise the spite, thereby using the head placement, did it unleash itself along with all the emotional energy bottled up with it.

As a by-product, Mrs Cook was left with a most powerful singing voice in the head range which she went on to develop, gradually softening its hardness with a little free air and singing in what turned out to be one of her many vocal characters, roles or sub-personalities.

# To Stay Forever Young

In Mrs Cook's case the child was an important archetype that was missing from her vocal spectrum and therefore from her immediate psychological field of vision. In the case of Sally Woods the reverse was true: her voice had become stuck in the timbre of a child and as a result the image of her personality which she communicated to others and to herself was a child-like one.

Up to the age of ten Sally Woods had led a so-called normal childhood, and suffered no accidents or severe illnesses, had shown no signs of psychological or emotional difficulties and had progressed in her education at a level average for her age. Then, shortly after her tenth birthday on a Sunday morning in spring, Sally walked straight into a stone pillar at her local church, where she had attended service with her mother. This trifling accident did not cause Sally anything more serious than a bruised forehead, but it marked the beginning of a number of similar collisions.

Over the next few years Sally bumped into objects with increasing frequency as though she had not noticed that they were there. In addition, she found that when indoors, particularly in poorly lit places, her vision was somewhat impaired and at school she had to strain to see to read and write. Sally Woods was going blind.

The doctors whom Sally visited were unable to provide any definitive diagnosis for this slow deterioration of her eyesight but told her that she should be prepared for an eventual total loss of vision. Sally later discovered that she had a form of retinitus pigmentosa.

When Sally became adolescent, she noticed that, unlike the other girls with whom she mixed, she was not developing breasts, neither was she menstruating. Sally needed to talk to someone about this but was isolated by the fact that neither her mother nor her father would voice their feelings, but instead tended to keep things 'brushed under the carpet'. The subject of Sally's blindness was hardly ever mentioned and her parents attempted to pretend that everything was 'normal'. When Sally finally approached her mother on the subject of her hormonal development, her mother briefly said that she should not worry, and that many girls were 'late developers'. However, when Sally turned sixteen, she still had not developed any breasts, and nor was she menstruating, and so they approached the doctor with a fresh problem.

Sally's mother had accompanied her to all her doctor's appointments and Sally had often sat without speaking, while the doctor spoke to Mrs Woods about her daughter, as though Sally was a 'vegetable'. The doctor now told Mrs Woods that the visual impairment and the hormonal problem were probably related and there followed several months of hospital tests. In addition to these problems, Sally had stopped growing in height after the age of fourteen and she remained therefore only 4 ft 8 in tall.

Eventually Sally was given drugs to encourage the growth of her breasts and to increase her height by several inches; but nothing has been done to bring on her menstruation.

After she had left school, Sally's father persuaded a friend to give Sally a job in a supermarket; he also opened for Sally a bank account in his name and took charge of all her finances. He was very protective towards her and both he and Sally's mother discouraged her from pursuing any social life for fear she would be ridiculed or shamed.

By the time Sally was nineteen she was completely blind. One evening her boss at the supermarket went behind her back to see her parents and to establish the fact that Sally would have to leave the job.

Sally was thirty-four when she came to work on her voice and had not worked since she was nineteen. I am normally very reticent about making a vocal analysis based on someone's speaking voice; it is not until you take the lid off and listen to the voice in its full non-verbal capacity that you can really hear what is going on, what is missing and what emotions dominate. However, Sally was an exception. When she spoke, the voice which emerged sounded like that of a twelve-year-old. It was light, wispy, without strength or weight and with timbres which we associate with a child who cannot get her own way.

When Sally came to sing and enter into the process of extended sound-making, her voice was confined to an exceedingly high pitch-range equivalent to the top half of the piano keyboard. It was capable of two main characteristics: a high-powered piercing scream, which soared right off the end of the piano at a height which only the occasional soprano has reached, and a childlike, soft and timid quality which wavered nervously as though she was out of breath. There was no 'bottom' to her voice, in two senses: there was no abdominal placement and there were no deep tones, as though Sally had no depth or maturity, no stability or wisdom; as though, in short, she were still a child – angry, frustrated and hurt.

A childlike voice often represents a psychological regression or return to childhood. In cases where childhood has been a happy time in which the parents nurtured and encouraged the child's expressive faculties, this regression is usually based on a deep-set desire to return to this glorious infancy when mother or father were there to listen and respond to every need. In such cases this regression is often precipitated by a feeling of not being heard as an adult and is a retreat from the competitive nature of 'grown-up' vocalisation or from the situation in which one's voice is not valued by husband, friends or children.

In cases where expression has not been nurtured in youth but has rather been thwarted and stifled, the childlike voice may derive from the process of being psychologically propelled back to childhood by the recurrence of an event or series of events which revive the memory of this insensitivity; as though childhood has been thrust upon the person once again. In both types of case the first thing to look at is the degree to which the person's present life-situation affords her the space to express herself.

In Sally's case a combination of both of these 'reasons for regression' were at work. On the one hand, her childhood had been a temptingly protective and satisfying time, where her every need had been taken care of by parents who were scared to let Sally take upon herself the tasks befitting her age lest she should get hurt. But on the other hand, she now recalled her childhood with a frustrated sense of irritation, recognising the fact that her parents had further contributed to the 'stunting of her growth' by their mollycoddling.

Unable to promote her self-image using the props available to a sighted person, such as different clothes and hair-styles, Sally relied upon the sound of her own voice to create an impression of who she was. But, because her voice was so steeped in childlike elements, her image of herself as a child had proved to be impossible to eliminate. And this is where our work began.

The first stage involved giving these two 'children', manifested in the two voices – one soft and hurt, the other wild and screaming – a chance to have their say, just as Mrs Cook had to play out her spite. Although Sally was small physically, the volume of the sounds which she produced would have led a listener to believe she was gigantic. However, this was also a problem. She found it very difficult to moderate both the volume and the intensity of affect contained in her voice, as though so much retaliatory impetus had been accumulated that, when given an opportunity for expression, it tended to burst forth without moderation. Sally believed this reflected her tendency to oscillate between being silent, ineffectual, polite and subservient to being overly emotional, vehement, irate and accusatory. These swings in mood seemed to have been a feature of her childhood, during which a general meek obedience towards her parents' over-protective attitude would be periodically perforated by 'temper tantrums', 'irritable fits' and bouts of 'wild screaming'.

In my work with Sally I began to bring the volume and intensity of affect into a lower pitch range and a lower placement, asking her to deepen the notes and imagine their resonation to occur in the womb. Because of her lack of menstruation, Sally felt she was not a 'real woman'. This, together with her problems in developing breasts and her general sense of impairment, meant that ideokinetic work centring on the womb was not immediately accessible or easy for Sally. But we continued to push for a sound of rounded depth, and eventually a whole new voice emerged, like a creature from the swamp.

This lower voice had a primitive, animality about it, combined with an audacity and confidence which exuded an inner certainty. Sally described it 'as though something has burst open and all the muck has come out'. This voice did not serve to soften or modify the huge degree of affect which was contained in the upper notes, but by placing the emotions in a deeper range and in a deeper placement, they began to sound more mature; more like a woman demanding her rights than a child pleading for attention.

The next stage of the therapy would be how to maintain access to this voice, how to allow it to infiltrate the phonational quality of her speaking voice.

Sally now works in her first full-time job since the days of the supermarket. She also attends psychotherapy sessions. We continue to work together, striving to awaken the 'swamp' voice on a regular basis, until it becomes a permanent feature of the overt personality.

# A Case of Stammering

Martin Coburn was thirty-six; he was married with two children and had driven a taxi for twelve years. He found it difficult to remember exactly when he developed a stammer, but he felt that it was around the age of eight. His stammer was irregular and vowels were equally affected as consonants. The most striking thing about Martin Coburn's speech-pattern was the involuntary jerking movements of his head and neck which accompanied vocalisation and which were particularly exaggerated during his stammering. His eyes closed, the head tilted backwards and to one side, the neck stiffened and his facial muscles contorted. His head would then jerk rhythmically and spasmodically for the duration of the stammered sound. The look upon his face during such episodes was one of tremendous fear.

Martin could not locate any single incident in his life which he could describe as severely traumatic. However, he spoke about his relationship to his father as having been a source of continuous trauma.

Mr Coburn senior was a professor of chemistry and his other two sons were both doctors. It had been clear from quite an early age that Martin was not going to reveal the same predisposition to academic activity as the rest of his family. Martin had been the brunt of jokes made by his peers at school and by his brothers at home, who called him 'bunny' because he had an involuntary twitch in his cheek.

Though Martin could not locate any single traumatic event, it became obvious over the period of our work together that his entire childhood had been a very unhappy one. Not only did he grow up in the shadow of his brothers' achievements, but he also had a mother who showed him little attention and no physical affection. He could not remember ever being held or cuddled or kissed by her; furthermore, he never saw his parents hold hands or show any physical signs of love to one another. The picture of his family life that emerged was an incredibly impotent one. Dry academic conversations, competitive brothers, meals at regular times often with guests who would parade their expert intellectual preoccupations, and a mother maintaining a cool and distant relationship with her sons and her husband.

When, in the first session, I had asked Martin if he had any other illnesses or difficulties apart from his stammer, he said that he had for many years suffered periodically from extreme headaches. He dealt with them by taking a variety of painkillers but these rarely alleviated the pain. On investigating further the genesis of these headaches, it was revealed that they worsened during times of extended verbal activity; the more he stammered, the more his head ached.

Martin liked his job as a taxi driver because 'on a bad day' he could 'get away' without talking to anyone – 'I just ask for the fare'. However, on a good day he would enjoy chatting to his customers and was frustrated intensely because he felt the stammer was preventing him from partaking in the social activities which he enjoyed. When asked to describe how he thought people perceived him when he stammered, Martin was adamant that he appeared stupid, or, to use his words, 'daft', 'idiotic', a 'moron' and a 'dim-wit'.

It emerged gradually that Martin had associated verbal proficiency with intelligence. The fact that he had not lived up to the academic standing of his father and brothers had made him feel stupid and his stammer further compounded this feeling and in many ways became a symbol for it.

It was also clear that Martin wanted sympathy for his condition, and indeed he responded very eagerly to a sympathetic attitude. In this respect he had very clear memories of his grandmother who had been an important figure in his life as a child and a single source of comfort, understanding and physical affection. She had also been very sympathetic about his stammer. Martin was prepared to admit that the onset of his stammer in childhood may have been, in part, a way of reaping affection and sympathy, and of excusing himself for his lack of academic achievement.

Despite our lengthy and in-depth analysis of the psychological implications of his stammer, it was clear from the early sessions that he was not going to recover fluent speech through psychotherapeutic analysis alone. His muscular activity needed retraining.

Martin's respiratory pattern was one which utilised thoracic expansion almost to the total exclusion of any abdominal movement. He breathed in short, sharp gasps and had a habit of drawing in breath through his teeth as though he had just witnessed something horrific. He said that he had acquired this habit from his mother.

Our physical work consisted first in retraining the respiratory musculature to utilise relaxed abdominal expansion. In addition, we slowly began to relieve the spasmodic movements which accompanied his stammer by using massage, manipulation and guided movement of the head, neck and upper back. After several weeks of this work, his headaches were relieved.

This physical work was integrated with a process of continual phonation on open vowels while opening and closing the lips to produce the following sounds: ma ma ma, me me me, moo moo moo, mi mi mi, moy moy moy, mow mow mow.

During this process we discovered that Martin had a beautiful bass voice and that he could sing the most complex linguistic phrases with complete fluency, not stammering on a single sound. While he sang, stammer-free, I continued to work physically with him and we gradually progressed to a chant-like form of vocalisation, mid-way between speaking and singing. Again this was completely free of any stammer. We slowly and methodically worked towards speaking, as though retracing the steps of childhood from the non-verbal state towards the acquisition of language. We succeeded in eradicating the stammer and the muscular spasms.

Most people who stammer can, like Martin, sing and chant with complete fluency. Learning to speak without stammering was successful in Martin's case because he committed himself to the process wholeheartedly and was prepared to view the curing of this stammer as part of a psychological retraining. Whether the same process can work for everyone is impossible to say.

## And the Loudest Voice Wins

Of the multitude of complaints with which patients attend the voice clinic one of the most frequent is aphonia or loss of voice. Of these cases very few indeed are seen to have any organic cause; both the vocal cords and the surrounding tissues are in a remarkable state of health, respiratory activity is normal and the patient exhibits no other signs of illness or dysfunction. Of all the cases of psychosomatic aphonia nearly 90 per cent are women.

There is another complaint which may be compared with psychosomatic aphonia; this is psychosomatic deafness. In psychosomatic deafness there is often a process of 'selective hearing' at work, by which the mind turns a 'deaf ear' to anything that belongs to a dominant complex; the patient simply doesn't hear words of phrases which provoke the memory of certain traumas or which revive the negative emotions associated with them. This unconscious selectivity can also occur as a vocal phenomenon, by which the voice is paralysed only in circumstances which are linked to negative memories and emotions. It is not uncommon for someone to lose his or her voice in response to a major traumatic experience, and in severe cases of psychosomatic recurrence the voice is repeatedly lost for an indefinite period whenever this person is disturbed by something which revives the affect of the original trauma. The voice becomes a physical expression of fear and retreat, and this is an extreme example of the common experience we all have of not being able to 'get our voices out' in the face of an impending catastrophe or nerve-wracking situation. Again we are reminded that so-called illness is only an exaggerated amount of 'dis-ease' which we all experience as part of our healthy life.

Aphonia is also often the only means a person has of declaring that she doesn't want to express herself, just as hysterical deafness means that the person doesn't want to hear; and in this respect aphonia is overtly 'feminine' in that its strength rests on passive rejection rather than aggressive expression. Aphonia represents the ultimate silence, and it frequently contains the only form of protest available to those who can withstand no more oppression. Often, then, the cause for the aphonic disturbance lies in the past or present suppression of the person's expressive rights.

Voice is a political phenomenon; it is the means by which a person expresses her rights; it claims her right to make a contribution to the way of things. In the nineteenth century, when Parliament came to put a vote to the people, it was called 'putting it to the voices', and 'voice' has ever since been used as a metaphorical description of political right. To suppress a person's voice is thus indicative of removing her rights, and to withdraw from using one's own voice is sometimes the only way one can continue to make a point in the face of such oppression.

Total loss of voice is one end of a spectrum of aphonic disorders, in the same way that the sense of hearing can vary from total loss to a minor reduction in volume. The partially aphonic voice is extremely quiet and barely audible; while it contains all the normal vocal expressive elements, it is weak and has a lot of free air.

Katherine Lane came to me suffering from an almost total aphonia which had persisted for nearly five weeks. She had lost her voice during a bout of influenza but had not regained it after all the other symptoms had subsided. The laryngologist had found nothing wrong with its organic functioning.

The most unusual thing about this case is that Mrs Lane's husband accompanied her to the first, the second and the third consultation. He appeared supportive, friendly, interested in the process as though genuinely concerned for his wife and eager for her health to be restored.

Katherine Lane admitted in the first five minutes to feeling a bit embarrassed by the fact there was nothing actually wrong with her voice and yet couldn't believe that it was all in her mind. She had a voice that was like grit or gravel, very quiet but just audible enough to hear each word when combined with watching her lip movements and hand gestures. There appeared to be no excessive muscular tension in her neck or upper back and her respiratory capacity was unhindered, though she did display a marked tendency to gasp inwards suddenly at periodic intervals.

She made repeated references to her husband during our work and was particularly concerned about 'wasting his time'. Whenever I suggested that she came alone, she would say, 'It's all right', or else she would explain that she could not drive. Neither of these reasons were in fact adequate because it wasn't 'all right' and there was an abundance of public transport to and from her home.

On the fourth consultation she did come alone as her husband was away working. By this time, however, her voice had almost fully re-emerged, not as a result of our work but of its own accord. When asked if this had ever happened before, she explained that this was at least the tenth occasion when her voice had vanished for a period and then returned suddenly and that she had only gone to the doctor on this occasion because she was worried that the added complication of the influenza might have caused a permanent loss.

The fact that Katherine was not accompanied by her husband on this occasion gave us the opportunity to speak intimately about her life, which she did with a tone that belied a gratitude for the fact that there was someone to talk to.

It emerged that Katherine Lane was deeply unhappy and felt suffocated by a marriage that was totally unfulfilling and without love. Her husband, though not physically violent, was an ill-tempered man and was completely uninterested in holding any sort of prolonged conversation with her. He expected from her the duties more appropriate to a Victorian servant than a wife of any era. Katherine had been forbidden to take a job, which not only stifled her mental faculties, but also meant that she had no money to spend on herself. Mr Lane provided what he called 'housekeeping' money on a weekly basis and the amount was barely enough for the provisions he expected her to buy. If there was ever the need for a larger, one-off purchase, they would always go together and he would pay for it by cheque.

Mr Lane often worked away from home and during these periods Katherine was at her happiest. She called these times her 'private holidays at home', during which she would arrange for her sister to visit, with whom she would speak about old times. Her sister refused to come when Mr Lane was at home.

When I asked her questions relating to my suspicion of a connection between the oppressive presence of her husband and her aphonic disorder, it emerged that in fact she had never experienced a loss of voice while her husband was away. When we went deeper into this, it further emerged that Katherine was almost leading two lives, one during her husband's absence and another when he was back home. She admitted that his presence stifled her and prevented any of her real character from 'coming through'. He kept her in a kind of prison which relied upon her lack of financial resources for its continued effect.

Katherine was always being encouraged to consider divorce by her sister but was extremely anxious about how she would survive on her own. As this session grew to a close, Katherine asked what we should do next time, when her husband was sure to be present, thus preventing us from furthering our discussion. The thought of her husband ever understanding or accepting his role in the genesis of her aphonia was to her utterly inconceivable.

We decided to discontinue our work temporarily and deliberately arranged a session when her husband was next away. By this time her aphonia had reappeared and she complained of being more aware of the effect of her husband's presence on her general physical well-being. She was somewhat disturbed.

Eventually Katherine gathered the courage to leave Mr Lane and she went to live with her sister. She then began to see me regularly, during which time we did work practically on the voice and also spoke together about how to reshape her life. Katherine Lane did not suffer from aphonia again.

Katherine Lane's case is one of the simplest and purest examples of social and psychological factors being the direct cause of a vocal problem. In this instance no practical work on the voice would have altered the circumstances which caused the disorder. Though this case is both simple and extreme, it demonstrates how a large number of vocal problems are caused by environmental pressures. Sometimes, however, a particular environment is so unlikely to change that something does have to be done to the voice in order that it may better stand up to it.

Another example of an environmental influence on the voice is a case reported by Jo Estill, one of the more creative voice therapists from Australia. Among her patients was a young boy aged ten who came to her with dysphonia. This was caused by his constant yelling, which in his home was the accepted way of communicating. If you did not yell, you simply were not heard. To retrain the voice to project itself in a moderate volume would thus have caused the boy to be unheard and yet the yelling would surely have caused permanent problems if it continued.

Consequently Estill taught the boy how to yell without generating the tissue friction that was causing the soreness. This entailed training in the same method of singing as used by Ethel Merman, a well-known exponent of the 'belting' style of singing popular on Broadway. Hence the boy was able to continue yelling without any negative side effects.

It is important to remember then that the voice is not only a political instrument representing the individual's right to expression; it is also a social phenomenon and as such it is affected by the quality of the environment. Any voice therapist who seeks to effect positive development in a pupil must necessarily take this into consideration, for no thorough understanding of a voice can be reached without an analysis of the social context in which it is used or misused.

# Traumatic Amnesia

A 8 o'clock in the evening on 6 November 1985 Lydia Philipson was shopping at her local supermarket. It was a cold evening. At 8.30 p.m. Mrs Philipson loaded up her estate car with the bags and drove home, whereupon she parked the vehicle in the driveway and went into her house through the back door to greet her husband and 'take a look in' at her daughter, whom she expected to be in bed. As the ground floor was deserted, she called up the stairs to her husband. He was on the telephone and interrupted his conversation to explain that he had sent their daughter to Lydia's mother's house for the night. An argument ensued.

At around 10.00 p.m. Mr Philipson went outside. A few moments later he shot a pistol through the window. The bullet entered the back of Lydia's head at the top of the neck. Mr Philipson then killed himself with the same gun.

The accident left Lydia paralysed from the waist down and with a permanent 'numbness' down the whole of one side of her body, a sensation which she described as an exaggerated form of the feeling 'which you get when you have an injection at the dentist'. The accident also rendered Lydia speechless; she did not utter a word for two years after the accident.

Eventually, with the aid of speech therapy, Lydia was able to speak again; but seven years after the accident Lydia was still very unhappy about her verbal and vocal proficiency. She complained of 'getting completely stuck for words' and of 'drifting off somewhere else during a conversation'. Lydia also recognised that her voice was very quiet and wondered if this was due to the disturbed hearing which she suffered as a result of damage caused by the gun wound. It was at this point that I met Lydia and our work together began.

Lydia had not spoken in any depth to anyone about her accident. She had had several sessions with 'a counsellor or psychologist or someone' shortly after regaining her speech, but from Lydia's description these appeared to be concerned with getting her 'on the road' to routine and stability rather than with subjecting the effect of the accident to any analysis. In the interim, between our first session and our next appointment, I asked Lydia to make a verbal note on a tape recorder of the times when this trance-like state of speechlessness occurred so that we might analyse those occasions. When we then came to listen to the tape, many of the situations in which she had 'stumbled' seemed to be connected with the notion of mobility. One situation was a conversation with a taxi driver with whom Lydia felt annoyed because he could not pick her up for some time; another was a conversation with a man who had telephoned her to express his gratitude to Lydia for having acted as a sponsorship manager for a county-wide marathon.

It transpired that Lydia was deeply embittered that she could no longer drive and that she had to rely on other people for her transport. It also transpired that most of the conversations which generated this speechless state occurred on the telephone, which she had hated to use since the accident.

Our next task was to set about discovering where these states originated and when they started. It did not take much digging.

After being shot by her husband, Lydia did not become unconscious but lay on the floor fully awake, 'in a stunned and completely removed state' for ten hours until she was found the following morning. She remained in this state for some months and it was not until early December that she was able to remember how she had received the injury and by whom it was inflicted.

It emerged that Lydia was still, seven years later, unable to remember very much detail from that night. I asked her to cast her mind back and try to visualise what had happened. We talked through the events slowly and methodically, starting with the shopping expedition.

Lydia recalled that she had tried to reach for the telephone but had seen blood all over the number pads and was 'for some reason unable to touch it'. As we began to excavate some of the details of this traumatic evening, it became clear that the states of speechless trance into which Lydia often plummeted were like microcosmic recollections of this terrible dumbstruck trance into which she was blasted by the bullet from the gun. Furthermore, the telephone had retained some of its horror, as though all telephones were somehow still covered in blood for her.

Lydia began to admit that there were in fact a number of phobic reactions which she had acquired since the accident and which we were able to trace to that night; for example, she hated the curtains to remain undrawn after dark, because they reminded her of the window through which she was shot.

Lydia continued to make tape recordings every day of her feelings and her thoughts and made notes of any disturbing situations, with particular reference to her speech. We discovered that the speechlessness not only occurred in conversations which made implicit or explicit reference to mobility, but occurred with a pattern that seemed to be unrelated to the content of the discourse. What they did seem to have in common, however, was a lack of importance or relevance in Lydia's mind. She was fine when she was involved in a conversation about a subject of a specific nature, but whenever the conversation became more rambling or 'just chit-chat', the silence set in.

It was obvious from Lydia's descriptions that she had a great fear of silence in conversations, as though it represented some failure or deficiency on her part. It eventually became apparent that what for many people might appear as a mildly embarrassing silence was for Lydia a subconscious recapitulation of the ten hours of inflicted silence which she experienced on that November night.

As Lydia continued to make tape recordings of her thoughts and feelings, the sophistication of her language and her vocal confidence increased and she began to raise questions and issues which she had not really considered before, and certainly had not previously spoken about. Many of these issues concerned the psychological adjustment which she had to make in order to come to terms with her disability and, more importantly, the way she was treated by most people because she was disabled: 'The way you get treated if you are in a wheelchair is like saying that, as soon as anyone sits down, their mind goes.'

Lydia was regularly asked by the local council to give speeches about the services available to people whose physical abilities have been to some degree reduced by accident or illness. At first, Lydia had been terribly uneasy about doing this because she was unconfident about her speech; but as she began to unravel the detail of the November night and understand where her phobic concerns originated, she was able to overcome them and start afresh. And the more she realised how widespread were the prejudice and condescension levied at so-called disabled people, the more angry she became and the more determined to speak out against it.

In Lydia's case a psychological motivation to develop and understand herself became coupled with a political motivation to effect social change; and our work together was focused on a primarily psychological investigation of her social predicament.

The importance of such an investigation for people whose physical condition is to some extent impaired cannot be underestimated. In all the psychotherapy journals throughout the world, there are hardly any cases of such patients. Those involved with helping disabled people are always so preoccupied with basic concerns – obtaining a wheelchair, organising ramps, acquiring social-service support and home-help – that no one stops to think of the person's psychological needs.

Voice movement therapy was able to help those people reported in the above case studies, and indeed it has been able to help many others. But not all of them have manifested symptoms or described life-situations as specifically traumatic or as needy as those described here. Others have pursued the work to mobilise psychological contents through vocal sound in order to enhance expressivity rather than to relieve aspects of a specific affliction.

Since my discovery of the pioneering work pursued by those practitioners discussed in this book and the beginning of my practical attempts to help people reach their inner selves through their voice, I have discovered many things, both about the voice and about the state of humanity for which the voice is an expression. But one point emerges particularly clearly. It is only possible to ignore something for so long. Endless case studies cited by therapists from diverse fields testify to the fact that the more deeply something is buried, the more powerful its impact will be when it inevitably resurfaces. This is no less true for the burying by society of whole modes of expression. And this includes the voice.

It is therefore inevitable that the importance of unimpeded vocal expression will be increasingly recognised. Already more and more people are showing interest in vocal work and voice workshops, tempted in many cases by the vision of achieving total physical and psychological well-being.

But I hope that, if I have done nothing else in this book, I have pointed to how complex and sophisticated the human voice is and consequently how respectful we must be of the detailed and complicated manner in which it reflects the psycho-physical state of the person in whom it resides. If we want to use the voice therapeutically, we must learn its own mode of functioning and ensure that we match our intellectual ideas with our practical experience.

There has been much research into the voice since the investigations carried out in the first half of the century, which is where my original impetus emanated and on which this book has focused. Recent technology, for example, has enabled us to plot with great precision acoustic patterns of pitch, timbre, volume, the degree of 'free air', shape of the vocal tract and so on. Meanwhile, artistically orientated singing teachers and vocal coaches search for more intuitive and image-based ways of encouraging liberated vocal function in students for whom scientific explanation would not necessarily help. This does not mean that voice practitioners of this type can afford to ignore science, but neither can clinicians ignore the intuitive, creative and analogical aspects of voice teaching and vocal rehabilitation.

In psychotherapy it is taken for granted that the ability of the therapist in comprehending a patient's predicament depends a great deal on the degree to which the therapist has investigated his or her own psychological material. However, the training of a voice clinician, such as a laryngologist, does not include vocal practice. Indeed, I have a colleague who is a well-respected speech therapist and whose basic training consisted of four years' full time study: but none of this time was spent working on her own voice! To understand the voice we must be prepared to use our own voice, to exercise it, nurture it and form an active relationship with it. When we have done this, we can and must sacrifice some of the seemingly infallible statistics provided by science for the direct experience gained from our own vocal function.

Voice movement therapy and its practitioners will, I hope, continue to forge links with professionals from other related fields which will be as rewarding as the informative and inspiring relationships which I have made during the years spent developing this discipline. However, although the discipline will continue to be enriched through the appropriation of established clinical and theoretical models of analysis, voice movement therapy will always remain rooted in action rather than words.

# Notes

All references to the work of Freud have been drawn from *The Standard Edition of the Complete Psychological Works* (abbreviated throughout the Notes to 'S.E.'), edited by James Strachey in collaboration with Anna Freud, assisted by Alix Strachey and Alan Tyson (London: Hogarth Press and the Institute of Psychoanalysis, 1953–74). Similarly, all references to the work of Jung have been taken from *The Collected Works of C. G. Jung* (abbreviated throughout to 'C.W.'), edited by H. Read, M. Fordham, G. Adler and W. McGuire (Princeton, New Jersey: Princeton University Press, and London: Routledge and Kegan Paul, 1953– ).

## INTRODUCTION
1 C. G. Jung, C.W., vol. 5, pp. 12–13

## CHAPTER ONE: ORIGINS – VOICE, MUSIC, LANGUAGE
1 O. Jesperson, *Language: Its Nature, Development and Origin* (London: Allen & Unwin, 1922), pp. 436–7.
2 H. Spencer, 'Essay on the Origin of Music', cited in O. Jesperson, op. cit., p. 434.
3 E. Kurth, *Musikpsychologie* (Berlin: M. Hesse, 1931), p. 291.
4 J. Ruesch and W. Kees, *Nonverbal Communication: Notes on the Visual Perception of Human Relations* (Berkeley and Los Angeles: University of California Press, 1956), p. 64.
5 See M. M. Lewis, *Early Response to Speech and Babbling in Infant Speech* (London: Kegan Paul, 1936).
6 M. Greene and J. Conway, *Learning to Talk: A Study in Sound of Infant Speech Development* (New York: Folkways Records, 1963), FX 6271.
7 See M. Greene and L. Mathieson, *The Voice and its Disorders*, 5th edn (London: Whurr, 1989), pp. 62–5.
8 See R. E. Stark and S. Nathanson, 'Unusual Features of Crying in an Infant Dying Suddenly and Unexpectedly', in J. Bosma and J. Showacre (eds.), *Development of Upper Respiratory Anatomy and Function: Implications for SID* (Washington: US Department of Health Education, 1975).
9 See M. Greene and L. Mathieson, op. cit., p. 64.
10 J. Harris, *Early Language Development: Implications for Clinical and Educational Practice* (London: Routledge, 1990), p. 8.
11 See D. Hymes, 'Competence and Performance in Linguistic Theory' in R. Husley and E. Ingram (eds.), *Language Acquisition: Models and Methods* (London: Academic Press, 1971).
12 See B. F. Skinner, *Verbal Behaviour* (New York: Appleton-Century-Crofts, 1957).
13 See P. Grunwell, *Clinical Phonology* (London: Croom Helm, 1982).
14 See P. Ostwald, 'Musical Behaviour in Early Childhood', *Developmental Medicine and Child Neurology*, 15 (1973), 367–75.
15 H. Gardner, 'Developmental Psychology after Piaget: An Approach in Terms of Symbolization', *Human Development*, 22 (1979), 73–88 (p. 76).
16 H. Gardner, *The Arts and Human Development* (New York: Wiley, 1973), p. 45.

17 See particularly E. Winner, *Invented Worlds: The Psychology of the Arts* (Cambridge, Massachusetts: Harvard University Press, 1982).

18 See J. Bamberger, 'Revisiting Children's Drawings of Simple Rhythms: A Function for Reflection-in-Action', in S. Strauss and R. Stavy (eds.) ,*U-shaped Behavioural Growth* (New York: Academic Press, 1982).

19 See H. Moog, *The Musical Experience of the Pre-school Child* (London: Schott, 1976).

20 See W. J. Dowling, 'Development of Musical Schemata in Children's Spontaneous Singing', in W. R. Crozier and A. J. Chapman (eds.), *Cognitive Processes in the Perception of Art* (Amsterdam: Elsevier, 1982).

21 See L. Davidson, 'Tonal Structures of Children's Early Songs', *Music Perception*, 2 (1985), 361–74.

22 J. C. Berryman with D. Hargreaves, M. Herbert and A. Taylor, *Development Psychology and You* (London: British Psychological Society/ Routledge, 1991), pp. 157–8.

23 S. K. Langer, *Philosophy in a New Key*, 3rd edn (Cambridge, Massachusetts: Harvard University Press, 1963), p. 88.

24 Ibid., pp. 260–61.

25 S. K. Langer, *Feeling and Form* (London: Routledge & Kegan Paul, 1953), p. 27.

26 Ibid.

27 S. K. Langer, *Philosophy in a New Key*, op. cit., pp. 246–7.

28 C. Clement, *Opera, or the Undoing of Women*, trans. by Betsy Wing (London: Virago, 1989).

29 See S. Freud, S. E., vol. 4, pp. 262–4.

30 W. B. Stanford, *Greek Tragedy and the Emotions* (London: Routledge & Kegan Paul, 1983), p. 57.

31 For a particularly in-depth analysis of the genesis and development of the Orpheus myth see J. Warden (ed.), *Orpheus: The Metamorphoses of a Myth* (Toronto: University of Toronto Press, 1985).

32 G. Stowell (ed.), *The Book of Knowledge*, vol. 5, p. 303.

33 J. Peri, preface to *Eurydice*, trans. by O. Strunk in *Source Readings in Music History* (London: Faber & Faber, 1952), p. 373. Cited in part in C. Headington, R. Westbrook and T. Barfoot, *Opera: A History* (London: Arrow Books, 1991), p. 22.

34 L. Manen, *Bel Canto: The Teaching of the Classical Italian Song-schools, its Decline and Restoration* (Oxford: Oxford University Press, 1989), p. 23.

35 See M. Eliade, *Shamanism: Archaic Techniques of Ecstasy* (London: Routledge & Kegan Paul, 1964).

36 See R. Windstadt, *The Malay Magician* (London: Routledge & Kegan Paul, 1951).

37 See K. Rasmussan, 'An Eskimo Shaman Purifies a Sick Person', in Lessa and Vogt (eds.), *Reader in Comparative Religion* (Evanston, Illinois: Row, Peterson, 1958), pp. 362–67.

38 See J. D. Frank, *Persuasion and Healing* (Baltimore: John Hopkins Press, 1961).

39 See K. Rasmussan, 'An Eskimo Shaman Purifies a Sick Person', in Lessa and Vogt (eds.), op. cit., pp. 362–7.

40 See J. Gillin, 'Magical Fright', in Lessa and Vogt (eds.), op. cit., pp. 353–62.

41 See W. LaBarre, 'Confession as Cathartic Therapy in American Indian

Tribes', in A. Kiev (ed.), *Magic Faith and Healing* (New York: Free Press of Glencoe, 1964), pp. 36–49.
42  See F. Densmore, 'The Use of Music in the Treatment of the Sick by American Indians', in D. M. Schullian and M. Schoen (eds.), *Music and Medicine* (New York: Henry Schuman, 1948), pp. 25–46.
43  See D. M. Schullian and M. Schoen (eds.), op. cit.

CHAPTER TWO:
PSYCHOTHERAPY AND THE MEDICINAL WONDER OF WORDS
1  S. Freud, S.E., vol. 2, pp. 6–7.
2  Ibid., vol. 3, p. 39.
3  Ibid., p. 35.
4  Ibid., p. 36.
5  Ibid., vol. 4, p. 101.
6  Ibid., vol. 5, p. 344.
7  Ibid.
8  Ibid., p. 339.
9  Ibid., p. 353.
10  Ibid., vol. 11, pp. 125–6.
11  Ibid., vol. 23, pp. 166–7.
12  Ibid., vol. 5, p. 352 (footnote).
13  Ibid., vol. 11, p. 143.
14  Ibid., vol. 23, p. 132.
15  C. G. Jung, C.W., vol. 2, p. 322.
16  Ibid., vol. 8, pp. 322–6.
17  Ibid., vol. 3, pp. 40 and 81.
18  Ibid., vol. 2, p. 601.
19  Ibid., vol. 3, p. 240.
20  Ibid., vol. 1, pp. 28–9.
21  Ibid., p. 47.
22  Ibid., vol. 3, p. 95.
23  Ibid.
24  Ibid.
25  This example is taken from J. Campbell, *The Masks of God: Primitive Mythology* (London: Arkana, 1991), p. 31.
26  C. G. Jung, C.W., vol. 8, pp. 133–4.
27  Ibid., p. 174.
28  Ibid., vol. 7, p. 201.
29  Ibid., vol. 9, pt 1. pp. 75–84.
30  Ibid., p. 152.
31  Ibid., p. 183.
32  Ibid., vol. 5, p. 292.

CHAPTER THREE:
THE PIONEERING FOUNDATIONS OF A SINGING CURE
1  W. Reich, *Character Analysis*, 3rd edn (London: Vision Press, 1948), p. 342.
2  Ibid., p. 341.
3  Ibid., p. 353.
4  Ibid., p. 47.
5  Ibid., p. 146.

6 Ibid., p. 48.
7 Ibid., p. 362.
8 A. Lowen, *Bioenergetics* (Harmondsworth: Penguin, 1976), p. 44.
9 Ibid., p. 62.
10 Ibid., p. 137.
11 Ibid., p. 43.
12 Ibid., p. 263.
13 Ibid.
14 Ibid., p. 99.
15 Ibid., p. 270.
16 Ibid., p. 271.
17 Ibid., p. 121.
18 Ibid.
19 Ibid.
20 Ibid., p. 273.
21 Ibid., p. 113.
22 See L. Wilma and others, 'Analysis and Interpretation of the Creative Work of John Sanders' (Confidential publication, Institute of Child Welfare, Study of Adolescence: University of California, 1942).
23 See H. E. Jones, 'The Analysis of Voice Records', *Journal of Consulting Psychology*, 6 (1942), 254–6 and *Development in Adolescence* (New York: Appleton-Century, 1943), pp. 122–3; P. J. Moses, 'The Study of Voice Records', *Journal of Consulting Psychology*, 6 (1942), 257–61 and *The Voice of Neurosis* (New York: Grune & Stratton, 1954), pp. 1–3.
24 P. J. Moses, 'Speech and Voice Therapy in Otolaryngology', *Eye, Ear, Nose and Throat Monthly*, 32, no. 7 (July 1953), 367–75 (pp. 369–70).
25 P. J. Moses, *The Voice of Neurosis*, op. cit., p. 15.
26 P. J. Moses, 'Reorientation of Concepts and Facts in Phonetics', *Logos* (1958) 45–51 (p. 45).
27 P. J. Moses, 'Speech and Voice Therapy in Otolaryngology', art. cit. (p. 367).
28 P. J. Moses, *The Voice of Neurosis*, op. cit., p. 6.
29 P. J. Moses, 'Speech and Voice Therapy in Otolaryngology', art. cit., pp. 370–71.
30 M. W. Brody, 'Neurotic Manifestations of the Voice', *Psychoanalytical Quarterly*, 12 (1943), 371–80 (p. 371).
31 Ibid. (p. 374).
32 Ibid. (pp. 375–6).
33 Ibid. (p. 379).
34 H. Stack Sullivan, *The Psychiatric Interview* (London: Tavistock, 1955), p. 5.
35 See R. E. Pittenger, C. F. Hockett and J. J. Danehy, *The First Five Minutes* (Ithaca, New York: Paul Martineau, 1960).
36 See P. J. Moses, *The Voice of Neurosis*, op. cit., pp. 15–20.
37 Ibid., p. 41.
38 P. J. Moses, letter to A. Wolfsohn, 16 April 1961. Repository: Alfred Wolfsohn Private Archives, Malérargues, France. Copyright © Marita Günther. Reprinted by permission.
39 A. Wolfsohn, 'Orpheus or The Way to a Mask', trans. by M. Günther (unpublished manuscript written in Berlin, 1936–8). Repository: Alfred

Wolfsohn Private Archives, Malérargues, France. Copyright © M. Günther. Reprinted by permission.

40  A. Wolfsohn, 'The Problem of Limitations', trans. by M. Günther (unpublished manuscript written in London, 1958). Repository: Alfred Wolfsohn Private Archives, Malérargues, France. Cited in Marita Günther, 'The Human Voice: On Alfred Wolfsohn', *Spring: A Journal of Archetype and Culture*, 50 (1990), 65–75 (p. 66).

41  A. Wolfsohn, 'The Biography of an Idea', trans. by M. Günther (unpublished handwritten fragment written in Germany, undated). Repository: Alfred Wolfsohn Private Archives, Malérargues, France. Copyright © Marita Günther. Reprinted by permission.

42  A. Wolfsohn, 'Notes on Orpheus', supplement to 'Orpheus or The Way to a Mask' (London, 1949). Posthumously published in *Spring: A Journal of Archetype and Culture*, 50 (1990), 76–9 (p. 77).

43  Ibid.

44  See C. Salomon, *Charlotte: Life or Theatre*, trans. by L. Vennewitz, ed. by U. G. Schwartz with a preface by C.E. Belinfante and an introduction by J. Herzberg (Harmondsworth: Allen Lane, Penguin, 1981).

45  M. Günther, 'The Human Voice: On Alfred Wolfsohn', art. cit. (p. 69).

46  A. Wolfsohn, 'Orpheus or The Way to a Mask', op. cit.

47  M. Günther, 'The Human Voice', paper read at the *National Conference on Dramatherapy*, Antioch University, San Francisco (November 1986). Published on audio tape by Roy Hart Theatre, Malérargues, France.

48  C. G. Jung, C.W., vol. 9, pt 1, p. 284.

49  Ibid., pt 2, pp. 233–4.

50  M. Günther, 'The Human Voice: On Alfred Wolfsohn', art. cit. (p. 71).

51  Ibid.

52  A. Wolfsohn cited in E. Weiser, 'Stimme ohne Fessel', trans. by I. Halcrow, *Die Weltwoche* (30 September 1955).

53  C. G. Jung, C.W., vol. 9, pt 1, p. 284.

54  M. Günther, 'The Human Voice: On Alfred Wolfsohn', art. cit. (pp. 70–71).

55  A. Wolfsohn, 'Orpheus or The Way to a Mask', op. cit.

56  See R. Luchsinger and C. L. Dubois, 'Phonetische und stroboskopische Untersuchungen an einem Stimmphänomen', *Folia Phoniatrica*, 8, no. 4 (1956), 201–10.

57  A. Wolfsohn cited in E. Weiser, art. cit.

58  E. Weiser, art. cit.

59  A. Wolfsohn cited in E. Weiser, art. cit.

60  Lionel Blue in interview with Paul Newham (1991). First published in P. Newham, 'Jung and Alfred Wolfsohn: Analytical Psychology and the Singing Voice', *Journal of Analytical Psychology*, 37 (1992), pp. 323–6.

61  See J. Roose-Evans, *Experimental Theatre: From Stanislavski to Peter Brook*, 4th edn (London: Routledge, 1989), pp. 180–81.

62  Ibid., p. 81.

63  Jerzy Grotowski, interview with Barrie Coghlan, David Goldsworthy and Noah Pikes, Karpacz, Poland (September 1979). Cited in 'Roy Hart Theatre: The Human Voice and the Aural Vision of the Soul', extended adaptation and revision of an unpublished paper read at the First International Conference on 'Scientific Aspects of Theatre' at Karpacz, Poland (September 1979), in 'Roy Hart Theatre', unpublished anthology of reviews, extracts from articles and

other material, compiled by Barrie Coghlan, with assistance from Noah Pikes (1979). Repository: Roy Hart Theatre Archives, Malérargues, France.

64 P. Brook, *The Shifting Point: Forty Years of Theatrical Exploration* (London: Methuen, 1988), p. 169.

65 See J. Martin, *Voice in Modern Theatre* (London and New York: Routledge, 1991), p. 63.

66 A. Artaud, *The Theatre and Its Double*, trans. by V. Corti (London: John Calder, 1981), p. 27.

67 Ibid., p. 29.

68 Ibid., p. 30.

69 Ibid., p. 58.

70 Ibid., p. 57.

71 Ibid., p. 52.

72 Ibid., p. 51.

73 Ibid., p. 58.

74 Ibid., p. 51.

75 Ibid., p. 18.

76 Ibid., p. 83.

77 Ibid.

78 Ibid., p. 20.

79 Ibid., p. 60.

80 Ibid., p. 21.

81 See C. Innes, *Holy Theatre: Ritual and the Avant Garde* (Cambridge: Massachusetts: Harvard University Press, 1981), p. 134.

82 See P. Brook, op. cit., p. 108.

83 J. Heilpern, *Conference of the Birds: The Story of Peter Brook in Africa* (London, Methuen, 1989), p. 191.

84 P. Brook, op. cit., p. 130.

85 J. Roose-Evans, op. cit., p. 175.

86 Ibid., p. 177.

87 J. Heilpern, op. cit., pp. 143–4.

88 L. Flaszen, '*Akropolis* – Treatment of the Text', in J. Grotowski (ed.), *Towards a Poor Theatre*, trans. by S. Sanzenbach (London: Methuen, 1975), 61–70 (p. 69).

89 A. Seymour, 'Revelations in Poland' ,*Plays and Players* (October 1963), 33–4. Cited in J. Kumiega, *The Theatre of Grotowski* (London: Methuen, 1987), p. 69.

90 J. Grotowski, 'Dziady jako model teatru nowoczesnego', *Wspolczesnosc*, 21 (1961), p. 8. Cited in J. Kumiega, op. cit., p. 36.

91 J. Kumiega, op. cit., p. 97.

92 Ibid., p. 130.

93 J. Grotowski, 'Theatre is an Encounter', in J. Grotowski (ed.), op. cit., 55–60, (p. 42).

94 J. Grotowski, 'Towards a Poor Theatre', in J. Grotowski (ed.), op. cit., 15–26, (p. 22).

95 L. Flaszen, 'Studium o Hamlecie', (Opole, March 1964). Cited in J. Kumiega, op. cit., p. 73.

96 J. Roose-Evans, op. cit., p. 166.

97 J. Grotowski, 'Towards a Poor Theatre', in J. Grotowski: (ed.), op. cit., (p. 21).

98 J. Grotowski, 'The Theatre's New Testament' in J. Grotowski (ed.), op. cit., 27–54 (p. 39).

99  J. Grotowski, 'Towards a Poor Theatre', in J. Grotowski (ed.), op. cit., (pp. 16–17).
100  J. Grotowski, 'The Theatre's New Testament', in J. Grotowski (ed.), op. cit., (p. 37).
101  J. Kumiega, op. cit. pp. 112–13.
102  J. Grotowski, 'The Theatre's New Testament', in J. Grotowski (ed.), op. cit., (p. 46).

CHAPTER FOUR: THE SCIENTIFIC PRINCIPLES OF VOCAL SOUND
1  See J. Sundberg, *The Science of the Singing Voice* (Illinois: Northern Illinois University Press, 1987), p. 50.
2  See O. Tosi, *Voice Identification: Theory and Legal Applications* (Baltimore: University Park Press, 1979).
3  See M. Greene and L. Mathieson, *The Voice and its Disorders*, 5th edn (London: Whurr, 1989), p. 57.
4  Ibid., pp. 197–8.
5  Ibid., p. 197.
6  M. Garcia, *Traité complet de l'art du chant* (Paris, 1840) and *Hints on Singing* (London, 1894).
7  See M. D. Stockley, 'Vocal Cord Paralyses', in M. Fawcus (ed.), *Voice Disorders and their Management*, pp. 259–71 and M. Greene and L. Mathieson, op. cit., pp. 293–307.
8  M. Greene and L. Mathieson, op. cit., pp. 309–32.
9  L. Heaver, 'Psychiatric Observations on the Personality Structure of Patients with Habitual Dysphonia', *Logos* (1958), 1–21. Cited in P. Bloch, 'New Limits of Vocal Analysis', *Folia Phoniatrica*, 12 (1960), 291–7 (p. 294).
10  See G. Arnold, 'Vocal Nodules and Polyps: Laryngeal Tissue Reaction to Habitual Hyperkinetic Dysphonia', *Journal of Speech Disorders*, 27 (1962), 205; R. Luchsinger and G. Arnold (eds.) *Voice, Speech and Language*; M. D. Morrison, H. Nichol and L. A. Rammage, 'Diagnostic Criteria in Functional Dysphonia', *Laryngoscope*, 94 (1986) 1.
11  P. Bloch, 'New Limits of Vocal Analysis', *Folia Phoniatrica*, op. cit. (p. 294).
12  F. S. Brodnitz, 'The Holistic Study of the Voice', *Quarterly Journal of Speech*, 48, no. 3 (1962), 280–84 (p. 283).
13  Ibid., (pp. 283–4).
14  D. A. Weiss, 'The Psychological Relations to One's Own Voice', *Folia Phoniatrica*, 7 (1955), 209–22 (p. 209).
15  Ibid. (p. 211).
16  Ibid. (p. 214).
17  Ibid. (p. 215).
18  Ibid.
19  A. Jellinek, 'Treatment of Vocal Disorders with Spontaneous Imagery', *Folia Phoniatrica*, 8 (1956), 70–84. (pp. 70–71).

CHAPTER FIVE: THE PRACTICAL ELEMENTS OF VOCAL LIBERATION
1  J. Rowland, *Inside Motion: An Anatomical Basis for Movement Education* (Amsterdam: John Roland, 1984), p. 10.
2  See M. E. Todd, *The Thinking Body: A Study of the Balancing Forces of Dynamic Man*, which has become a seminal work in the field.
3  M. E. Todd, *The Balancing of Forces in the Human Being: Its Application to*

*Postural Patterns* (New York: Mabel Todd, 1929), p. 49. Cited in L. E. Sweigard, *Human Movement Potential: Its Ideokinetic Facilitation* (New York: Dodd, Mead & Co., 1974), p. 6.

4 See B. Clark, *Body Proportion Needs Depth* (Illinois: Barbara Clark, 1975).

5 See L. E. Sweigard, op. cit.

6 See L. Bonpensiere, *New Pathways to Piano Technique: A Study of the Relations Between Mind and Body with Special Reference to Piano Playing* (New York: Philosophical Library, 1953).

7 See M. Fulkerson, *The Move to Stillness* (Dartington Theatre Papers, Fourth Series, 1981–2).

8 W. B. Faulkner, Jnr, 'The Effect of the Emotions Upon Diaphragmatic Function: Observations in Five Patients', *Psychosomatic Medicine*, 3, no. 2 (April 1942), 187–9 (p. 189).

9 A. Jellinek, 'Observations on the Therapeutic Use of Spontaneous Imagery in Speech Therapy', *Folia Phoniatrica*, 5, no. 1 (1953), 166–182 and 'Treatment of Vocal Disorders with Spontaneous Imagery', *Folia Phoniatrica*, 8 (1956), 70–84.

10 A. Jellinek, 'Observations on the Therapeutic Use of Spontaneous Imagery in Speech Therapy', art. cit. (p. 167).

11 Ibid, (p. 173).

12 Ibid.

13 See R. Assagioli, *Psychosynthesis: A Manual of Principles and Techniques* (Wellingborough: Crucible, 1990).

14 See C. G. Jung, C.W., vol. 8, pp. 322–6.

15 See P. J. Moses *The Voice of Neurosis* (New York: Grune & Stratton, 1954), pp. 37 and 104, and 'Vocal Analysis', *Archives of Otolaryngology*, vol. 48 (1948), 171–86 (p. 177).

16 See, for example, the description of air-flow measurement in M. Gordon, 'Assessment of the Dysphonic Patient', in M. Fawcus, op. cit., pp. 39–72.

17 M. Kustow, 'Ludens Mysterium Tremendum et Fascinoscum', *Encore* (October 1963), 9–14 (p. 12). Cited in J. Kumiega, *The Theatre of Grotowski* (London and New York: Methuen, 1987), p. 40.

18 See C. F. Lindsley, 'The Psycho-physical Determinants of Voice Quality', *Speech Monograph*, 1 (1934), 79–116.

19 See K. Linklater, *Freeing the Natural Voice* (New York: Drama Book, 1976).

20 D. Bless, 'Voice Assessment: The Need for Standards', paper read at the British Voice Association International Symposium, University College, London (June 1991).

21 D. Juhan, *Job's Body: A Handbook for Bodywork* (New York: Station Hill, 1987) p. 164.

22 A. Hollings, 'The Aims of Singing Versus Speech and the Therapeutic Potential', newsletter of the Voice Research Society (now the British Voice Association), vol. 4, no. 1 (August 1989), 6–14 (p. 6–7).

23 A. Wolfsohn, *Vox Humana: Alfred Wolfsohn's Experiments in Extension of Human Vocal Range* (New York: Folkways Records, 1956), FX 123.

24 For further reference see D. Juhan, op. cit., the eloquence and practical relevance of which cannot be overstated.

25 M. H. Duncan, 'An Experimental Study of some of the Relationships between Voice and Personality among Students of Speech', *Speech Monograph*, M107, 47–60 (p. 49).

26 See S. Paxton, *Contact Improvisation* (Dartington Theatre Papers, Fourth Series, 1981–2).

27 See A. Kilcoyne, 'Common Sense: Making Use of the Sense of Touch', *The British Journal of Visual Impairment*, 9, no. 2 (July 1991), 47–9.
28 For an introduction to the background of this work see Ida Rolf, *Rolfing and Physical Reality* (Rochester: Healing Arts Press, 1990).

CHAPTER SIX: THE LIBERATED VOICE
1 J. Kovel, *A Complete Guide to Therapy: From Psychoanalysis to Behaviour Modification* (Harmondsworth: Penguin, 1991), p. 216.
2 Ibid., p. 215.
3 C. G. Jung, C.W. vol. 7, p. 201.
4 Ibid., vol. 8, pp. 97–8.
5 Ibid., vol. 5, p. 368.
6 Ibid.
7 Ibid., vol. 7, p. 238.
8 C. G. Jung cited in Miguel Serrano, *C. G. Jung and Herman Hesse: A Record of Two Friendships*, trans. by F. MacShane (London: Routledge & Kegan Paul, 1968), p. 50.
9 M. Fordham, *Explorations into the Self*, Library of Analytical Psychology, vol. 7 (London: Academic Press, 1985), pp. 118–19.
10 J. Redfearn, *My Self, My Many Selves*, Library of Analytical Psychology, vol. 6 (London: Academic Press, 1985), p. 131.
11 J. Hillman, Re-visioning Psychology (New York: Harper & Row, 1977), p. 88
12 Ibid., p. 32.
13 Ibid., p. 24.
14 R. Aldridge-Morris, *Multiple Personality: An Exercise in Deception* (London: Erlbaum, 1989).
15 J. Redfearn, op. cit., vol. 6, p. 95.
16 Ibid., p. 117.
17 C. Case and T. Dalley, *The Handbook of Art Therapy* (London: Routledge, 1992), p. 6.
18 See D. Walker, *Becoming a Profession: The History of Art Therapy in Britain 1940–82* (London: Tavistock/Routledge, 1991) and J. Alvin, *Music Therapy* (London: Stainer & Bell, 1991).
19 See J. L. Moreno, *Psychodrama*, vols. 1 and 2 (New York: Beacon House, 1946).
20 See F. Perls, *Gestalt Therapy Verbatim* (Utah: Real People Press, 1969).
21 M. H. Davies, 'Dramatherapy and Psychodrama' in S. Jennings (ed.), *Dramatherapy: Theory and Practice for Teachers and Clinicians* (London: Routledge, 1987), pp. 104–23.
22 See M. Klein, *Contributions to Psychoanalysis* (London: Hogarth Press, 1948).
23 C. Case and T. Dalley, op. cit., p. 62.
24 M. Naumberg, 'Art Therapy: Its Scope and Function', in E. F. Hammer (ed.) *Clinical Applications of Projective Drawings* (Springfield: C. C. Thomas, 1958), p. 511.
25 C. Case and T. Dalley, op. cit., p. 68.
26 See P. Heimann, 'Counter Transference', *International Journal of Psychoanalysis*, 31 (1960), 81–4.
27 S. Freud, S.E. vol. 7, p. 116.

NOTES

28 See S. Jennings (ed.), op. cit. and *Dramatherapy: Theory and Practice 2* (London: Routledge, 1992).
29 See H. Payne (ed.), *Dance Movement Therapy: Theory and Practice* (London: Tavistock/Routledge, 1992).
30 See M. S. Whitehouse, 'C.G. Jung and Dance Therapy: Two Major Principles', in P. L. Bernstein (ed.), *Eight Theoretical Approaches in Dance-movement Therapy*, vol. 1 (Dubuque: Kendall/Hunt, 1979), pp. 51–70.
31 See J. Chodorow, *Dance Therapy and Depth Psychology* (London: Routledge, 1991).
32 See A. Noack, 'On a Jungian Approach to Dance Movement Therapy', in H. Payne (ed.), op. cit., pp. 182–201.
33 See S. Mitchell, 'Therapeutic Theatre: A Para-theatrical Model of Dramatherapy', in S. Jennings (ed.), op. cit., pp. 51–67.
34 See B. Meekums, 'Dance Movement Therapy in a Family Service Unit' and M. Steiner, 'Alternatives in Psychiatry: Dance Movement Therapy in the Community', in H. Payne (ed.), op. cit.
35 A. Samuels, *Jung and the Post-Jungians* (London: Routledge, 1985), p. 12.
36 I first suggested this term as a result of discussions with D. Garfield-Davies. See P. Newham, 'Jung abnd Alfred Wolfsohn: Analytical Psychology and the Singing Voice', *Journal of Analytical Psychology*, 37 (1992), 323–6 (p. 335).
37 C. G. Jung, C.W., vol. 11, p. 544.
38 Ibid., pp. 325–6.
39 Ibid., vol. 6, p. 63.
40 D. W. Winnicott, *Playing and Reality* (Harmondsworth: Penguin, 1988), p. 44.
41 See C. Case and T. Dalley, op. cit.
42 J. Hillman, 'Further Notes on Images', *Spring: A Journal of Archetypal Psychology and Jungian Thought*, 39 (1978), 152–82 (pp. 158–9).
43 Ibid. (p. 170).
44 Ibid. (p. 165).
45 Ibid.
46 See P. Kugler, 'Image and Sound: An Archetypal Approach to Language', *Spring: A Journal of Archetypal Psychology and Jungian Thought*, 39 (1978), 136–51 and 'The Phonetic Imagination', *Spring: A Journal of Archetypal Psychology and Jungian Thought*, 40 (1979), 118–29.
47 J. Hillman, 'An Inquiry into Image', *Spring: Journal of Archetypal Psychology and Jungian Thought*, 38 (1977), 130–43 (p. 82).
48 J. Hillman, 'Further Notes on Images', art. cit. (pp. 170–71).
49 J. Hillman, 'An Inquiry into Image', art. cit. (p. 66).
50 Ibid. (p. 69).
51 J. Hillman, 'Further Notes on Images', art. cit. (p. 162).
52 *Svenska Dagbladet* (July 1982), cited in J. Martin, *The Voice in Modern Theatre* (London: Routledge, 1991), p. 67.
53 E. Pardo, 'Dis-membering Dionysus: Image and Theatre', *Spring: A Journal of Archetypal Psychology and Jungian Thought*, 45 (1984) 163–79 (p. 166).

CHAPTER SEVEN:
FROM SONG TO SPEECH – THE MUSCLE BENEATH THE SKIN
1 See F. S. Brodnitz, *Keep Your Voice Healthy* (USA: College Hill, 1988).
2 Compare, for example, M. Morrison, *Clear Speech* (London: A. & C. Black, 1977) and M. Bunch, *Speak with Confidence* (London: Kogan Page, 1989).

253

3 See, for example, J. Clifford Turner, *Voice and Speech in the Theatre* (London: Pitman, 1977) and J. Laver, *Phonetic Description of Voice* (Cambridge: Cambridge University Press, 1980).

4 Among his most interesting writings are *The Alchemy of Voice* (London: Robert Hale, 1965) and *Vocal Truth* (London: Robert Hale, 1969).

5 See J. Rush, *The Philosophy of the Human Voice: Embracing its Physiological History; Together with a System of Principles, by which Criticism in the Art of Elocution may be Rendered Intelligible, and Instruction, Definite and Comprehensive. To which is Added a Brief Analysis of Song and Recitative* (Philadelphia, 1827). For an overview of Rush's life and work see L. L. Hale, 'Dr James Rush – Psychologist and Voice Scientist', *Quarterly Journal of Speech*, 35, no. 4 (1949), 448–55.

6 See, for example, W. B. Jenks, 'Speech Training as a Means of Training Maladjustments of Personality' (unpublished doctoral thesis, University of Chicago, 1932) and P. E. Kauffman, 'An Investigation of Some Psychological Stimulus Properties of Speech Behaviour' (unpublished doctoral thesis, University of Chicago, 1954).

7 See C. Berry, *Voice and the Actor* (London: Harrap, 1973) and *The Actor and his Text* (London: Harrap, 1987).

8 P. Rodenburg, *The Right to Speak: Working with the Voice* (London: Methuen, 1992), pp. 106–7.

9 Ibid., p. 107.

10 Ibid., pp. 74–8.

11 Ibid., pp. 64–5.

12 Ibid., p. 86.

13 Ibid., p. 71.

14 Ibid., p. 87.

15 Ibid., pp. 91–2.

16 Ibid., p. 17.

17 E. Sapir, 'Speech as a Personality Trait', *American Journal of Sociology*, 32 (1927), 892–905.

18 J. R. Davitz and L. J. Davitz, 'The Communication of Feelings by Content-free Speech', *Journal of Communication*, 9 (1959), 6–13.

19 See W. F. Soskin, 'Some Aspects of Communication and Interpretation in Psychotherapy', paper read at American Psychological Association (Panel on Communication in the Counselling Situation) (Cleveland: September 1953).

20 See B. F. Skinner, *Verbal Behaviour* (New York: Appleton-Century-Crofts, 1957).

21 See P. F. Ostwald, 'Human Sounds', in D. A. Barbara (ed.), *Psychological and Psychiatric Aspects of Speech and Hearing* (Springfield, Illinois: Charles C. Thomas, 1960).

22 See P. E. Kauffman, op. cit.

23 P. J. Moses, *The Voice of Neurosis* (New York: Grune & Stratton, 1954), p. 5.

24 Ibid., p. 8.

25 See J. Harris, *Early Language Development: Implications for Clinical and Educational Practice* (London: Routledge, 1990), p. 46.

26 See G. Bateson, *Steps to an Ecology of Mind* (USA: Aronson, 1987).

27 See J. Lotz, *Linguistics: Symbols Make Humans* (New York: Language and Communication Research Centre, Columbia University, 1955).

28  F. McGehee, 'The Reliability of the Identification of the Human Voice', *Journal of General Psychology*, 17 (1937), 249–71 (p. 251).

29  T. H. Pear, *Radio Times* (14 January 1927).

30  T. H. Pear, *Voice and Personality* (London: Chapman & Hall, 1931).

31  See H. Herzog, 'Stimme under Persönlichkeit', *Zeitschrift für Psychologie*, 130 (1933), 300–379.

32  See G. W. Allport and H. Cantril, *Study of Values: A Scale for Measuring the Dominant Interests in Personality* (Boston: Houghton Mifflin, 1931) and P. E. Vernon and G. W. Allport, 'A Test for Personal Values', *Journal of Abnormal Social Psychology* 26 (1931), 231–48.

33  G. W. Allport and H. Cantril, 'Judging Personality with the Voice', *Journal of Solial Psychology*, 5 (1934), 37–55. (p. 53). Also in *The Psychology of Radio* (New York: Harper & Brothers, 1935), 109–58 (p. 109).

34  See P. J. Fay and W. C. Middleton, 'Judgment of Spranger Personality Types from the Voice as Transmitted Over a Public Address System', *Character and Personality* 8 (1939), 144–55.

35  See E. Spranger, *Types of Men* (Halle (Saale): Niemeyer, 1928), p. 402.

36  P. J. Fay and W. C. Middleton, art. cit. (p. 154).

37  E. R. Skinner, 'A Calibrated Recording and Analysis of the Pitch, Force and Quality of Vocal Tones Expressing Happiness and Sadness', *Speech Monograph*, MIZ vol. 2 (1935).

38  See P. E. Kauffman, op. cit.

39  See J. A. Starkweather, 'The Communication Value of Content-free Speech', *American Journal of Psychology* 69 (1956), 121–3 and 'Content-free Speech as a Source of Information about the Speaker', *Journal of Abnormal Psychology*, 52 (1956), 394–402.

40  W.F. Soskin and P.E. Kauffman, 'Judgment of Emotion in Word-free Voice Samples, *Journal of Communication*, 11, no. 2 (June 1961), 73–80 (p. 80).

41  P. Rodenburg, op. cit., p. 4.

42  R. Stagner, 'Judgments of Voice and Personality', *Journal of Educational Psychology*, 27 (1936), pp. 276–7.

43  P. Rodenburg, op. cit., p. 54.

44  S. Richards, *Sonic Harvest: Towards Musical Democracy* (Oxford: Amber Lane Press, 1992), p. 91.

45  K. Linklater, *Freeing the Natural Voice* (New York: Drama Book, 1976), p. 2.

Excerpt from *The Psychiatric Interview* by H. S. Sullivan (London, Tavistock, 1955) reproduced by kind permission of W. W. Norton & Company, Inc., New York.

Excerpts from *The Shifting Point* by Peter Brook; from *Conference of the Birds* by J. Heilpern; from *The Theatre of Grotowski* by J. Kumiega and from *The Rights to Speak* by P. Rodenburg reproduced by kind permission of Reed International Books, London.

Exceprts from *The Standard Edition of The Complete Psychological Works of Sigmund Freud*, translated and edited by James Strachey, reproduced by kind permission of Random House UK Ltd., London.

Excerpts from *The Standard Edition of The Complete Psychological Works of Sigmund Freud*, translated and edited by James Strachey, reproduced by kind permission of Random House UK Ltd., London.

Excerpt from *Bel Canto: The Teaching of the Classical Italian Song-Schools, Its*